D0132413

# CAREERS
## BY DESIGN

**THIRD EDITION**

ALLWORTH PRESS
NEW YORK

© 2001 Roz Goldfarb

All rights reserved. Copyright under Berne Copyright Convention, Universal Copyright
Convention, and Pan-American Copyright Convention. No part of this book may be reproduced,
stored in a retrieval system, or transmitted in any form, or by any means, electronic, mechanical,
photocopying, recording, or otherwise, without prior permission of the publisher.

05    04    03    02    01              5    4    3    2    1

Copublished with The Graphic Artists Guild
Published by Allworth Press
An imprint of Allworth Communications
10 East 23rd Street, New York, NY 10010

Cover design by Jennifer Moore, James Victore, Inc.
Page design by Jennifer Moore
Page composition by CA Brandes


Printed in Canada

Library of Congress Cataloging-in-Publication Data:

Goldfarb, Roz.
Careers by design: a business guide for graphic designers/by Roz Goldfarb.—3rd ed.
    p.cm.
Includes bibliographical references and index.
ISBN 1-58115-205-1
    1. Commercial Art. 2. Vocational guidance—United States. I. Title.
NC1001. G65 2002
745.4'023'73—dc21
                2001006181

# Table of Contents

# AN INTRODUCTION TO
# A SPECIAL WORLD

The world of design is many things to many people, and efforts to characterize that world and the attributes of those who inhabit it have often been attempted. If anything, design is an emotional terrain. Those people who are creative, or who work with designers, find themselves within a landscape of professionals incredibly dedicated to the craft of design in its various applications, and committed to it in a way that often defies logic. Successful designers share a passion for design that is an essential component of their lives. This is true of most serious creative people practicing in any of the arts, but if this book has only one message, it is that design is a business, driven by many motivating business factors. Its applications are very practical. Therefore, today's successful designers require a whole other set of skills to survive in this complicated technological and global business climate. Keeping issues in context, it should be remembered that designers have been accused of not being able to see the "big picture," of being too focused on the detail of the design, of being so engrossed in the design as to forget the business requirements of the projects. Often, designers have been accused of being an introverted clique, talking to themselves and not communicating with the outside world.

However, the reality is that the designer's role is highly extroverted, for the graphic designer holds a unique position in our expanding world of communications. While the field of design has grown and matured substantially in the United States, the general public is only beginning to recognize its impact on our everyday existence. Simply put, everything we wear, touch, read in traditional or interactive media, ride in, or live in has been created by a designer. Our newspapers, magazines, and books; our activities on the Internet; e-commerce, research, and entertainment; our household appliances and automobiles; the packages that cover every object imaginable and entice us to buy; the graphic images, logotypes, and signs in stores and restaurants, as well as their identity, menus, and, sometimes, even their names; the computers, cell phones, PDAs, and their interface screens; the amusement parks we take our children to; the famous cartoon characters we become attached to, and the licensed products we buy with their logos or images; the shapes of cosmetic jars, bottles, lipsticks, and their packaging; the gift wrap and cards for presents; the incalculable numbers of brochures, annual reports, and corporate literature—all have been developed or designed by graphic, architectural, and industrial designers. The list is endless.

This book is all about the business of design. It is a guide through the boundaries of design, how these companies are structured, the roles people play, and what business or communications problems they are required to solve. It is also about how to find one's way, build a career, and get a job.

There is so little information about the business of design that this book became an instant success when it was first published in 1992. As we approach the third revised edition, it confirms the need for periodic changes, for this is a business always in transition. Tracking transition is always difficult, for the question of how to define a new direction versus identifying something that is perhaps only trendy is very tricky. And in this fast-paced world, one always has the sinking feeling that the minute something is put to print, it is obsolete. Nonetheless, this guide has proven very valuable for those who are entering this arena from colleges, or those who are transitioning from other fields, or those who just want to learn more about the world of design. These pages are also peppered with the comments of many professionals whose day-to-day challenges require knowledge and insight to help guide the way. Their contributions are extremely valuable as they give a special sort of timely reality check.

*Careers by Design* also looks at the history—the development of the business with perhaps a sense of where it is going. In that light, all my colleagues agree. The business has changed; it's different. Casual conversations over lunch or chance meetings on the street all focus on this point. "What's new?" one asks. "Everything. The business surely is different . . . it's just not the same," is the answer, said sometimes wistfully, sometimes in frustration. These remarks were written for the revised edition of this book in 1995 and now, at the beginning of 2001, they are still true, but the difference at the beginning of this millennium is not just in computerization or a sentimental wish for the way things were. The differences refer to a profound shift as to what design can mean, being defined as both a tangible designed object as well as a process of thinking. Technology has force-fed new ways of thinking about systems and structure, and has created the ability to produce at speeds not always healthy for considered thought. In fact, if there is any common complaint, it is the insatiable request for speed. Shorten timelines and the concept of 24/7 has become the bane of many designers' existence.

As said, *Careers by Design* was originally published in 1992. The World Wide Web only came into practical usage in 1994. In 2001, we cannot imagine life without the resources of the Internet, our fast computers, the frustrations in search of broadband access, our PDAs, cell phones, and the obvious advent of wireless technology which is so advanced in countries other than the United States. The state of business today is digital, global, infinitely more complicated, sophisticated, and, without question, exciting. Our society has changed at a pace unparalleled in history and the graphic designer's role is not only integrally connected but often on the cutting edge of these continuing changes. Nonetheless, many of the "basics" of design fundamentals do not change. It is important to keep perspective, for the utilization of systems and technology do not replace the fundamental requirements of design, composition, typography, taste, and talent. And technology has given us an enhanced understanding of the importance of content as well as the necessity of the art of communication. What better an environment could a designer ask for? This world of content, visual, and systems solutions for communication is an environment that requires design on every front. The nature of analytical thinking and design-based problem solving is a clear requirement for solutions.

In reviewing the editions of *Careers by Design*—1992, 1997, and now 2002—an interesting history develops outlining the shifting market and technological factors affecting the design business. The first edition, with its subsequent revisions, produced a commentary of the design field, tracing its growth, maturation, and ultimate acceptance of design the mainstream of commerce. And yet. . .so much remains the same. People still need to carve out goals and directions in their lives; design is a destination for an increasing number of individuals, and information that is clear, concise, and offers insight into this expanding field is all the more needed. It is important to remember that this work is a business guide to graphic design as well as a career guide. In my mind the two are inseparable, for to succeed as a graphic designer requires an understanding of the business.

Design, like any business sector of the economic picture, is subject to the vicissitudes of the economy. In fact, it usually anticipates downturns as well as rebounds. Anyone who needed to hire staff was subjected to the most intense talent shortage imaginable by the year 2000. By the last few years of the 1990s, the impact of the dot com world had created a concentrated and insatiable demand for talent, leaving more jobs available than there were qualified people. This was in the face of a continued increase in the number of people entering the design business. The economic boom of the end of the twentieth century added many new businesses and created the need for adding on or extending the regional offices of existing businesses, all requiring large numbers of new people in addition to the existing demands of traditional media. At the beginning of 2001, the inevitable consolidations occurred, many interactive businesses merged or closed, and while many people lost their jobs, the need for talent with substance has traditionally always been at a premium. By mid-2001 there were a large number of designers unemployed. However, talented individuals will always survive these economic storms provided they can be flexible and have business savvy. And who has the talent and business savvy and what does this mean? Clearly, the value judgment on what qualifies as talent is highly subjective, but there are also standards of business sophistication and aesthetic savvy that are necessary for a successful career. Hopefully, this book will help designers learn that while it may be the first requirement, talent alone is not enough.

And while change may be a constant, work-related criteria have not changed at all. The need for excellence and creativity in the workplace, be it in design or in business strategy, never changes. A strong work ethic combined with sensitivity to human values is always a necessary commitment. The need to focus on lifestyle and family needs remains and will always remain. My case in point, one more time, is that while everything seems new and different, the core values never change.

Life is a series of choices. To my mind, choice is the key to the game of life. Being able to make informed choices means having freedom. It means having the freedom to choose and direct the course of your future, the freedom to change directions, and the freedom to feel in control of your actions. This kind of freedom does not come easily. It requires a commitment to work, to research, and to yourself. Truthfully, I also think it requires a certain amount of luck. But if you are worldly and aware, it is amazing how luck can find you. There are people who make their opportunities happen and those who wouldn't recognize an opportunity if it stared them in the face. The information required to function with "freedom of choice" falls into three categories.

- ☛ You must have the proper education—exposure to the concepts and tools necessary for your personal development.
- ☛ You must have the ambition and commitment to want to do

your personal best.

☞ You must be knowledgeable and informed about your chosen career and the world at large.

After a long career in design placement, education, and career management, I'm totally convinced that broad-based career information is the key to making informed decisions. To achieve success in a career, a requirement is an understanding of the structure of the business and how its various components, along with the people who make it happen, interrelate with each other as well as with graphic design as a whole. It's the ability to see the forest and be able to discern different species of trees. This is the kind of information that would enable professionals, students, career counselors, and educators to make important life choices. For some people, these initial choices, made early in life, often determine unalterable courses. I often refer to my "Smorgasbord Theory of Choice" on speaking engagements. It's an obvious metaphor to guide our decision making. The theory goes like this: Assume you're at a wedding reception where you are presented with a very long smorgasbord. Most importantly, you are only allowed one plate. Therefore, you get in line, take a plate, and start to fill it with wonderful, delicious food. The only problem is, as your plate fills up, you realize you haven't reached the end of the table. As you approach the end, you see the selection is better and you'd prefer that food—but you have no more room on your dish! Had you only known! You now realize it would have been wiser to have scanned the length of the table before getting in line. Although life does not allow us to scan the length of our table before getting in line, there are some things we can control through knowledge and preparation. Choosing a career or making a career change at least affords us an opportunity for research and introspection. I sincerely hope the information in this book will afford a much broader concept of what lies ahead on that wonderful smorgasbord of life.

Too often, I have interviewed people well on in their careers who have only a vague notion of which paths their careers might travel. Early on they were propelled by only an intuitive recognition that they were talented and lacked any real sense of the field they wished to enter. Creative talent usually surfaces very early in life. Most creative people first recognize that part of their personality when they are young children and in later years acknowledge a need to find a practical application of their abilities. When that interest turns to design it is a rare person who has an informed, realistic picture of what graphic design is about, or how it relates to advertising or interactive media, and where in the scheme of things is the gratification and fit—for most people it's totally vague.

Accessing proper information is clearly the goal. What is unique and special is the kind of information a recruiter is exposed to year after year. As a recruiter, and as president of Roz Goldfarb Associates, I'm subjected daily to the vicissitudes of hiring criteria and firing practices, to the demands hundreds of employers place on their staff, and to the frustrations people experience in the workplace on both sides of the fence. Furthermore, we are exposed to a huge variety of firms, their business plans, personalities, and structure. The savvy individual seeking career information will surf the Web, research different professional organizations, or hopefully have informative interviews with professionals. High school students and their parents will seek out help from guidance counselors and art teachers. Colleges rely on their faculty, placement offices, and alumni. Unfortunately, few of these individuals have the breadth of information we do. Their own education and life experience have not given them enough exposure. My conversations with educators have most often proved to be an eye-opener, for many teachers, guidance counselors, or art teachers have little access to relevant or pragmatic industry information. There are a number of professional design colleges in this country which have a distinct advantage (see chapter 16), but it should be indicated that most of them have a somewhat specific rather than broad educational point of view and specialization within their curricula.

As it is easy for someone to offer opinions, it is important for the readers of this book to know how and why my opinions were formed. In 1979, after nearly ten years as an administrator and educator at Pratt Institute, I joined an executive recruitment firm and became a specialist in placing designers and art directors. While at Pratt I became aware of the urgent need for proper career information—something I never had. At that time my efforts were directed toward developing courses, workshops, and seminars for high school and college level students and teachers. As an individual who established my own firm, I have had the opportunity to deal with real business issues, my own and my clients', I have been a witness, on the ground floor, of the emergence of new technologies, new visions, and the development of new ventures. I have also been given the unique opportunity of observing careers in the making, as well as careers that flounder. As I indicated, we see these occurrences from a very special vantage point, for we are the consultants whose very existence depends on our ability to keep a confidence. Our clients range from the design gurus—the movers and shakers whose fame precedes them—to small entrepreneurs and all others who recognize that the success of their business depends on the quality of their creative and business personnel. Both our clients (those who pay our fees to find them the "perfect person") and our candidates (those who wish for another career opportunity and position) confide their motivations to us, knowing that information is necessary for us to function accurately, and knowing it will be kept in confidence. The vast number of negotiations—the hard decisions and profound, fundamental choices we experience in the daily drama of our office—by far outstrip the person who has probably (and hopefully) changed jobs less than ten times in a lifetime, even though the lifespan of a job is now measured in dog-years.

In providing any overview of design, clear distinctions must be made between design and other related areas. The types of jobs that will lead to realistic careers must be discussed, as well as what one can expect to earn in these positions, and what kind of a lifestyle that may dictate. With proper information, and more than a little good luck, an informed decision for a life choice or career change is possible. I hope we can provide a guide to a fascinating world and some of its opportunities. As I've mentioned, you can't make a decision if you don't know what the choices are. Too often, we're asked to do just that! Often at Pratt, I would encounter an irate parent, who strongly believed that the investment of time and money into an art education was impractical and wasteful. I'll never forget the student applying to Pratt Institute who tearfully told me why he couldn't accept our offer of admission and partial scholarship. His father, a teacher, would have gladly paid for his education if he were to become an accountant or the like, but would never contribute his hard-earned money to further a design education. Nor would the father allow me the opportunity to explain that one could earn a respectful and sometimes highly compensated income in design and that his son could achieve the personal gratification necessary for a complete life.

Yes, it is possible to achieve both and one can expect economic and personal compensation. When business objectives are combined with creative goals we enter a unique realm and the financial and personal rewards are there. It requires a sophistication of business knowledge and real talent. The following chapters will outline how this plays out in different sectors. All design must reflect a responsiveness to market factors, and designers must be knowledgeable about sociological and economic trends. Today we all are well aware of being members of a global economic community. The design community, as part of the business community, has played an integral part in these developments. Many firms have an international reach through their Web sites, branch offices, or a multinational client base. Anyone entering these fields must recognize the need to participate in the core of the business to be in a position to make the important decisions. All these factors contribute to the ability to make career and life choices.

This book's goal is to identify the distinctions between various areas of specialization, to analyze the talent and personality most apt to thrive, to point to the newer, developing areas where increased opportunity may lie, and to give an approximation of the salary levels currently prevalent in these fields. Generalizations are always dangerous, but this book will try to discern the characteristics of major market segments, as well as look to the future.

In defining graphic design, I have included the roles of marketing executives, strategic planners, account services, and production personnel as key players working with designers and the final creative deliverable product. I have also included discussions about advertising, architecture, and industrial design only in its relationship to graphic design. I have eliminated the associated fields of photography and illustration. Both are formidable creative areas practiced by many designers. However, while graphic designers may utilize photography and illustration in their own work, or art direct photographers and illustrators, the converse is rarely true. Photographers and illustrators are rarely graphic designers. The exceptional people who do it all are legendary. This book is geared toward all those considering a career in design: the student, the young professional, the established professional seeking change, as well as the art educator. It is written from a point of view acquired through years of dealing with everyday, real life experience, and designed to inform in a concise manner.

No one works in a vacuum and I am very fortunate to be surrounded by a company of wonderful people who have contributed their knowledge and energy. The recruiters of RGA have had a significant role in the updating of this book. Chapter 9 in particular is team-authored by Rita Armstrong and Jessica Goldfarb with contributions by the RGA's interactive recruitment department—Amy Fried, Joanne Kivlahan, and Penny Burrow. Joanne Kivlahan and Tara DeConigilio have authored much of the chapter on production. Margot Jacqz has contributed her significant expertise to the chapter on environmental design. Sylvia Laniado, Connie Kail Wolf, Penny Burrow, and Frank Dahill have contributed their advertising expertise; Deborah DiFronzo provided information on packaging design; and Marion Thunberg has shared her excellent insights in print design. I also want to thank Linda Bowen for helping me with researching and assembling this material. I also have to give a very special "thank you" to those individuals who agreed to be our "guests" and offer their valuable opinions and insights. They are: Patrick Baglee, Kenneth Cooke, Eric Chan, Myrna Davis, Pam DeCeasar, Jean-Michael Ekeblad, Patrick Gallagher, M. Arthur Gensler, Jr., Michael Gerke, Marc Gobé, Sarah Haun, Jim Hatch, Scott Kraft, Helen Keyes, Hans Neubert, Brent Oppenheimer, Peter Phillips, Hayes Roth, Simon Williams, and Tucker Viemeister.

On a personal note: Those who know me know that, as much as I love my work, I am nothing without my family. I count myself very fortunate that I have always had the support and love of my husband Ben, our three daughters—Meryl, Leslie, and Jessica (now my partner)—and the joy of grandchildren: Matthew, Marc, and—? Lastly, I have always found my mother to be the strongest influence in my life. She instille in me the ethic of living and working to one's fullest, striving simply to be the best. She was a woman who had run her own business in the most difficult of times, long before the women's movement was a concept. Her legacy is one I can only hope to equal.

Ultimately, we are the sum of our experiences. My professional life has been enriched continually through the fellowship of many very talented and sometimes brilliant people of vastly different viewpoints. This diversity itself has educated me, for I have always been fascinated by their life experiences and business philosophies. By keeping an open mind, listening intently, evaluating, accepting, and rejecting, I have formulated my own opinions. While it is not possible for me to thank all those who have given me this opportunity to learn, I will close with a toast to them and to those of you who will be a part of my future, for we all need to continue to learn.

Roz Goldfarb
*February 2001*

# What Is Graphic Design?

**H**ow many people can indeed give a reasonable definition of graphic design? It's not a profession that has a clear identity in the mind of the general public. Design is a much used word, and can mean many things. Fortunately, the general perception is changing, albeit confused, in this wired and product driven world. In the past, when people referred to designers they may have had a generalized notion of fashion design or engineering design, as well as automotive, product, and architectural design, and perhaps industrial design. But graphic design has been grouped with that ubiquitous term "advertising." Advertising is, after all, well known. We have seen it in film and fiction and, while graphic designers are beginning to appear as characters in stories, it is doubtful that anyone really understands what this person is doing. Tell someone at a party you're a graphic designer and you'll probably find they will consider you part of the advertising world or confuse your job with graphic reproduction and the printing industries. Designers are so absorbed with themselves that they rarely think about how little the world understands the field. Hopefully, change is in the wind. The public believes it knows what architecture, interior design, or advertising are about, but graphic design remains a mystery. It's interesting to note, and disappointing, the amount of confusion among educators and other professionals as well. Few can identify the difference between an industrial designer, environmental designer, or graphic designer. Fortunately, the wide visibility of Web design has focused a great deal of attention onto the look and feel of the sites and the role design plays in their success. Therefore, we need to begin by taking a look at the graphic designer's role, and the attributes and tenets of graphic design.

## THE DESIGNER'S ROLE IN SOCIETY AND BUSINESS

While design has traditionally been one of the somewhat hidden professions, recognition may be on the way to the anonymous designer. Achieving acceptance has been a long struggle. Design became a media topic in the 1990s. A hallmark was when business publications started to focus on the correlation between design and the success of product launches. Every year *Business Week* offered a cover story on industrial design. A special moment in time was their issue of August 23, 1990, themed, "Innovation: The Global Race." The editors predicted: "Design is to the '90s what finance was to the '80s, and marketing to the '70s: It is the corporate buzz-word for the new decade." Unfortunately, as I write this in 2001, this perception is not yet the rule, although we can add many new buzzwords for our branded and digital world. Various professional organizations have tried to promote the importance of design to the business community and even included discussions about the value of licensing graphic designers as a method of influencing public recognition. As said, the advent of interactive media and Web design has probably put more focus on design than ever before. The public's appreciation of new products and their design are enormous. Design is finally "paying off" to the business community. Designers in interactive media have become the focus of working in a field that is new, exciting, constantly innovative, and sexy and clearly not only the domain of nerds. But this is only a small, highly visible sector of the world of graphic design.

The effect of good, functional design in the marketplace has long been recognized in other parts of the world. We all are aware of the impact of German, Italian, and Japanese design in product and the automotive field; Italian and Scandinavian design in home furnishings; Italian lighting, French or Italian fashion, and Scandinavian design in silver and now in telecommunications. It's a sad commentary that only some sectors of corporate America are at last recognizing that good design can sell. This recognition is shedding new light on the profession of design and advancing the perception of the graphic designer's contribution to the "bottom line." The comparative recent escalation in the value of branding as a function of a corporation's image and products has forced a new evaluation of the role of design along with design's ability to construct organizational information. Graduate schools are slowly incorporating into their curriculum a recognition of design's role in product development and information architecture, and are emphasizing that it is an essential tool for a strategic process towards branding. The London Business School had been on the leading edge of this move in education. Today, Columbia, Harvard, and many others have joined. The effects of utilizing design as a strategic business tool are on the agenda of many business conferences and publications, and the Design Management Institute as well as the Corporate Design Foundation seek to promote the relationship between effective design and the successful corporation.

While the graphic designer's role today may not yet be as readily identifiable to the average individual as it is to the sophisticated corporation, it is worthwhile to point out the enormous impact the designer has on our society. Designers create the look and feel of our world. They are the arbiters of taste and establish, as well as lead the way, to how we perceive what's good, tasteful, stylish—or not, as the case may be. Virtually everything around us is created through design. The diversity and global reach of the designer's influence, through traditional and new media, is so vast it can be difficult to comprehend. Therefore, it certainly must not be overlooked or undervalued. Designers create and interpret sociological trends. They create the mood and shape of our world. Designers, therefore, must be worldly in the true sense of the word. They must be aware of all things that affect change and style. Politics and finance, entertainment and literature, fine arts and history, food and music—all play important roles in our constantly transforming environment. In other words, they must observe and, perhaps, partake in all facets of life. No one entering this field should be content with a confining definition of creativity. Creativity is not just the action of the imagination and a particular skill such as drawing, writing, or composing. You must also have the ability to analyze, assimilate, and interpret the past and present structures of society in order to interpret the present, as well as foretell the future.

As there is little in our daily experience that is not designed by designers, the graphic designer has an unusual opportunity to make a personal contribution to our world in this expanding business environment. As a designer, you can derive creative fulfillment from your efforts and still earn a reasonable, and in some cases sizable, income from those efforts. The combination of personal and economic satisfaction offers many individuals a gratifying avenue to apply their talent. Graphic designers, by and large, may sometimes complain about long hours and, perhaps, their pay scale, but mostly, they are a committed and satisfied group because they can always see a tangible result of their work effort. Importantly, I have never met a committed designer who did not feel passionately about their work and put the quality of their work before financial considerations.

And design is a field that is expanding. It's an exciting time to be in graphic design. Design firms are growing in their complexity and size. Like advertising, design is increasingly a global business. Many of the products and services marketed by the clients of large design consultancies are done so on a global basis. Cross-cultural design and marketing is an increasingly important aspect of communications. Another aspect of globalization is the effect of industry-wide mergers, joint ventures, and international expansion, all of which have combined to produce companies that are viable in the international arena.

While many firms have expanded through acquisition—such as buying out another design firm in another city—in the past few years many design firms have been acquired by advertising agencies. This is because of the recognition in the profitability of "below the line" companies as well as the understanding that these services are an integral component to the entire communications "package." The term "below the line" refers to companies without media placement. Agencies traditionally derive income from a percentage markup of media placement—meaning a markup on the dollars spent for their clients in buying time and space in broadcast (television and radio) or in print publications. New media and interactive media are redefining all concepts of media placement.

## CLEARING UP SOME CONFUSION ABOUT ADVERTISING AND DESIGN

Advertising differs from design in many ways. Advertising is always a visual and written solution to a marketing strategy. The message is to sell or market a product or service. The key word here is "sell." Never underestimate that intent. Whether it's television, print advertisements found in newspapers and magazines, direct mail, or direct response ads, it is all there to send the message "buy me."

In most agencies the key players are the creative team working in conjunction with the marketing account executives and planners (jokingly known as the "suits"). The creative team is composed of art directors and copywriters, who work in tandem. This combined team of creative and marketing talent devises the advertising strategy with and for the client. Each point of view offers another expertise to form the final direction. It is the media department who makes the necessary decisions for placement of the advertising in print and broadcast because they buy the space and time. In addition, the agencies have added to this mix their ownership or relationships with interactive media agencies to carry the message online or to wireless broadcast. Advertising is a huge business whose budgets dwarf those allocated to the design field. And as we all know, advertising is a powerful force in our media intensive society, saturating us with concepts like the Energizer Bunny or "Do you Yahoo?" which, when successful, become a part of our lexicon.

It is important to note that the business of advertising (as well as design) is ultimately its creative product. It is the art directors and the copywriters who "make" advertising. It is this creative concept that makes advertising, and the various areas of design, a unique business. And these are service businesses, another special characteristic. They are dependent upon the quality of their product and dependent on business relationships that "buy into" or believe in the power of the work as an effective business practice. Some advertising can be tracked to be made accountable, especially direct marketing and online advertising. Mostly, however, it is far more intangible—really a perception of success.

In any discussion of advertising and design, it should be noted that it is in sales promotion that the two disciplines meet. While sales promotion will be discussed at length in chapter 7, let it suffice to say now that the brochures, marketing tools, and point-of-sale products developed by the sales promotional divisions within advertising agencies need talent that can work with design values and marketing-driven concepts. These promotion groups, at their best, offer designers opportunities to work on a variety of diversified assignments not always available in studio environments.

Therefore, the two immediate distinctions between advertising and design are (1) design firms, while they may work in interactive media, by definition, do not place traditional media, and (2) designers generally do not create print advertising and television campaigns. When firms place media, they are considered, by definition, an agency. In recruiting talent for our clients, the ability for a designer to work with copy can frequently be a key ingredient in the job description. To work with copy means the designer must be able to visually interpret the copy concepts. Many graphic designers are more comfortable working strictly with graphic symbols, visual images, and systems design without incorporating headline concepts or detailed copy.

Designers produce product and image-driven visual solutions and tools for goods and services. Design, like advertising, can be produced on any scale or budget. Designers produce solutions for multinational firms, as well as export their expertise in image marketing all over the world. For example, consumer product corporations such as Avon or Colgate produce product design and packaging design to be sold throughout the world. The designs of these products may have to be altered for the cultural/marketing conditions of the geographical area, and in some cases, that may mean changing the name as well. An annual report or corporate brochure may be produced in many languages; a retail chain will need its graphic imaging subtly defined for another culture.

## DESIGN'S IMPACT ON STYLE

As the importance of design receives ever-increasing acknowledgment from the media, its impact can also be seen in the emergence of specialty gift shops marketing "design savvy" products as a sales tool. Design departments in museums have been highlighting the important role of graphic and industrial design for years. The Museum of Modern Art in New York, for example, has had a seminal role in design appreciation and has now mastered the art of merchandising chosen products through its store, catalogs and Web site. All of this attention bodes well for the growing prestige of the designer. It is a direct response to the proven influence design has on business profitability and an affirmation that design has created the look and feel of our world. Apple's design-driven products have created a culture of their own and influenced a host of products utilizing clear plastic and color. Design determines how we perceive what's good, tasteful, and stylish—or not—as the case may be. As noted earlier, corporate America is recognizing that design is good business and big business, and that it drives the marketing efforts for success. Good design sells, and a well-designed package can sell a product. A well-designed retail image will move shoppers and merchandise. An excellent corporate identity program can affect the entire perception of the company, even on Wall Street.

## SUCCESSFUL DESIGN IS A SUCCESSFUL BUSINESS SOLUTION

So the bottom line is the bottom line! The importance of the graphic designer and graphic design as a profession is ultimately its impact on business. Therefore, although graphic design incorporates an aesthetic experience and is a creative endeavor, it is its alliance to business, its ability to service clients' needs, that defines its place and status in today's economy. The art student pursuing a graphic design education must acknowledge design's role in the business community. Not to recognize this factor could only be an act of unnecessary idealism, as well as a foolhardy conclusion. Without question, the overriding common denominator of the most successful people in graphic design is their ability to maintain the highest creative standards without losing sight of their role as creators of business solutions.

I've often thought it a shame that fundamental business courses are not taught within the standard curriculum found in professional art colleges. Business insight is necessary to run your own business, to understand your clients' businesses, and to understand how to solve your client's problems. For most, it has been on-the-job training. If you are going to design an annual report, you'd better be able to understand what the financial data in the back of the book represents. If you're going to design a corporate identity program, you should have the knowledge of how that corporation functions in the marketplace, what you need to convey in terms of its image, and how that image will affect the company's internal structure as well as its external communications. In short, you need to know how the business community operates.

For many designers, much of their assimilation into business initiatives is achieved through working in collaboration with strategic planners, account executives, and marketing personnel within design firms. In fact, most large design firms define themselves as "Marketing Communications Consultants," and the creative head counts within these firms are less a percentage than the business management personnel. While these roles will be discussed in chapter 4, I now want to emphasize the necessity for the student or design professional to appreciate how important it is not to think of utilizing your creative instincts in the naïve vacuum of creating to make things "look wonderful." The role of the professional graphic designer is to identify the client's communication problems and to create solutions that are aesthetically pleasing, to communicate a proper message to the public, and to do so in a timely manner and on budget. Most hiring requests today emphasize the need for someone who is not only supremely talented, but someone "smart;" someone who understands the business needs of the firm and can verbally, as well as visually, communicate them.

## IS DESIGN FOR YOU?

The individual determined to seek a career in the creative arts often seems to recognize this goal from a relatively early age. The ability to draw is always admired in children and the encouragement often elicits the spoken ambition of becoming an "artist." Obviously, it's a long road from those origins to identifying graphic design as the chosen path. The roots, however, are important, but out of those roots must evolve a designer with a love of typography, color, and materials, with a desire to communicate through visual media. The designer must be a committed individual with a strong, determined desire to do good work. This book will point out the paths through the maze of choices within graphic design.

The designer must also become a sophisticated person, knowledgeable and articulate about politics, business, and all the arts—music, painting, history, food, and travel. The designer is a communicator. After all, how can one successfully communicate to a society without being a full-fledged citizen of that society? To compound the issue, our society is now global, and, therefore, everything needed on a national basis is now a global issue.

These are the characteristics of a successful designer. The profession is stimulating in its vast breadth and exposure to every sector of the global business community. The individual who desires this direction must be prepared to enter this community with the knowledge and skills required to make a contribution.

Finally, is graphic design for you? Only you can say for sure, but you can expose yourself through this book and other resources to allow yourself an educated decision. If you have the motivation, go for it. Having a passion for your work is critical, whatever that work may be. Many people change careers during their adult lifetime. Many do not end up doing what they thought they would. It is always fascinating to ask individuals you admire what they thought they would become. The answers are often surprising.

# The Structure of Graphic Design

2 &#9432;

**W**e have just examined the essential nature of graphic design and familiarized ourselves with the role of the designer in our society. It is now time to consider the nature of the creative product and how it services the marketing needs of business, and to discover the many parts which form the whole of graphic design. What may have seemed a simple classification is, in fact, an umbrella term for a sophisticated network of graphic-based communications disciplines. It is important to distinguish between these fields of endeavor for a clear understanding of the interrelationships within graphic design. A structural knowledge of the differing aspects of design is critical because although these aspects interface with each other individually, they connect and correlate with the whole. In addition, they characteristically define the role of the professional. This perspective needs to be seen with some historical context as well, for with the passage of time and the refinement of the business, we shall see how these fragments of graphic design have often branched off to form areas of specialization.

Therefore, the perspective offered in this and the next chapters should help people realize their career goals as well as more completely understand the essential nature of graphic design. And what are we talking about when we say graphic design? Classically, we mean the broad concept of branding, incorporating:

- Brand identity and packaging design
- Corporate identity—as applied to all visual identifiers, traditional and new media, logotype, and naming (or nomenclature)
- Corporate communications and corporate literature—including corporate promotion and annual reports
- Design for interactive media
- Editorial and publication design
- Environmental design—two- and three-dimensional design of a space, including architecture, branded environments or retail identity, and exhibition design (also considered a part of industrial design)
- Sales promotion (can be an adjunct to advertising)

Ask most people participating in these fields to name their profession within traditional media and they'll probably respond, graphic design. Within interactive media there are those who will refer to themselves as Web designers and/or information architects. These people are, of course, correct, but all that they do stems from graphic design training. Information architects produce the organizational structure and navigational flow, so while the product is not "graphic," the thinking that allows for this structure often comes from solving graphic communication systems. Web design and its applications are a graphic discipline. Information technologists (IT) are the specialists who make it happen but whose contribution to the projects are not the graphic visuals.

## THE RISE OF SPECIALIZATION AND THE RECENT CONVERGENCE OF MEDIA

In order to discuss these areas of specialization, as they relate to the whole and as individual fields of endeavor, let us use an old, but appropriate, metaphor. Consider this image: we are observing a large river with many smaller rivers and streams flowing into the main estuary. Can you visualize the great main waterway, its vitality and its bustling river traffic? We'll name this river Graphic Design. Now let us look at its tributaries. We will call them branding, Web design, packaging, publishing, and promotion, all flowing into and merging together to form Graphic Design. The river pilots of these tributaries understand how their water conditions are interrelated with the main river body, but they know their branch best. The pilots of the main riverboats have far-reaching itineraries, traveling up and down all the branching rivers. These pilots enjoy the ever-changing vista and are quite flexible; however, they may have to familiarize themselves anew with waters not often traveled or they may consult with the local experts. The branch river specialists, however, while aware of the total terrain, find that by limiting themselves to servicing their own river they have gained an increased knowledge of its waters. And whenever a traveler needs specific information about their river, they know they can be available for consultation.

This metaphor describes how specialization has evolved within graphic design. In most instances the specialization of these segments has become so highly refined that they have become design businesses with their own strong self-image and marketing strategy. Their strength is that they are experts in their specific knowledge base. These firms have become in many instances design/marketing consultancies and the emphasis is on the consulting aspects of their work. The globalization of trade and reach of communications beyond geographical considerations and into cyberspace has created a need to combine specialists. The convergence of media and experts to work together is producing working relationships not yet completely defined. Teams of specialists from every spectrum are working together on aspects of complicated projects and creating both a virtual and existing workplace that is most exciting, the detail of which we will discuss in the following chapters.

## MEETING THE CLIENT'S NEEDS

How specialization developed by responding to clients' requirements and how it now expands to encompass a variety of needed information specialists can be demonstrated by the following hypothetical example. It demonstrates the essential issue: that creating business solutions for clients becomes the driver for growth of services. And as our world of communications becomes more complex, so do the solutions.

Graphic design began with and still has many firms practicing a variety of disciplines. For example, let us consider a basic business scenario. We'll assume that graphic design firm A + B Associates, has a client, The Widget Corporation. TWC (as The Widget Corporation likes to be called) believes a new logotype to promote the introduction of its new line of improved widgets will benefit TWC's product introduction as well as the corporate image. A + B Associates creates the new widget identity, along with promotional brochures for TWC's sales personnel and customers, in-store banners, posters, counter cards, tee shirts, and buttons with the new logo for employees. It has also created the packaging system for the new widget line that will be responsive to the needs of warehouse storage systems. Everything is so successful that TWC asks A + B Associates to develop an advertising program that will keep the widget identity firmly in place in the public's mind and compliment the new design system. In addition, new dealer's sales sheets and parts catalog are assigned to A + B Associates. It's an excellent client/design firm relationship. Every time The Widget Corporation needs anything done, they know just who to call.

That's wonderful, you say. What could possibly be wrong with this picture? Well, nothing. There are many firms that have managed to maintain this sometimes enviable diversity of work. Some of these firms are internationally famous, and many are found in smaller cities such as Seattle or Atlanta. However, the motivating factors producing the current climate of specialization have always been the forces that drive the needs of business. When business has grown to certain proportions, many large corporations have a greater comfort level in choosing specialized design firms.

Let us once again turn our attention to The Widget Corporation. Eight highly successful years have passed. TWC has increased its output and manufactures fifty-three different consumer products. It also has "gone public" and now is listed on the New York Stock Exchange. TWC has recently diversified by acquiring several other corporations. TWC learns that it needs to court the financial community for funding. It is through the vehicles of its annual reports and quarterly reports that TWC can position the company properly with respect to the stock brokerage houses and the banks. The Widget Corporation's board of directors now believes it may serve the corporation's best interests to seek out a design firm that has a proven track record in dealing with the subtleties of producing such corporate literature. TWC has, additionally, discovered some of its products are losing their market share in the now more complex marketplace. After a consumer research study, TWC's market research firm has recommended a new packaging system that will allow their products to be more visually competitive. TWC clearly needs a firm that understands the research studies, their value and how to interpret the visual criteria and develop a creative strategy that will distinguish TWC's product from the competition. It will seek out a graphic design firm specializing in packaging design. And when TWC comes to believe that their corporate identity system no longer is appropriate for their new position in the marketplace, it seeks out a marketing communications specialist. After strategic analysis, this specialist may not only redesign the old TWC logo, but recommend changing TWC's name to something that will not be identified only with widgets but also can be easily adapted to the stock market ticker quotation requirements, adding to its recognition factor. The firm will recommend a total analysis of the branding program to insure that the communication of the identity program is consistent over all media, including its subsidiary firms and regional offices around the globe. All media means tradition and interaction so the program will include the need for a Web site to communicate its image, services, and products to the business community and consumer.

As you can see, this will require another level of sophistication in corporate communications, solved by either a company who has grown to include specialized departments, personnel who can interact, or working relationships with outside specialists. This combination or convergence of specializations is fed by the expanding methodology of communications and communication systems. As indicated, some of these systems require developing a structural analysis of the program to include a strategy, indicating how to choose methods or styles of communication.

Design is entering new areas of involvement. Experience design is being heralded as a way of identifying the reality of design in an age where all professions function in a cross-disciplinary way. Therefore, while the age of specialization is very much with us for many functional reasons, the interrelationships of these design-based functions become a critical component. Traditionally, firms that have limited their activities to certain areas of expertise discovered this limitation to be extremely advantageous to their own business, as it established them as the experts who solve specific problems. Thus, their reputation grew, identifying them as having the know-how required to fulfill a client's needs, and they in turn became finer-tuned within their specialization. So the restrictions feed upon themselves—setting up the dictum: The more specialized work you do, the more you become expert, the more specialized work you get. The difference today is that they often have to team in cross-functional efforts with other firms.

And what happened to the design firm that started working with TWC? It may be relegated to clients with simpler communication requirements or it may become part of a larger organization. Ultimately it cannot compete with the large globally-based communication design firms developed in the last fifteen years to service global corporations. Of the many challenges facing designers who service these large corporations, understanding and fully comprehending their global requirements can be the most compelling test. Brent Oppenheimer, partner and creative director of OH & CO in New York, states: "Globalism is something that we are also going to have to deal with. Some corporations have earnings that are larger than many of the economies of entire countries in other parts of the world. They now have a greater responsibility to communicate to their constituencies than they ever had before. Design is in the center of this enormous management task and is responsible for articulating what the position of the company is and where they stand."

## EXPERIENCE DESIGN

In the volume 1, number 1, 2000 issue of *Gain*, (*www.gain.aiga.org*), Richard Grefé, executive director of the AIGA declared, "A new discipline of design is emerging from the needs and forms of communication in the network economy. 'Experience Design' is a discipline created by the reality of communication today, when no point of contact has a simple beginning and end and all points of contact must have meaning embedded in them." The AIGA defines experience design as the formula (Form + Content + Context) - Time = Experience Design. The coverage goes on to include a fascinating chart designed by Clement Mok of Sapient (see below), describing the skills and professional specialties that compose this cross-disciplinary teaming. The value of this diagram is that it visually describes the diversity of design functions as well as the complexity of their interrelationships.

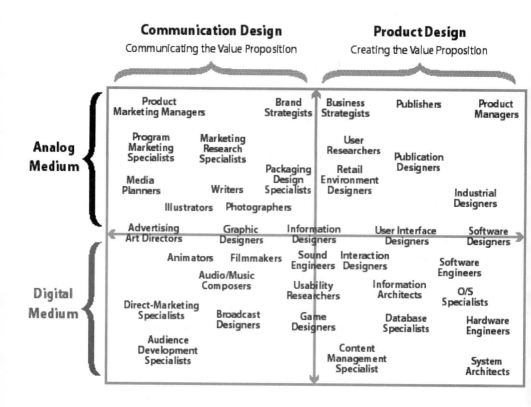

Source: Clement Mok for AIGA Experience Design

# THE EFFECTS OF MEDIA CONVERGENCE

The AIGA's concept of experience design points out their recognition of a need for definition. If it will become the defining method of describing this cross-discipline method of solving communication needs, only time will tell. It does point a way to what has up to now been described as media convergence. The TWC example offers a demonstration of this paradigm shift: the combination or synergy between these specializations, providing a cohesive brand vision for the client. Graphic design is changing at a rapid pace. Convergence, or experience design, reflects the need to communicate across various media platforms, and thus bring together specialists with a common goal. The expansion of media choices for communication and the need to service clients across all medias can be easily traced when one considers the growth of possibilities available: print, broadcast, Internet, intranet, and wireless. It also reflects the technological convergence as software systems become more ubiquitous. A sidebar to these changes is the business activity in mergers and the establishment of larger holding companies, developed to consolidate a multifaceted offering of services.

With these ever-expanding complexities factored in to solve communications needs and develop products, design firms have, in recent years, developed into very sophisticated strategic companies. They have had to be very resourceful, utilizing new analytical methods and technologies to stay responsive to a chaotic business climate. Design is also being recognized as a controlling force in communications. As Richard Grefé wrote in *Gain*, "When communication leaps across media at the speed of electrons, meaning is the only true currency. Design does not add value to this economy— design creates value." Remembering the Widget Corporation as our role-model client, we will now analyze the individual regions of graphic design with a look to the future.

# Branding and Design Management

## 3

The core message of this survey is the fact that graphic design is a business, and the various sectors of design are utilized as strategic marketing tools. The design business is unusual due to several factors: It is a service business, its product is creative, and it has no inventory. This statement requires the caveat that in reality, all business is creative and the generalization holds true that any successful business is probably directed by a very creative, entrepreneurial, and innovative individual. Most designers are so caught up in their own creative powers that they fail to recognize this reality. The particularly appealing element of the graphic design business is its output. The product of the service is creative and it is the quality of the design that is the driving force.

With recognition of the vigor and vitality of these factors influencing the business of graphic design, let's now immerse ourselves in the domain of graphic design.

## BRANDING

Branding as a concept of a method of communicating a product or service has been around for a long time. But the recognition of its value as a strategic device has escalated tremendously in the last five years. While we will not get into the various concepts and strategies of branding (see bibliography) this discussion will focus on the various roles the designer assumes in this important process.

Distinguishing the differences between branding and identity can be confusing, but one is the larger concept of the other and they can be used almost equally in this context. Identity or branding refers to image. Branding, in usage, refers to the large holistic concept of developing a brand by a method of how it is used. If there is one essential word we could attach to any part of graphic design or advertising, it is image. We are all in the image business in one way or another. We build and contribute value to the image of goods and services for every business imaginable. We do it through perception of the company's graphic "look" and we do it through hard or soft sell, advertising in print and various media. Identity is utilized as a strategic business tool. In graphic design, it falls into three basic categories. They are:

- Corporate branding/corporate identity
- Retail branding/branded environments
- Consumer product branding/packaging design

Additionally, there are components in any discussion of branding that must be included: the use and role of design management in the process and experiential/emotional branding as a concept to include all aspects of traditional and new applications. Marc Gobe, president, CEO, and executive creative director of d/g★ (Desgrippes Gobe), in New York puts it this way:

> The changes in our business have first come with the concept of Branding. Designers are asked to give a personality to products, companies, and people. We are expected to provide a different viewpoint on how a company can communicate. The arrival of the Internet and digital communication has brought a new set of opportunities to designers, allowing them to expand their skills beyond flat two-dimensional design to 3D, animation, and multisensorial experiences. We are living in a much more complex world where communication needs to work harder. The vehicles that carry communication, TV, posters, print, have now become digital and portable, entertaining and emotional. The role of today's designer has been expanded and now we have also to be solution-providers. We are not just creators of pretty design; we must be able to articulate a message accessible to many different media and relevant to many audiences.

## CORPORATE BRANDING AND CORPORATE IDENTITY

The methodology of corporate branding is the strategic positioning and creative impact of a company's image. Again, the use of the term branding or identity is almost synonymous, its use subject to how companies wish to position themselves. Branding has become the more popular description, as the connotation is broader in application than identity, and that is the term we will use. The usage of corporate branding refers to how the name and visual equity is assimilated by the viewer and all the socioeconomic associations incurred by that brand. How that brand is perceived by its clients, public, stockholders, and employees is a crucial element, and corporate branding is a key marketing tool in every facet of the company's communications. The branding/identity program affects all printed matter, advertising, interactive/digital media applications, building signage, trucks, uniforms, promotion materials, packaging, and any other possible conveyance of the corporate image.

Many design firms, large and small, take on identity assignments, and many designers consider themselves practitioners of corporate identity when they create logos and stationery systems. The large and/or highly specialized firms have the capability to stress in greater detail, and at a far more sophisticated level, the strategic planning components of corporate branding utilizing their teams of consultants, nomenclature experts, and account services staff, always starting with investigative research. (See chapter 4.) The scope of these comprehensive and fully realized programs are long-term projects often taking several years to complete. Such a program would require intensive study, which includes customer research, positioning the corporation within its competitive arena, of its internal corporate culture, including the firm's past, present, and future perceptions of itself. The process allows the consultant to recommend a strategy which will include evaluation of the company's name, its positioning in the marketplace, future trends analysis, and, finally, its visual image. One should note that the visual image is the final result of the strategic positioning, not the first step, as most designers would imagine.

Therefore, a sophisticated corporate branding practice includes an intensive period of strategic planning, assessment, and inventory of the internal and external operations of the corporation. This "audit" is accomplished by teams composed of the management group as mentioned: consultants, naming and branding experts, account executives, project managers, planners, and graphic designers, which can fluctuate, depending on the personnel available within the consulting firm. In structuring themselves as strategic consultants, many firms utilize a team of key executives comprised of their management consultant group, including the marketing staff (who initiated the client contact and sold the project) and the creative director to develop the core positioning strategy during this "phase 1" (development) period of the project. (In some firms the creative department may be excluded from the first phase of project definition altogether.) For other companies, the structure can mean the creative directors assume the account function without any other staff, or other variations of teams are created on an as-needed basis with independent consultants. The complexity and sophistication of these company structures and the strategic focus towards consulting can offer a vastly different perspective to the graphic designer who tends to think of corporate identity strictly in terms of the visual image. As these companies mature in their practice they tend to hire more consultant level personnel than designers (see chapter 4).

Ultimately, the structure and the environment of these firms have changed. For designers it means interfacing with a host of M.B.A. and account managers and being able to be a part of the team, often in client presentations and the ability to communicate with them. Designers have to stretch themselves intellectually, working with non-designers, all of whom have the same goal: to service the client with unique solutions. What this means to the designer and how the designer functions in this environment is accurately articulated by Kenneth Cooke, chief creative officer of Siegelgale.

> Rarely, if ever, does a client contemplate updating or completely changing their corporate or brand identity for purely, aesthetic reasons. Typically, there is an underlying business need or objective that is driving the project. Often, the problem, as presented by the client, is not really the problem. Brand strategists and/or consultants are responsible for uncovering the existing weaknesses in a client's brand strategy, developing new strategies, rationalizing or consolidating complex brand architectures, and generally keeping creatives honest by representing the client's point of view. This frees the creative group to focus on how to solve the problem instead of spending time trying to figure out what the problem is.

> I view brand strategists and consultants as members of the creative team, not as outsiders. They are critical in establishing performance criteria the creative must meet or exceed. Sometimes, creative people create for other creative people rather than the audiences who will be actually experiencing a product or service. Not having a vested interest in a particular execution allows brand strategists and consultants to question the validity of a concept or if it's actually communicating or not.

Most of these "noncreative" folk, the planners or brand strategists, are focused on the audit and phase 1 period of the process which develops surveys of all of the corporation's existing visual materials in current operation. The audit tracks inconsistencies in the materials, and perhaps, inconsistencies in logotypes. It is not uncommon for large corporations to have so many divisions functioning independently that over the years the logomark, color, and type can have many variations. It produces a contradictory and disjointed visual message weakening the entire impression of the corporate image. The audit's other purpose is to analyze the internal corporate mission. It is as if the audit takes the temperature of the company. By interviewing staff at different levels, the audit learns what the firm thinks of itself, what it believes it wants to accomplish, and what it believes it wants to communicate. Much of this focuses around the problems relating to the positioning of the corporation in the marketplace and creating a brand that delivers and supports its "brand promise" to the public. The brand strategists or planners concentrate on the perception of the corporation's brand and image, how that may need to be changed and how to deliver that change. Change management becomes an important part of this process when corporations merge or need to redefine themselves. The end result of the audit should be an extensive profile of the company, offering an assessment of the firm from within and from without. The process can then address the problem-solving requirements of the new and/or updated image and how to communicate this revitalized message with clarity and in a unique manner. The sheer number of people involved in this process attest to its complicated nature and the critical need to "get it right," as so much is at stake.

## THE DESIGN PROCESS

What then is the role of the designer in this process? When do the designer's skills begin to play into this complex process? Helen Keyes, managing director, creative at Enterprise IG in New York, helps us understand how the creative brief is developed and how designers work to maintain a consistency of image. Helen writes,

> From the agreed strategic positioning further research is carried out to test the viability of the thinking. When these results are gathered and the customer/consumer audience has "given the company/product permission" to move in that direction a comprehensive brief is created and socialized around both client and consultancy. Results may vary in the discovery phase of a project, some companies/product brands may need to be revitalized at every touch point with the exception of the logo element—some may need to be completely reinvented/repositioned within the marketplace. Mergers, acquisitions, and takeovers have contributed to the number of major brand renaming and repositioning projects that have happened in recent years, i.e., Bank of America was formerly Nations Banks and Bank America. So with audience permission to change a company/product the client will have

the key components of a design and communications brief in front of them.

At this point the brand and identity consultant will have a scope of work, timetable, launch initiative, ongoing implementation, and communications plans in place for the client. Some clients have urgent requirements due to legal constraints, i.e., mergers and others have 2-5 year plans in place because they will look at the cost versus impact for their brand introduction. Shareholders are a high consideration in any branding exercise and the cost to a company can be significant in implementation and socialization.

With an agreed brief and scope of work the brand and identity consultant will start the creative process alongside the strategic planning and communications initiatives that need to be carried out. In the case of a brand name change, the lengthy creative process will begin involving all parts of the consultancy. Brainstorming ideas, putting together long lists, editing, searching, linguistics, availability, and getting to a shortlist for presentation to the client for final choice approval and usage.

Meanwhile, the design process will begin working with the approved names and design brief. Numerous images and ideas will be created that capture the vision of the new brand. Mood boards, image criteria, and symbol generation, as well as typographic exercises, will begin and these ideas will be reviewed and organized for presentation to the creative director. Design routes will be pursued to reflect the thinking behind the brand and these will be presented to the client several times over until a shortlist of contenders is agreed upon. These designs will be tested with the appropriate audiences to gauge the acceptability of the new designs with them, as well as finding out if there are any negative connotations associated with the work. It is important to remember people are always uncomfortable with any new concept—especially when a familiar brand or brands are being replaced. It is human nature to want to hang on to the old and familiar —even though progress is inevitable and, more importantly, expected by the marketplace.

Having agreed upon a new name or logo to represent a brand, the job of "selling it in" to the internal audience has to be done. The brand and identity consultant will organize with the client the task of communicating the new brand and the thinking behind it. This may take the initial form of pinpointing brand integrators and creating brand ambassadors within an organization (people senior enough to have the respect of their employees), who will back and reinforce the need for change and build ownership of the new brand leading by their example and actions.

An internal launch will be organized, sometimes having to touch hundreds of thousands of employees in one event across the globe. This is a time when the client can be met with hostile employees who may be scared of change and not wish to embrace another belief system/ vision within their workplace. Communication and brand leadership is key at this point and much time and effort should be spent on employees. They are, after all, the true embodiment of any brand—a rude FedEx delivery person will shatter your expectations as effectively as a late package.

With everyone on board, a public/customer launch is planned and organized. This may take some time if a brand is going to go public; many things have to be in place for that day, from stationery and forms to signs for a financial institution, to new vehicle livery, plane interiors, meal tray designs, in-flight entertainment, to airport signage for an airline. The type of business a client is in dictates the numerous design and communications initiatives faced by a brand and identity consultant on a day to-day-basis.

Having organized a launch, successfully gone public, and invested in a sometimes massive communication program with advertising and public relations agencies, the huge task of building brand awareness and internal ownership continues. "A brand is for life"—it needs to be nurtured, cared for, loved, and have a driving passion for success behind it. This must all come from within an organization. If you do not believe in your brand or product and cannot deliver on its promise it is less likely to succeed.

## BRAND ARCHITECTURE AND DESIGN IMPLEMENTATION

Brand architects are most often design trained systems specialists who can analytically design a matrix of how a brand is distributed to companies that perhaps have a common holding company and/or different divisions within a corporation. Wherever the brand would have a logical usage, where the brand "lives," the designer has to structure a brand architecture for those applications. It is easy to understand that where the brand should exist can be an important strategic and marketing decision.

To formulate how the implementation and application of the visual image is made, standards are developed for use by all designers, advertising agencies, corporate offices in other cities/countries, and for any vendors using the visual elements of the brand. In other words, anyone can have the proper guidelines to work from. These guidelines set the standards and criteria for all who need to access information in utilizing the identity for any application, such as stationery systems, Web sites, publications, transportation vehicles, signage, retail environments, advertising, packaging, or the like. The key, goal is to maintain strong visual brand language that can be delivered appropriately in the marketplace. Servicing the brand and the audience and using the brand in an intelligent way is mandatory, and while consistency is key it is not an inflexible methodology, but a system that can be difficult to maintain without such design standards.

Before the ability to disseminate information by means of Web sites, Zip discs, and CD-ROMs, an extensive identity manual would be required, most often produced in a series of ring binders of hundreds of pages. Today, that process has been streamlined, condensed, and information pinpointed to a particular user utilizing a variety of media, and the use of intranet manuals have revolutionized this practice for internal corporate communications. Identity standards continue to be critical in controlling and maintaining visual consistency for corporate communications, and are particularly effective when large corporations require this uniformity on an international scale or throughout complex organizational structures of holding companies and/or subsidiary firms.

## NOMENCLATURE/NAMING

Nomenclature is the art of naming as applied to the branding of corporations, services, or products. Within the product categories, naming is most often applied to new products coming to market. These products can include any consumer goods products, from food to automobiles. The emphasis has been on new products being brought to market, and there has been an explosion of new products in the pharmaceutical and health and beauty aids (HBA) categories and the multitude of names developed for the explosion of dot com companies (i.e., Yahoo!). These are, by definition, totally new names, creatively developed from the lexicon. A few examples would be Nissan, Vioxx, Origins, and Viagra. There are thousands all around you. This process of naming requires a tremendous effort in legal search to determine if these names do not exist on a global basis and if the names do not have any negative connotations in different languages. Names, like colors, can mean different things in different cultures. Additionally, any naming and its branding implications must be viewed in context to the applicability to Web site URLs and their availability.

The first phase of the new or revised vision of the corporation will address the firm's name. Does the name still communicate what the consensus believes the company represents? Should the name be changed subtly or dramatically? The issue of "equity" is a most significant factor. Equity means how readily a name, its logotype, and corporate message are recognized by the public. If the recognition factor is very strong there may be less tampering with its intrinsic character and emphasis may be placed on modernization or establishing an updated look. The protection of the equity is a fundamental consideration in any name or image change. These are the essential questions that must be answered at this stage. Naming is the key component to the corporate branding process and the process is most often identified as nomenclature. Name changes are common with mergers, and mergers represent a key market for new corporate identity business. When companies are merged or acquired, something, if not everything, will need to be changed. Nomenclature is part of a corporate identity firm's services and the firm either employs a staff expert or works with other independent nomenclature consultancies who function as naming and branding consultants.

There are some interesting examples of excellent work by the nomenclature experts, and some extremely bad choices as well. Citicorp is an interesting example. It originally was the City Bank of New York until it determined its mission was to become an international bank. Today, Citicorp continues to use that name (you can find its Web site at *www.citicorp.com*) and uses the Citi logo but is also know as Citigroup (who uses its own name as a Web site *www.citigroup.com*). Citigroup includes Citibank, Salomon Smith Barney, Travelers Insurance, and PrimeAmerica Financial Services, in addition to others, which they advertise as "strong brands," and, of course, they continue to expand through acquisition. Sometimes name changes are required to differentiate between divisions of large global corporations or to create a separation, and a company's need to position itself in the changing marketplace can mandate a new brand.

A high-profile and controversial example of a rebranding program is that of Andersen Consulting, who after a legal battle to break free from its global parent, Andersen Worldwide, and sister company, Arthur Andersen, the accounting firm, needed to create a name change. A company program called BrainStorming produced almost 2,700 entries from its employees in forty-two countries, and the result was Accenture, "suggesting the consulting firm's accent on the future" (effective January 1, 2001) as reported in the *Wall Street Journal* of October 27, 2000. An indication of the complexity of such a change facing a global firm is indicated in the Accenture press release which reads:

> Accenture was selected after an intensive three-month research and analysis process involving thousands of candidate names. A shortlist group of about 50 names, all of which met the positioning and personality criteria for the firm, was evaluated globally for trademark and

URL availability, possible cultural sensitivities, and local market pronunciation. The initiative was led by Andersen Consulting's global marketing team and supported by the international branding and identity firm Landor Associates, as well as law firms in more than 49 countries, who conducted the more than 3,000 trademark searches required under the project's tight deadline. In choosing the name, every effort was made to tap into the creativity of the people who know the firm best—its 65,000 professionals.

Another recent example of a name change was the establishment of Verizon from Bell Atlantic. Some names are developed in response to their symbol on the stock market. Nobody refers to IBM as International Business Machines. Spin-offs cause the need for new names and identities. Lucent Technologies represents a spin-off of AT&T. How these identities are managed throughout the system is a complex process that is mirrored in many other similar corporations. These are a few corporate examples. The naming of products and the relationship to new product development dovetails with branding efforts. As new products, branding for consumer products, corporations, or business services are developed and introduced, their chosen name is the essential component of the recognition factor.

It is only after all of these studies that the graphic designer can begin to delve into the visual systems that will create the solutions needed. Systems design is what a lot of identity design is all about. It is the operable visual systems that will bring clarity and order to the strategy of image. Another important advantage of establishing a workable solution is the cost savings to the company. The elimination of duplications in forms and printed materials often save enough money over the long run to justify much of the cost of the CI program. However, this is not the sole motivating factor in a firm's decision to take this route. The reordering of image is far more profound.

## DESIGN MANAGEMENT

Design management has grown as a profession and is now an acknowledged, integral part of the process for any corporation who is concerned about how their brand is managed and/or whose product focuses on consumer goods. Classically the role of a design manager falls into two categories: those working with consumer products and those working on maintaining the corporate brand (the logo cops, as they are sometime, smilingly referred to). While we will cover the design managers as they relate to packaging in that section, here the discussion will be restricted to corporate branding.

Once the system is designed, the paramount need is to implement the program with adequate quality control. If the program is not scrupulously administered by the corporation, it will eventually fall into disarray and create many of the same problems that triggered the corporate branding program's initiation. Should the firm be large and widespread, controlling the identity program can be a full-time task. The design firm responsible for a rebranding program may introduce training programs for various managers within the company and will probably suggest the need for a design management director for corporate identity (if there isn't a person in place already). Often, this experience will provide designers with a career segue to the corporate side as design managers.

The problems incurred in the management of identity programs can often be closely linked to rebranding. In October 2000, Reto Ruppeiner, director, Novartis International AG, presented an excellent case study at the Design Management Institute's (DMI) annual conference, which, for our purposes, highlights the dimensions and linkage of the nomenclature process and design management challenges inherent in a "mega-merger." The Novartis International example is most interesting, for in 1997, the Swiss multinationals Sandoz and Ciba created the largest corporate merger to date. As outlined in the DMI conference manual, "Instead of combining the names of the two proud companies, as had been the case in the pharmaceutical industry, they chose to create something completely new. The challenges of gaining external and internal acceptance for the new Novartis name and logo were enormous. The logistics of implementing a new global branding strategy for a wide variety of products and independent companies with various degrees of corporate integration were daunting." The case study goes on to analyze the lessons learned, the problem incurred in developing a new visual identity, and how that identity was implemented throughout the corporation. This implementation includes dealing with the requirements of intranet and Internet communication as it applies to e-commerce.

Maintaining corporate standards and communicating the role of the branding program within the corporation is often a difficult role. Additionally, design managers must interface with upper management and people more classically trained in marketing. When I asked Peter Phillips, a design management consultant, his view on the changing role of design managers, he responded:

> For a great number of years, a corporate design manager could be successful simply by being a good administrator, a good mentor and motivator to his or her design staff, and a good designer. But all of that is no longer enough. Today, the successful corporate design manager has to be proficient in all of the above plus considerably more. Today's design manager must become a truly strategic business partner for every function in the organization. The design function can no longer be

perceived as simply a "service" organization. One can argue that design groups do provide a service, but the law department, human resources, procurement, finance, marketing, sales, and nearly every other function in the organization also provide services. The difference is that those other functions have not traditionally been viewed as strictly service groups. Most of them have been involved in developing overall business strategy for years while design has not.

There are many reasons for this phenomenon, but I believe the core issue is that design groups have charged hourly fees for services while the others have not. It is very easy for senior management to perceive a group that does work for a fee as expendable. After all, you could easily buy that service externally. Design managers have often complained that they are not participants in various processes at an early enough stage of a project. This is usually because they are not considered contributors to the overall business strategy of the organization and, therefore only need to be called in when actual design work is needed.

Today's design manager must become involved in all aspects of the company's business strategy. They must minimize the perception that they simply "provide a service." To do this they must become far more proactive as business "partners." They must network effectively throughout the organization. They must focus more on the overall effort to increase market share, shorten time to market, increase shareholder wealth, and develop a powerful competitive advantage. They need to talk less about aesthetics and design and more about how design is a problem solving discipline geared toward increasing profitability. Unfortunately, most design schools have not offered much to students in these "business" areas. Design managers must find ways to educate themselves in the business of business. They must also learn how to effectively present the value of design in non-design terminology. The most successful new design managers I have met in the last few years have told me they have pursued graduate degrees in business administration or enrolled in executive education programs simply to survive in a corporate environment. I wholeheartedly endorse these activities for design managers.

Since the design manager is often coming to this position as a creatively educated individual, the success of their endeavor often rests on the individual's, own innate management skills. Educational programs developing the skill bases required for these senior management people have been increasing and organizations such as the Design Management Institute (*www.dmi.org*) have been very effective.

## RETAIL IDENTITY

Retail identity (RI) works in the same manner as corporate identity and is often a part of a comprehensive CI program. In recent years, it has been separated as a specialized area because of the rise of an important and large market in specialty retailing. Initially, retail was considered just another form of CI and much of its business was (and in some cases still is) funneled through standard CI departments. While most people generally associate retail with shops and stores, it can also mean gas stations, banking centers, ATMs (automatic teller machine stations), and anything you would find in a shopping mall or airport.

This form of identity establishes the marketing image of the retail environment. Environmental design strongly dovetails and sometimes includes retail identity. It duplicates the strategic planning of corporate identity, but the specialized focus is on retail marketing. Therefore, how the retail image is designed and marketed to the public is the designer's mission. Companies that have a public space, such as retailers or banks or airlines, work to define their brand in all area of consumer interface. Designers work to apply the strategic positioning to the environments consistent with the brand through the appropriate choice of furniture, materials, colors, lighting, and graphics. An airline lounge should speak as clearly about their identity as the plane.

Retailers are the most aggressive at fully integrating the brand program. Marketing success is dependent on customer recognition and comfort. The experience in the store should be an extension of the marketing program. The Gap is often cited as the most successful in an integrated expression of their identity, from advertising to store design and merchandising to packaging. Cosmetics companies are another group identified with their selling environments. These shops or counters highlight graphics related to the marketing and advertising programs; the shapes or materials are related to the product packaging; all are designed to attract a recognized demographic target audience. In banks, a brand "eye" will be looking at the overall feel of the public space, the displays of brochures, the ATM surrounds, and the interface design to ensure a consistent customer experience.

Creative solutions for retail environments are strongly influenced by buyers and merchandisers, as well as marketing and advertising firms. At the high end visual stylists like Simon Doonan at Barneys are practically rock stars. But this need to be immediately identifiable in an increasing "noisy" world means new extensions of a brand presence. We are seeing increasing reach of consumer product brands into the environment driven by promotional activity. Frito-Lay is working on promotions that "brand" a supermarket aisle through floor supergraphics, systems of shelf talkers or end caps and co-displays of soda and chips. Although the design may start with a logotype, it will ultimately extend to the layout of the environment (again, possibly working with environmental designers), banners, shopping bags, signage and packaging. For a full description of branded environments, see chapter 6.

## BRAND IDENTITY AND PACKAGING DESIGN

Branding and packaging can rarely be separated. Traditionally, many packaging design firms were only involved with the package itself. As the significance of the design's effect on the product's marketing was recognized, design firms began to participate with the total image of the product (hence, designing the brand image). For our purposes, however, let's separate the two.

Branding or brand identity (BI) simply deals with the logotype and naming of the product. However, it is a far from simple imaging problem, for the brand equity (the same "equity" factor as discussed in corporate identity) is the most important instrument of the marketing strategy. If that equity is to be changed, it has to be done in a manner that will not destroy, but enhance, the history of that equity. A classic example would be a study of the Coca-Cola or Pepsi-Cola logo and how each has slowly and gradually changed over the years. These visual images are the icons of our culture. The subtle changes are testimony to how incremental the updates are over the years and, most importantly, the need to make changes without the public's awareness and yet with their acceptance as thinking of the product as contemporary. The manner in which these changes are achieved to update an image without changing the equity of the old is the key to branding. Sometimes changes to the visual image are a result of a marketing strategy in trouble. When Pepsi developed its campaign of a young, trendy drink (The Pepsi Generation), making Coke look stodgy, Coke responded with Classic Coke. It resulted in one of the best marketing/branding solutions possible. And while the packaging returned updated variations of the original bottle, the strategy also allowed for an enormous variety in Coke packaging design.

It is usually estimated that a brand and package has a life span of perhaps eight years, with shorter time periods depending on the market, at which point it may need to be updated. Those guidelines have been re-analyzed in our fast and faster society and products are being updated on a quicker timetable. The significant word that must be clearly stressed is "update."

The equity of a product and name is the reputation and goodwill of that product. The equity of a corporation or product is the essential marketing tool challenging the designer. You can be sure the corporation's product managers are very cautious to protect any changes that might challenge the image's equity as revealed in the product's positioning and market share. Graphic designers must learn the company's marketing strategy before they can begin to tamper with the design. They must be able to communicate on equal terms with the brand and product managers. These are the classic M.B.A. (Master of Business Administration) folk who, chances are, have never taken a design course, just as designers rarely have access to marketing in their undergraduate curricula. While the problems inherent in this situation are clear, these two constituents are in partnership and must work as a team to bring the solutions to fruition. The graphic designer must recognize and have an understanding of a design brief with its marketing objectives as well as the strongest points of the brand's equity and understand that the path to success requires communication with the marketing and business powers that be. These skills are imperative to the process. While both designer and marketer should learn in this process, the designer must aggressively absorb the appropriate marketing language and savvy to achieve the established goals.

Packaging design has had a powerful impact on the advertising and marketing of consumer products, since it has long been recognized as the last point of communication with the consumer. Advertising's role is to condition the individual's product perception (for example, how you feel about a product). This is often achieved through the study of focus groups and the use of quantitative and qualitative analysis. It also establishes its status and identifies its audience. Advertising can promote a product or offer incentives to buy the product. It is packaging, however, that performs the former (the product must be ready to show in the ads) and latter tasks of presentation to the consumer.

The package communicates in advertising when an image of it is displayed in tandem with the advertising copy in print ads. However, its strongest impact is on the shelf. It is in the retailer's arena that the package must stand out against its competition. The marketing researcher's role is to control the focus groups and research studies to determine how the product is perceived and accepted by the public. Does the package (and the advertising) send the message determined by the corporate marketing and product managers? Is the color, design, size, and positioning of the branding correct? The designer's priority is to manipulate these elements to solve and precisely communicate these objectives. The package becomes a three-dimensional advertisement and it operates at the last place of consumer resistance or impulse—the crucial moment the consumer reaches for the product on the shelf. The designer's challenge is to consider shelf impact: Does it communicate at the point of purchase (POP)?

Packaging design also consists of many technical elements that the graphic designer needs to know. There is the physical structure of the package itself. The materials, printing, and engineering are some of the elements tangential to the design. Product or industrial designers can provide the three-dimensional design needed as well as packaging engineers. In addition, the designer is currently faced with concerns about ecology, and must decide how to eliminate unnecessary boxes and how to use environmentally safe materials and printing processes. Corporations are beginning to embrace the concept, and consumer awareness of ecological needs is rising. Public conscious raising on ecologically safe packing products has still not proven to be a successful marketing strategy. Delays in retooling are caused by uncertainty of consumer acceptance along with the costs of the necessary changes in production. Federal regulations have also mandated changes in packaging labeling. How the size, actual content, nutritional elements, and ingredients are displayed are now controlled under the Nutrition Labeling and Education Act of 1990, which mandated compliance by 1994. All these factors challenge the graphic designer's ability to create a successful design that is responsive to the criteria established by the client.

Packaging design, like all the divisions of graphic design, has experienced rapid computerization, and therefore the restructuring of their workforce. The Apple Macintosh environment is the market standard, and design firms are online. They are able to complete color and layout variations at speeds unknown before. They are also very successful in implementing the line extensions as required. Line extensions contain the modifications for a product's variations, such as a jam line whose label will change color with different flavors, or a shampoo that requires different labels for dry or oily, scented or unscented.

The computerization of design firms has created another, more substantive change in the emerging character of these firms, which divides them into two distinct groups. First, firms that can manage the required strategic planning and product positioning are moving to the forefront of industry leadership. These firms' projects are the large national and multinational brands with many SKUs (Stock Keeping Units, a count of every unit of change in a product's size or line extension, such as how many units are spun off a single product). Second, there are many small design groups, perhaps less than ten people, who work on smaller brands or less complicated projects. Computerization has made these firms fast and nimble. There are also numerous individuals who, with their own computer installations, can work from home either on freelance projects or work for other design firms, often transmitting the work by modem. This is a particular boon to those with young families. Flextime exists in design management as well as in design firms, especially at this time in the market, with a shortage of really knowledgeable designers. Computerization has also caused a particular challenge to the field in relationship to changes in the pricing structures. The pricing of projects and the demand for speed has the negative effect of turning the work of these firms into a commodity, an item that is purchased on the premise of delivery on time for the lowest price. The positive result of this challenge has forced larger firms to offer the value-added services associated with strategic planning along with the graphic expertise, through their staffing of consultants and account services. These firms, therefore, become powerful marketing consultancies, offering a broader range and far more important role in the development of a product than simply design.

Packaging design has the enviable attribute of being almost recession-proof. In difficult economic times, corporations may not earmark funds for research, development, and new products, and they may cut back on their advertising budgets. But they do recognize that certain products will be bought, no matter what. How will they command control of the consumer at the point of purchase? Through the package! History has proven that while design firms can be downsized, they rarely let go of their prized designers. They find other ways to economize. My experience has shown there has always been a market for excellent packaging design talent.

## PACKAGING DESIGN MANAGEMENT

Successful packaging designers develop such savvy in marketing that their career paths become quite flexible with many options. After years of apprenticeship and experience in design firms, many find their futures may include not only becoming a key player with possible equity in their firm, but the ability to transfer their skills to the corporate sector. They can assume positions within corporations in design management. Design management positions usually entail managing product lines from the creative point of view within the corporation. Design managers rarely have hands-on creative responsibilities, but rather manage the process by working in liaison with the corporation's product and marketing groups, as well as controlling the creative process by supervising design studios and vendors. Design managers must be able to make critical taste judgments, articulate marketing objectives, and work within the corporate environment. Some other designers go on from their creative responsibilities to take the management positions stressing strategic planning, account services, or new business development. Some prefer to operate small independent design firms or to become permanent freelancers. The required skill and specialized knowledge of packaging establishes their value, whichever direction they choose.

I asked Pamela DeCeasar, director of packaging and brand design at

Kraft, as an experienced design manager, to describe the skills required by corporations today. She characterized them thusly:

Package design management requires a unique blend of right and left brain thinking, skills, and actions. Managers of a creative process within a corporate environment need to possess a knowledge and understanding of all aspects of creative development, as well as skills to create win-win partnerships and navigate design through what is often a complex and subjective business environment.

Excellent design management begins with having and articulating a vision for the brand that can successfully support the brand's business objectives. This starts with an intuitive or right brain understanding of how the brand currently functions within the marketplace and how it must change or be enhanced to communicate its core essence to consumers and induce sales. It is inexorably linked to consumer's perceptions, trends, the competitive mix, and ultimately, business goals.

But having a brand vision is just a starting point in design management. When action is called for, it must be defined, communicated, and planned through layers and players within a corporation whose responsibility it is to provide functional insight and support. Most corporations have established methods for managing brand design; they are always tactical and in the best case tactical and strategic. Access to key decision-makers that can champion out of the box aligned with every image the consumer experiences. Great vision, know thinking, and innovative design processes pave the way for the greatest strategic brand design success.

Finally, having a vision for the brand and knowledge of how to navigate though the twists and turns of process is not complete without external partners—brand design firms—to support the vision. Design management truly comes to life with external partners whose role it is to collaborate on the brand vision and bring it to life with great creative solutions. The best, most relevant brands are those that present their brand face to consumers in a seamlessly integrated manner across all communication media. Design management excellence is the ability to create brand images that truly reflect the core essence of the brand, and are flawlessly how supportive relationships can make it happen.

Additionally, Deborah DiFronzo, Roz Goldfarb Associates recruiter for packaging, offers this advice to those in this field: "With current conditions, more and more find having a hands-on approach is needed, including an understanding of the programs used to create work in order to direct freelance and staff or be able to pinch hit in a crisis." And Deborah adds as advice to all designers:

First, it obviously helps if you have a passion for good design, and that can mean different things to different people. Whether on the design or the corporate side, you want your work to be the best it can be, as well as answer the client's needs and fulfill their objectives. You should be a very detail-oriented, well organized person as well as a good communicator—these skills are essential. Today, designers are not only packaging and branding for shelf impact, but also for the Web. How these packages are perceived digitally as well as in print has opened an exciting new area and created additional demand for package designers presently and in the future. I also believe that it is to both the designer and design manager's advantage to walk in each other's shoes, in order to understand the processes, demands, and requirements of each others job! Lastly, I would advise designers to learn as much as possible from engineers, printers, and industrial designers in regards to structure and the ability to produce a cost-efficient and functional product and bring it to market in a timely manner.

# Design Consulting Services: The Business Side

## 4

In the previous chapter we reviewed the importance of the relationship between designers and the consultants working within creative companies. This chapter will expand on that theme, discussing an area of tremendous growth opportunity for people interested in working within a company where the deliverable is a creative product. Marketing communications firms and advertising agencies have long recognized the need for individuals who can assist their clients with the day-to-day tactical requirements of maintaining and servicing the account. Strategic planning and strategic branding have added new aspects to the substance of a design firm's services. By presenting clients with strategic solutions, using standard business analysis practices, quantitative and qualitative, have produced companies that are consultants to their clients in all aspects of the strategy and structure of a creative solution. The result is a company that can provide a client with an enrichment of thought and process far beyond the visual solution. Unfortunately, those firms who cannot provide strategic counseling find their work and business becoming a commodity for hire.

Carbone Smolan is an excellent example of a design firm that recognized the limitations of only delivering visual solutions. Leslie Smolan, partner, has observed many changes in the twenty-five years that she and Ken Carbone have had an office.

> Every day the design business becomes more about servicing. One major change is that recently we have added an account staff to our

firm. The account person becomes an objective advocate for both sides and takes care of the administration work on the project as well as the relationship with the client. In the past five years they have become an essential part of both the business and the creative team. In the past we used to think that our work spoke for itself and never made any sales effort. We were successful without one and 99 percent of our business came from referrals. But with the formation of the new business group, we are dedicated to a more proactive approach; we've worked on our presentation, developed our own brand, and now have people out selling. CSA has evolved into a hybrid agency; changing our name from "Carbone Smolan Associates" to "Carbone Smolan Agency" made a huge difference in how we were perceived. We keep tinkering with the business; this is how we stay fresh and relevant.

My advice to someone who wants to work in account management or new business development is to bring something more, some knowledge base that a design firm does not have experience in. Being a client first and then changing sides is one way to do this. For those who are still students or just starting out, you need to educate yourself about the management side of the business. Understand the financial aspect of the work including proposals, estimates, and budgets. Develop your communication skills. Switch your brain over to the client side and know the strategy, challenge, and results of the projects. The information is there if you want to find it.

Ken Carbone found this in a fortune cookie and it has since become our company motto: "The road to success is always under construction."

## TITLES, TITLES, TITLES

While titles vary tremendously from firm to firm, the business and noncreative personnel in a creative firm generally consist of individuals described as follows:

- ☛ Account executives
- ☛ Account services
- ☛ Project managers
- ☛ Implementation managers
- ☛ Consultants
- ☛ Strategic planners
- ☛ Brand strategists
- ☛ Researchers
- ☛ Marketing
- ☛ Marketing/sales

In each category there exists a hierarchy relating to experience and responsibilities. Therefore, within each area there are assistant, associate, senior, manager, director, vice president, executive vice president, and principal or partner level positions. As an example, if we are discussing "Consultants," there can be associate consultant, managing consultant, and senior consultant positions. At the top of this hierarchy exists the managing director and the "C" people: the CFO (chief financial officer), the COO (chief operating officer), CMO (chief marketing officer), CEO (chief executive officer), and CSO (chief strategy officer). These designations have become very popular and we may experience more "Cs" to come.

## BUSINESS ROLES

Account executive titles are more common in advertising agencies. Account services, project managers/directors, and implementation people usually find their day-to-day activity in servicing the projects, liaising between clients, creative, possibly working in production, and having responsibility for scheduling and delivering the project on time and on budget.

Consultants', strategic planners', and brand strategists' responsibilities fall more into the problem solving areas, working on concepts before the creative work and usually very closely with the creative staff. The researchers provide the data and investigative materials for the projects.

Marketing, marketing sales, and business development talent are always the key players in this business mix, providing the leads generation and marketing strategy to propel a company forward. There are no general guidelines for marketing/sales structures within companies. Firms existed (and still do) by reputation. The past years have seen an expansion of the aggressive marketing of design services. Most firms no longer simply rely on the referral process or on the sole ability of the principals to develop business. To many, aggressive marketing can include a combination of researchers, telemarketing, account services personnel, and marketing executives solely devoted to the new business effort. Sometimes these individuals are multi-tasked, responsible for everything from cold-calling to closing on a client. More often, in larger firms, there is a department that will control not only the new business function but also the marketing of the firm's image through public relations efforts. That would include a voice in how the firm is marketed through its printed materials and Web site. Growth is always mandated and this is a highly compensated area for those who are able to represent and market a creative product or service company. The ability to successfully market a creative service is the most important component to any design business. Bringing in the business is, of course, critical to any firm's survival. In the past most new clients came to design offices through the referral process.

Some of these marketing executives enter design with an MBA degree. They may have had prior experience as a product manager in a corporation or worked in an advertising agency on an account team. However, many of these executives started their careers in design and found they had a knack for the business side. Some moved into this area as designers who became account services executives. Some designers went on to get their M.B.A.s.

Directors of communications positions exist in many agencies as well as corporations. These individuals' job descriptions can vary considerably, stretching the emphasis from those people who seem to function as advertising or design managers responsible for the control of the quality and content of corporate communications and the creative image, to those whose function is closer to controlling the public relations and marketing effort. One of those individuals is Sarah Haun, who worked at Pentagram before joining Red Sky Interactive as director of communications. Her perspective offers a reality check on what it takes to succeed in such a position.

> Great communications skills, of course—writing and talking and listening—are essential. Creativity and a sense of humor are top traits for this job, too, especially when you're crafting messages, pitching stories, and participating in the development of collateral, site copy, presentations, and other communications. You also need to have sensitive "antennae" for newsworthy issues and what will and won't get past a typical reporter's sensitive BS detector. (This is why many of the best people in PR are former journalists.) It helps to be diplomatic. In putting together a story or promotion piece, a communicator will often discover discrepancies between the sanctioned corporate message and what's really going on. It takes a lot of tact and persistence to get to the bottom of these issues without ruffling feathers. It's also important to be thick-skinned and levelheaded. When management doesn't heed your advice, an editor turns down your pitch, or a reporter slams your company in black and white, it can be especially tough going. Since your career depends on good long-term relationships, you are often the one who has to take the heat—and then go explain the situation to other parties involved. Finally, and perhaps most importantly, you have to be honest and straightforward to earn the trust and respect of your colleagues and clients.

Sarah goes on to offer insight into her job and working within a design-based firm:

> I'm pleased to say the job has gotten much better and more interesting because of three major trends: 1) the increasing public awareness of

design, 2) the greater sophistication of the designer as a PR "client," and 3) the heightened importance of Internet activity on brand. Another positive trend in recent years is that designers and design firms. . . are becoming more aware of the value of good communications. Most of the good ones are fanatical about employee communications—since the sensitivity that makes designers open to new ideas also makes them fragile to criticism, creatives tend to be high-maintenance employees—so that is usually a matter of refinement as opposed to starting from scratch. But designers have traditionally kept to themselves and stayed out of the public light. Now many are more aware of the opportunities to make their value known to the world, and eager to take advantage of them... In handling media relations, my job used to be nine parts explaining what design was and why it was important to business, and one part making a specific pitch. Now the formula is reversed. Just think how many times the word "brand" has appeared on the cover of a business magazine in the past couple of years! That's great progress for the design profession, but also makes the arena more competitive. It has also opened it up to marketers and consultants of every stripe to co-opt (and often eclipse) the designer's contribution.

## HEAD-COUNT DOMINANCE

To point out the growth of head-counts for these "noncreative" individuals in design firms, and while statistics in the United States are not readily available, the London-based periodical *Design Week* has an annual survey that offers an interesting insight into the structure and ranking of design firms. As most of the top twenty firms are global, the information is applicable to the United States offices of these firms. The April 1, 2000 issue noted that:

> This management consultant type structure has been gradually expanding for a number of years and presents one of the largest growth areas for personnel. Companies are incorporating in their personnel mix executives whose professional experience includes management consulting firms, corporate branding, advertising, and many with M.B.A.s. Logically, these executives hold significant positions within the firm and they work in tandem with the creative group. While the ratio of account services people to creative will vary from firm to firm, and in many large companies the balance is tipped away from creative, it must be remembered that these firms are still deliver a creative product. Their own image as "Marketing Communications" consultants in this instance means operating as image and planning consultants with the visual solution to be determined and executed at the conclusion of the process.

The above statement is completely applicable to the United States, as organizational structures in both countries are so similar. Company organizational structures, methodologies, approaches to pitching business, and general business, philosophy are closely tied on both sides of the Atlantic. From time to time, one may create change in the other but with the consolidation of global design firms, the similarities far outweigh the differences. *Design Week* continues: "It is, however, surprising to see designers accounting for only 36 percent of the team at INS (Interbrand in the United States), given its design heritage in the former Newell and Sorrell. It shows how much such a business has changed over recent years, moving away from pure design work towards more consultancy business...although the number of other staff far outweighs designers, design patently has a significant place in their culture. At Wolff Olins the percentage of designers is even less—32 percent." In the United States, as indicated, exact figures are not available, but the designer entering these companies must understand that they will be interfacing with a wide variety of individuals, not designers, who they might not have anticipated. Furthermore, the most significant part of this is that in many design-driven firms, where the final product is a creative solution, the actual number of people who are designers is a far smaller percentage than most people would expect.

## KEYS TO SUCCESS

What are the key factors for success in these often highly compensated positions? Usually firms require a business degree and M.B.A.s are highly valued. However, there are many who have succeeded in transitioning from various parts of the business sectors, advertising, in-house positions in corporations, and, sometimes, creative positions. The strongest background would be someone who has worked in traditional consulting companies. Beyond the experiential requirements, there are the personal requirements. On average, the culture of these companies is very entrepreneurial and very fast paced. They require that special blend of personality who has a lot of structure is very good at detail and is a self-starter. That does not negate the importance of working in a team environment in that is most cases flexible depending on the assignment. For the designer making a career segue, they will find this an important niche in design, for the account team is an integral part of the creative process. Account services offer the opportunity to work with the client in the initial stages of project development, setting the strategy and criteria. It is an intellectually stimulating period in the scope of the project. The account people are often responsible for translating these criteria to the creative staff and all the follow-up liaison work between client and creative. They usually have project responsibility for writing proposals and monitoring budgets. While these positions are not necessarily filled by people with a creative education, they do offer opportunities to designers looking for a career change. These companies are, above all, service companies even though much of what they do is analytical. The client is the prime priority. There tend to be a lot of difficult travel schedules and long hours. One needs, as in all work, to have the desire and passion to withstand the rigors.

It is interesting to learn from several professionals as they talk about the challenges of business development, the marketing of a creative company, the kind of person who works well in the strategic arena, and marketing a company with a public relations point of view.

Scott Kraft is a partner at Sterling in New York. He writes:

In new business development the sales cycles are much faster, which doesn't make it easier; it involves a greater amount of strategic planning. It used to be about four months from contact to contract; now it's about two. Our clients are the CMO and higher executives who share in the ownership of the product and are more involved in the projects. In packaging, for example, the design process must succeed for global applications as well. Clients are looking for long-term relationships, not single projects. The business is very competitive, with lots of companies offering the same services.

The skills we look for in marketing people begin with a generalist knowledge. These people must be able to think about our company as a brand, develop a strategy to target new clients, and know how to work with creatives. Understanding of the creative process inside the office makes it possible to write an intelligent proposal. New business is driven from the outside in, and you have to know what the marketplace is looking for, and have a sense of what's happening. You also have to be single-minded about the area you are in, very focused. One of the most important things to me is the ability to do numbers. We want disciplined individuals who have an organized way of doing business, and the ability to make long-range plans, and, who can trace their steps. This person is goal-oriented and has established, for example, that twelve meetings a month will yield four solicited proposals, resulting in one new job. Management skills are required to oversee the support staff that executes the plan. There is no ideal salesperson. Salespeople sell best to people who are like them. Very aggressive salesmen sell to very aggressive clients; thoughtful, boisterous, chummy, geeky, or hard-nose, seek out their counterparts. Diversity is important. For the more bureaucratic companies like AT&T, a very conservative, slow, persistent person who knows all the rules is the right person. For the high tech industry it must be a young sales force. You have to have a match. A design company principal should hire someone unlike himself.

My advice to someone who wants to work in marketing and business development is take courses, anything that has to do with numbers. This will give you discipline and power. The power lies within the budget, which equals control. If you know the budget and can explain the process, the costs, and the profit you have leverage as well as credibility.

We asked Hayes Roth, vice president of Americas Marketing at Landor Associates to offer his ideas on the linkage between design and strategy, as well as comment on the type of people who excel in this environment: "Design plays an immensely important role in the brand experience, as does strategy. How do we get people to live the brand? Two years after the introduction of a brand, we are asked to survey and analyze to results. There is a growing business in this area called cultural change; we are now doing business in a different way. How do we do business globally, with cultures that are different from our own? This creates huge design and strategy issues."

On how to be effective in New Business Development, Hayes continues:

You have to love presenting. No matter how good a person is as a designer, he has to be able to articulate what he does and get people excited about it. This is a showmanship business, and those who are really successful can sell it as well as do it. You have to be a quick study, read a room very quickly, figure out who the decision-makers are, and listen very well. In terms of gender, I don't think it makes a difference; some of our best people are women, so that's not an issue. This is a nonjudgmental, totally creative business, you can be of all or any persuasions, and it doesn't matter. Unlike the ad business where you have maybe two big pitches a month, in a design firm you may have seven a week. With cold-calling and proactive marketing you try to get a buzz going, and keep your name out there, but if there isn't a need, there's nothing you can do. Interactive has become very important because it provides ways of developing relationships for specific projects. The day-to-day operation of new business is gathering the right information, keeping it fresh, and making sure that your people are presenting well. It's an exceedingly competitive marketplace.

And on hiring,

Although we obviously hire a lot of people with advertising backgrounds, Landor is interested in individuals with a broad general knowledge. You have to be interested in how design affects people's lives, to love the end product. The ability to communicate effectively is critical; you have to be able to build a back story, a rationale to sell the new name or the design. Can you handle a dozen projects at a time, amazing deadlines, and a lot of pressure? The typical job is three months, maybe six months at most; you have to be able to get deep, fast. In our office people have to do what they say they are going to do; they have to deliver. The sooner you get the client to buy into the idea the faster you get to where you're going, and you're less likely to make mistakes.

This chapter has presented the rationale for the inclusion of business professionals in the creative arena. It also offers a glimpse of the views of a few professionals as to the methods and challenges of marketing a creative product or service. Be it the development of new business, the promotional activities in creating a public relations effort, or the teams creating the strategic solutions and account management, these contributions to the creative whole have become critical for a firm's success in the marketplace. The challenge remains for these talents, coming from different viewpoints and training, to work together in cohesive teams and create the integrated solutions that result in unique solutions for their clients.

# Print Design

## 5

**T**his is a vast area, attracting designers who love the printed work, the feel of paper, and a commitment to typography. Some of the tools of the trade include a deep consideration of the aesthetics of page layout (which can also be applied to Web layout) and the utilization and/or art direction of illustration and photography. Designers have to have a knowledge of the printing process, understand materials, inks and papers, and are often required to go on press checks.

Any discussion of design, and therefore print design, must at some point focus on typography. Typography is the heart and soul of design. Without typography there is no written message, just image. It is a universal fact that at the core of all design functions, the art and knowledge of typography is primary. But what about the designer who has to grapple with the multitude of digital and media choices easily confusing his or her clarity? What is the importance of typography as it applies to the real-world challenges facing designers today? I asked Patrick Baglee, who is the chair of England's *Typographic Circle* and creative director of London's Realtime Studio, to give us his thoughts. Patrick writes,

> Thoughtful, user-focused typography is as important now as it ever has been. Despite the proliferation of devices and channels, written information still sits at the core of the majority of communications. That being the case, intelligent typography (and type design) is the difference between confusion and communication. The obvious act of tak-

ing documents that previously lived in print and placing them in new types of media demands careful consideration. Putting annual reports online and weather reports on palmtops or phones offers a myriad of richly layered (often beneficial) possibilities, but without intelligent interpretation of the information and the medium, the product and its typographic integrity is shovelled and not shaped. Placing the least possible interference between message and recipient should be typography's aim. Irrespective of the medium, long may that remain the case.

Print design has suffered in recent years from the stigma of being too "design-y," designers make things look too "pretty." Indeed, there have been many examples of design becoming so precious and so self-involved that it fails to communicate. The challenge is to overcome the perception that designers are only communicating with their peers. The obsession with texture or typography manipulated by computer to the point of illegibility helps support this observation. Trendy design clichés rarely solve real and pragmatic communications problems, although many experimental designers have produced a body of work that can influence others to newer ways of expression. When the visual does not communicate the message, the public and the designer's clients can become confused or dissatisfied. Designers may have pursued a cutting-edge image but if the work didn't serve basic communication needs, the chances were the client would move on.

The use of information in a substantive way is now an essential part of the designer's responsibility. In today's competitive and heavily traveled information superhighway, meaningful content has become critical to print communications. The designer must develop the skills necessary to analyze and conceive what the message should be. In order to achieve this goal a designer needs to be concerned with all aspects of the message, not just the visual. The designer has the ability to provide the pivotal role by recommending concept, content, and strategy along with design. Copy is the vehicle through which information and the message is often delivered. Copy is the conceptual partner to the visual solution and copy is the key component with which designers must work. In the past, copy was associated only with advertising. Not so today.

There is an old perception among advertising agency folk that designers are not conceptual. In their viewpoint designers only know how to make things look good (and, of course, they know all about typefaces and computers) but they are basically not conceptual the way advertising is. The concept is not often expressed to designers, and when it is, it is greeted with understandable shock. This notion is perhaps admissible for some of the purer elements of design. It certainly is not valid for the designer who understands the value, meaning, and necessity of copy as the motivating force that sets the direction for visual interpretation. The newer branding and communications groups within advertising agencies, albeit a smaller segment of the agency picture, are proving that design and advertising can meld in productive ways. Another aspect of this parochial view is the differentiation within advertising between art and copy. While they both are integral functions of the creative, and while art directors and copywriters work as teams, advertising has traditionally been copy-driven. When an agency needs to hire a creative director, their request will often acknowledge ambivalence as to whether the person has an art or copy background. But, in fact, when the decision-making process is over, the position usually goes to the copywriter. It's a bewildering fact to most art directors. Why does this happen? Because the message, and therefore the essential concept, is most often in the copy. The sooner art directors and designers begin to think of this total picture of integrated art and copy, the better.

In its simplest form, print design includes any printed materials that are two-dimensional, such as pamphlets, brochures, posters, and various other published materials. The semantics of the communication fields can sometimes be confusing. In advertising, "print" refers to ads—print advertising—as opposed to advertising on television or film. And in advertising, "collateral" refers to projects that are not ads but what designers call "print," such as brochures and other printed materials.

For our purposes, the following areas are included in the context of print design: corporate literature, information and systems design, annual reports, corporate communications, editorial design, magazine promotion, book design, and catalogs.

## CORPORATE LITERATURE

Corporate literature is so broad it can include every and all forms of brochures, annual reports, sales tools, and promotional print. It includes companies whose products may be business-to-business services, financial or technical services, or consumer products. It speaks to all sectors of the economy. Editorial design plays a role as well, as many firms have company magazines and newsletters. The field of corporate communications is dominated by the need to produce a vast variety of print materials whose audience is both within and without the corporation.

## INFORMATION AND SYSTEMS DESIGN

Information design is an interesting career option, a combination of print design and systems design. Information systems and systems design have been applied to the design of forms, legal documents, and publications stressing facts. Guidebooks, instruction manuals, charts, graphs, newspapers, and television informational visuals are important regions for this work, and easily apply to the interactive forms of media, user interface, and software design as described in chapter 9. This growing area of graphic design offers the tremendous benefit of clarity in a society on information overload. It also demands and requires the analysis of information, and for that to be designed and delivered in a clear logical manner. The needs of the audience must always be served and the information kept "consumer friendly."

The New York design firm Siegelgale (previously Siegel & Gale) opened a new frontier in graphic design when it developed Language Simplification in 1975. It came as a response to a need for clarity of business forms, both in their visual appearance as well as the written language. Alan Siegel was the first to recognize the opportunity to pair the work of graphic designers with attorneys to produce loan forms, all kinds of applications, and even the redesign of federal tax forms for the United States and Canadian governments. The work has proven fascinating to designers who have an interest in combining their typographical skills with systems design, and Language Simplification has also benefited the public in a measurable way.

Systems design is most appropriate for designers who thrive on analytical and organizational systems and typography. While it is twenty-five years since Siegelgale's inception, the long-term effects of this highly analytical visual approach to systems design has had many ramifications, not the least of which is Web site design, and these systems can also be transferred and utilized in exhibition design.

## ANNUAL REPORTS

This highly specialized field is another example of an area that is constantly requiring creative talent skilled to meet the needs of marketing corporate communications. The annual report is a mandated corporate year-end report and has grown into a significant marketing tool for those publicly held corporations that need to attract investors. The Federal Security and Exchange Commission mandates that all publicly held corporations issue annual reports to their stockholders. In addition, many choose to issue quarterly reports.

These materials have become informational guidebooks to the corporation. They not only communicate the image and economic health of the organization, but also have come to express how the organization feels about itself and its future. The annual report is significant not only because it is distributed to the stockholders, but because it is a marketing tool to the financial sector (Wall Street) and to future investors and employees. It is an instrument of research for anyone who wants in-depth information on the company. The annual report can perhaps convey a story line or interviews with employees or customers. Since the report's role so strongly relies on image, it has become one of the corporation's most significant communications devices. The point of view in the written copy as well as the visual image can narrate a far more focused message than reading the mandatory financials in the back of the book. It's the company's annual opportunity to communicate its story. Even a superficial look at a random selection of annual reports will quickly reveal their vastly divergent viewpoints. A closer look will confirm that this is a highly sophisticated medium of corporate communications.

The financial information submitted by the corporation has to be scrutinized carefully for accuracy. The overriding message as well as the company's depiction has to be approved by the CEO and president. Sometimes the very nature of the annual report can trigger an overly obsessive case of collective corporate paranoia. I remember a time when a designer had to insert and remove a single comma some fifteen times. The designer is in partnership with the top echelon of the firm and the whole enterprise's responsibility rests on a few shoulders. It can be a tense time, with the designer in a pivotal position.

Annual reports have also come to be a design status symbol for the corporation. For some companies, much emphasis is placed on the quality of the image they wish to portray. When reports win coveted prizes, the prize goes to the corporation as well as the design firm. While the pressure exists to get the job done right and on time, the freedom to use the report as a creative medium is considerable in some cases. Huge budgets can be riding on large printings. Only the very best photographers and illustrators will do. The quality of paper and printing became paramount. These priorities can be hard to duplicate in other avenues of print design. The result is often an enviable work. The online version of the annual report has become increasingly important. No longer a novel, additional option in today's business climate, this is necessary for communications.

Turning to an established practitioner of this art form, I asked Jim Hatch, executive vice president/creative director at Straightline International, who has been working with annual reports for at least two decades, to give us his views. His response:

> We have seen the annual report go from dry financial document to go-go excess to brand-building tool. The current landscape is amusing because all those forms are still out there. While the best reports have always been brand-focused, defining or extending a company's existing image, the establishment of the Internet as a high-profile medium for

corporate communications has really put the annual report in its place. Increasingly, the report is understood as one, integral part of a company's overall brand imaging. As a legal document it has a unique obligation to reflect the rational and responsible side of that image. The designer's first challenge is to communicate within this context. That requires the resources to establish a broad understanding of the company's existing messaging, as a foundation for creative recommendations. The second challenge is to conceive for interactive and print formats at the same time.

Graphic designers who work within this area can realize a meaningful and well-compensated career. The key is having the staying power, for too often there is a significant burnout factor. This is caused by changes in content, delays, and the fact that the majority of annual reports are subject to strict deadlines. Reports coincide with the company's annual meeting and usually appear early in March. As a consequence, these deadlines produce a fairly seasonal business in which the bulk of the work is done between Labor Day and April 15th. Most firms are attempting to structure their businesses into a twelve-month year. Some annuals do not have the April 15th deadline and firms are also able to develop other design products. During these deadline periods studios can work very long hours, six to seven days a week. Then there is the need to go "on press," to supervise the printing, make any last-minute decisions, and make sure it is as "perfect" as possible. While press time is reserved in advance, of course, there are always last minute emergencies. It seems everyone I have ever known has ended up on press at two a.m. in some small town somewhere in the United States. You can understand why people get burned out and may want to leave this specialized field. But when you look at the really great reports, you can also understand why there are those who are totally dedicated to this work. The level of design required at the better annual report firms provides designers in this area with an easy transition into other areas of top corporate communications design. In my experience, however, many annual report people become hooked and stay with it.

## CORPORATE COMMUNICATIONS

This identifier is usually used for corporate materials that are often, but not exclusively, accomplished by an in-house corporate staff. These are the communications products that serve to promote the corporation. They can include, but are not limited to, capability brochures, annual reports, company newsletters, sales tools, internal company forms, posters, invitations, special events, logomarks for subsidiary divisions, multimedia materials, sales meeting materials, incentive awards, and company magazines. The communications sector of a corporation may also work with the assigned advertising agency if there is not one in-house. Few corporations do their own advertising.

Designers working within a corporation usually have a very different experience than those working for a marketing communications firm or design studio. The biggest difference is that, while the designer may have many corporate divisions as "clients," there is really only one client. This is one of those good news/bad news trade-offs. The diversity of many clients is found in design consultancies but chances are it will be a specialized consultancy. The corporation may offer only one very large client and the diversity comes from having to do virtually everything for that client.

Working for a corporation used to mean substantial job security. While that notion has changed with the economic turmoil of the last decade, the turnover in corporate positions is still much lower than in the offices of design consultants. Corporations are slower to hire and slower to fire. The atmosphere is traditionally conservative. Corporate positions are highly prized for their excellent benefit programs, including sign-on bonuses, higher year end bonuses, and, very often, stock options, as well as shorter workweeks and relative security, which makes this an appealing choice for people with families. Obviously, since corporations are located all over the country, the ability to relocate is a necessity.

## EDITORIAL DESIGN

Editorial design refers to the design of magazines. It must be remembered that magazines currently appear in print as well as in online media. The publishing field is not the only market for editorial designers, as many special interest groups and corporations will develop books and magazines as part of their corporate communications efforts. It works much like other areas we have discussed, except the "client" is the publisher and/or editor. The audience is the public at large.

Publishing is, of course, the core for editorial design and it is a field in which the publishers and editors make the primary decisions relating to the focus, concept, and marketing of the product. They hire the creative director and/or art directors who can work with them to visualize their publication's point of view. A creative director is usually necessary when a publication is very large or there are several publications within a group. Otherwise, the top creative title is usually senior art director or art director. Under the creative head is a creative group whose size depends again on the size of the publication and how often it is published. A weekly publication requires more effort than a monthly. This group may, therefore, include an associate art director, assistant art director, designers, and production artists. It is always valuable to check the mastheads of magazines, for they will credit the staff and this allows you to see the structure. The creative director or art director will be responsible for hiring the staff, which can also include photo stylists or photo editors. The distinction between an art director's responsibility and a designer's is reflected in their roles. The art director "directs" the creative team on staff as well as photo shoots, art directs illustrators, and generally functions as a person who makes creative decisions in a supervisory manner. The designer is primarily involved with the hands-on implementation of those decisions working on the layout (mostly with software programs), and perhaps makes some of the type and visuals decisions. The designer's responsibilities will vary depending upon the size of the staff and how much the art director may wish to delegate. If the publication's staff is small enough, the art director may be asked to do the work of a designer as well. Designers are hired because of their ability to understand the subject matter and visually realize the magazine editor's focus. When designers change jobs it is also easier to move within a subject matter. For example, high fashion and financial based publications are so far apart in their content that most often a switch from one to the other is not possible. Publication design can be a somewhat stifling area because once a magazine has been formatted, creativity is bound by very tight parameters. There is an established grid and usually the choice of typefaces is restricted. An interesting test of the success of a magazine's identity is to open it without looking at the cover and try to recognize it solely by the visual identity.

Magazines fall into specialized business categories. They are:

- Lifestyle (such as a regional, like *New York* magazine)
- Fashion
- Business
- Trade (not found on newsstands)
- High tech (computers, science)
- Consumer and special interest (computers, automotive, children, education, travel, health and fitness, entertainment, financial)

## MAGAZINE PROMOTION

The promotional department is a totally separate entity within a magazine, and often the people in one department have no contact with the people in the other. Magazine promotion offers an interesting variety of work. Several creative services departments in a large publishing company will handle as many as twenty magazines. Often the staff works on several publications simultaneously with the exciting challenge of maintaining the individual identity of each, switching gears at every turn. The work includes: invitations, 3D promotions, advertising for clients, advertorials (articles that appear to be editorials but are actually advertisements, as indicated in the top margins), as well as rate cards, media kits, etc. The revenue from the advertisers, not subscriptions and readership, determines the financial success of a magazine. Magazine promotion is marketing the product to potential and repeat advertisers. Magazine promotion can mean designing rate cards, subscription inserts, and promotional brochures, computer floppy disks, and kits geared to attract advertisers. While we discuss promotion separately, it is necessary to point out how often it is closely linked with the editorial. The publisher will, of necessity, have a keen interest in the magazine's effective promotion. In addition, on small publications, the art direction staff may be called upon to design or supervise the promotion as well as the magazine.

## BOOK DESIGN

Book design is often perceived in relation to the design of book jackets. While this is the most visible, and in some ways splashy, manifestation of the design work, it is far from the whole story. The layout of the total book is a subject that requires insight into the character and purpose of the book. It requires establishing in the layout a sensitivity towards systems design and informational design, as well as a deep concern for typography. Often the design responsibilities will be separated, with one person responsible for the cover and another person for the interior. Art directors will originate the overall concept and then source the appropriate illustrators, photographers, and typographers to achieve their vision.

The book publishing field falls into many specialized categories as well, within the separations of hardcover, softcover, and paperback. They include:

- Textbooks
- Fiction/nonfiction
- Children's publications
- Trade publications
- Special interest (travel, cookbooks, etc.)

Book packagers occupy an interesting corner of the publishing field. They sometimes group publications together based on compatibility of subject matter or perhaps package a promotional device along with the book. A common example of a packaged publication grouping would be "The Collected Works of..." More inventive packages can offer an aligned product such as the well known illustrator Geoffrey Moss's wonderful children's book, *Henry's Moon* (packaged by Sommerville House in conjunction with Little, Brown Publishing), which included a night-light with a shade that was an illustration from the book.

Publishing's utilization of new technologies has created several important new directions. The CD-ROM offers the interactive form of publishing, offering not only a replica of the print version but the ability to involve the reader and allow the reader to be an active decision-maker in choosing information in a dialogue with the subject not otherwise possible. It is, after all, nothing more than taking existing published material and putting it on an interactive screen, but the inherent qualities of the interactive process and how it involves the participant produces a wonderful learning device. How to play better tennis, visit a museum, or learn about history can be more effective in this format. This business has created many new jobs for designers, as each option on the screen requires another layout. Within the textbook area, it is now possible to customize textbooks to meet teachers' specialized requirements. Books are being designed with flexible formats so that an instructor can request a text containing specific chapters from perhaps different sourcebooks. The final customized text can be delivered on short notice and with the instructor's name on the cover. A new advent to publishing is the e-book which is beginning to move into our world and, while in its infancy in 2001, there should be wonderful applications available with the expansion of wireless and PDAs.

Book design positions exist primarily within publishing firms, but a large number of assignments are distributed to small studios and freelancers. The practice of creative directors or art directors to assign projects allows for the type of design flexibility required by vastly different subject matter. The sourcing of outside talent allows total design adaptability.

## CATALOGS

Catalogs are no longer the stepchild of the industry, as shown by the sheer volume of publications landing almost daily on your doorstep. They provide an opportunity to create an exceptional selling tool for a client. If a designer is interested in photography and art direction, as well as a more editorial approach to design, this is an excellent venue. Since people have become accustomed to purchasing even expensive items through the mail, the high quality of catalogs has given new status and credibility to what once was considered "trash mail." This area creates an attractive option for people who are in editorial design or print advertising. Salaries are higher than in editorial and it is an easy transition from here to online catalog design.

In summing up and assessing the current state of the marketplace, Marion Thunberg, who is an associate of Roz Goldfarb Associates specializing in print design, talks about the many changes:

In the past five years the needs and scope of the design industry, particularly print, have broadened, making it more multidisciplinary. No longer will designers of "print" deal exclusively with print on paper. They will be expected to work in Web, packaging, and three-dimensional design like retail. Clients are beginning to look for design firms who can handle all aspects of their needs rather than only a specific area. It is entirely possible that the trend of acquiring and merging design firms will continue and we will see fewer small offices in the future. Many firms have become design consultancies who advise their clients on strategic aspects of their business, including marketing and planning.

A first job after graduation is as important as the fifth one. The company you decide to work for will determine your portfolio after a year. When interviewing, ask to see the company's current work. Money should be the least important factor at this point. The most important consideration is to work with someone whose work you respect and aspire to, someone who can be a mentor. Don't be impressed solely by the name recognition of a potential employer. There are many excellent firms who maintain a low profile but whose work is wonderful. The advice I give people entering the design arena is to keep an open mind, explore all possibilities, but never lose sight of your end goal.

# Environmental Design

## 6

**A**s an amalgam of two- and three-dimensional design, environmental design is extremely diverse in its variety of applications. Thus, it offers an opportunity for industrial designers, architects, and interior designers, as well as graphic designers, to work as a team on various projects. Environmental design represents a mosaic of design specialties, and, therefore, stands alone, unique in this capacity. The identifier "environmental" does not pertain to ecological concerns. This is a semantic confusion that sometimes causes the mistaken belief that an environmental designer is working on projects to clean up our environment. In all discussions of environmental branding the reader must cross-reference to chapter 3, "Branding and Design Management" as the two areas overlap significantly.

As RGA associate for environments and architecture, Margot Jacqz is especially knowledgeable about the quality and diversity of opportunities within environmental design. Here is her assessment of this fascinating part of design.

## ENVIRONMENTS BRANDED AND OTHERWISE, RETAIL AND ENTERTAINMENT: A DEFINITION
*Margot Jacqz*

Environmental design is not landscaping or ecological engineering but the accepted description of a discipline that comprises a broad range of design activities and places that designers have influence over.

Environments are, by definition, surroundings. Designers are drawn to these projects comprising two- and three-dimensional thinking from several directions—as architects who want to work on a more intimate scale, industrial designers who are interested in a larger scale, or graphic designers who are able to work beyond print.

Environments include retail stores, offices, hotel spaces, museum exhibits, theme parks, hospitals, and airports. Professionals with training in architecture and interior, industrial, and graphic design affect the final design of these places, and, increasingly, we see truly integrated teams with these different designers communicating with each other early in the project phases.

Environmental design is gaining recognition as a specialized design field as designers gain experience with the specific problems encountered in working on environmental projects.

## WHERE ENVIRONMENTAL DESIGNERS WORK

Most offices specializing in environments such as museum exhibits or retail stores are small (fewer than twenty-five employees). However, many identity and brand consulting offices develop environmental applications as part of the program—such as for banks or airlines—and so have multidisciplinary project teams. Many marketing and advertising agencies are also adding teams that have environmental design deliverables such as vendor shops, exhibits, or events.

Corporations vested in consumer activities such as merchants or entertainers have in-house staff and teams dedicated to their environments. Walt Disney's Imagineering division in Burbank, California, is an early example, employing a very large staff of designers and conceptualizers who work in a think tank environment. There are architects, materials specialists, ride and exhibition designers, storyboarders, illustrators, model makers and visualizers, urban planners, graphic designers, industrial designers, and signage specialists. Traditional retailers have store design and construction departments, and marketing and merchandising divisions. These are less divided than in the past, with all visual aspects of a store image coming under a single creative director. Thus, graphic designers, whether in advertising, marketing, promotions, or merchandising may be working at least in passing with store designers or industrial designers on in-store shops.

In any discussion of environmental design the relationship to industrial design and industrial design education is very important. Industrial designers are found in retail, point-of-purchase, and fixture design, exhibit, entertainment, and environmental graphic design teams. (Please see chapter 8, "Industrial Design.")

## SAMPLE PROJECTS

A look at the 2000 Society of Environmental Graphic Designers' (SEGD) award-winning projects is a way to understand the scope of environmental design. This list indicates not only the range of the projects but also the scale. The awards for design honors and merit included: Muvieco Paradise24 Theater; The Endurance: Shackleton's Antarctic Expedition; Levi's Mothership Trade Show Exhibit; Apple at CompUSA; Kansas City Board of Trade Sculpture; Aveda Retail Prototype; Grand Central Retail Map and Metro North Map; Ducati Showroom Prototype; Paradise Valley Mall Children's Playcourt; USAID exhibit; Corning Museum of Glass: Glass Innovation Center; Nike World Campus; Downtown Indianapolis signage program; Monsanto Childcare Center; Concord Mills; Michael Jordan's Steak House; and Teledesic Headquarters, interior and exterior signage.

Branded environments are the key to the expansion of environmental design. The extension of the brand into the three-dimensional applications is a natural extension of branding as detailed in chapter 3. Branding as a concept of advertising and merchandising is at home in any retail or entertainment application. Experiencing the brand by being inside the brand is a comparatively new method of brand extension.

Margot continues to expand on how that can be played out.

We have seen in the past five or ten years an increasing sophistication brought to environmental design due to the increased sophistication in understanding the user and the way people respond to the spaces they are in whether as workers, travelers, purchasers, or learners. The most noted changes recently have been in retail design and what we call "branded environments." In retail we have the growth of specialty stores in malls and cities around the world. Merchants like the Gap or Brookstone or Polo/Ralph Lauren have concentrated efforts on the design of their stores so that they are immediately recognizable worldwide.

Perhaps this started with yellow arches found near the first McDonald's, appropriated for the identity and now a powerful graphic symbol worldwide. The arches are supported by other signs, the shape of the roof, the materials of the restaurant, the in-store signs, the menu boards, and the packaging. This consistency, just like the hamburgers, is the McDonald's brand image. Or, perhaps, it started with gas stations across the country that needed to identify themselves to motorists with large, highway-scaled signs such as the Mobil horse, and later, complete enclosures like the Texaco stations of the 1980s. Now stations incorporate attached convenience stores designed in components chosen to fit the specific sites.

Banks are another more recently maturing example. As they grow, banks are striving to identify themselves to customers internationally. Not only do they have signs outside, they also have ATM lobbies, with machines and an interactive interface, and interiors with opportunities for other kinds of communications. These are all opportunities for reinforcing the identity of the institution.

Designers in retail may be expected to work on a wide range of identity applications, as well as site-specific or event-specific information. And, of course, not all retail is chain stores. The individual shop requires equal versatility from a designer. The most important aspect of any retail program is the ability to maintain the integrity of an identity while adapting it to different media, dimensions, and scale. In a successful retail program all the elements of an environment are directed toward the same vision and the customer's experience of the product is seamless from the advertising to the store to the packaging.

Starbucks is a fine example: Originally a coffee shop, the ubiquitous chain is noted less for its coffee than for the experience of going there and even the chance to sit down on a busy day and listen to jazz for twenty minutes. Creative services design team efforts are directed at bringing you into that experience (advertising, store graphics), supporting it (menu boards, fixtures, game table graphics), and extending it (developing private label products a customer can take home).

For reinforcing the presence of a brand we can also look at vendor shops or merchandising environments that are not stand-alone. Cosmetics companies create mini-environments in department stores, using fixtures, display, and graphics to distinguish themselves for the appreciative customer. Frito-Lay is looking at how to brand a supermarket aisle gathering all their product—drinks, chips, and dips—under one banner, over a floor graphic, or in a distinctive gondola fixture. Sprint has created its own section at Radio Shack that is both compatible and distinct.

Similar to retail are business-to-business environments such as trade show exhibits. At a trade show a corporation needs to make an immediate impression in the midst of intense competition. While the bulk of this exhibit work is done by architects and industrial designers because of the space making and structural components, graphic designers are critical to the process in adapting the brand image to the booth and the communications, both preshow and on-site.

Other consumer environments that have evolved significantly are entertainment venues and exhibits, including museums, zoos, or national parks.

"Entertainment" covers a multitude of possibilities and can be seen as a continuation of retail except that customers are not necessarily buying physical products, but spending money on experiences. These require integrated teams, like the Imagineers, to write the story and then to implement and adapt the applications. Designers with theatrical imaginations thrive in entertainment and highly themed retailing, where the primary goal is to create an activity and engage a visitor in an experience they will want not only to repeat but to share with friends. Entertainment venues are increasingly part of corporate brand strategies. Examples that come first to mind are Walt Disney World or Universal Studios in Orlando, Florida, but what used to be easily distinguished theme parks have evolved into other kinds of urban projects like Universal CityWalk, Sony Metreon Center, or the NBC Experience, which provides interactive engagement and product to sell. This product, of course, dovetails with the licensing experience as described in chapter 7. Opportunities abound for brand communications in print, signage, and video.

The porous border between retail and entertainment is broached in the other direction by the early NikeTowns. These stores were designed to provide a consumer experience, to reinforce the Nike sporting/lifestyle image, and to leave an impression. As stores they are not wildly successful on a dollars per square foot basis, but as brand elements they are hugely successful. While not being entertainment in the traditional themed, storytelling, or media sense, they have become tourist destinations. The brand experience delivered through the 'entertainment' portal has the overarching effect of creating a brand that can be sold in many other venues at satisfying price points. In other words, a NikeTown store may not be a financial success but Nike will sell a host of products with an enhanced brand recognition and on a global basis. In chapter 3, we learned of the branding mantra of the brand as a promise. In this case, the promise is an experience.

## LEARNING ENVIRONMENTS

Historical exhibits, zoos, and parks intend to engage visitors at a more educational level. Yet, we see techniques and technologies learned in consumer entertainment brought to these experiences as well. Stories are told using the full range of graphic expression, from print brochures and artifact information labels to interactive educational experiences and full 3-D animated videos found in many museums of science. The challenge for designers at a project like the 2000 Congo Gorilla exhibit at the Wildlife Conservation Society in New York is to put information where it is relevant and add detail where it can be absorbed at different levels without detracting from the natural setting or impeding the thousands of daily visitors.

Designers often become engaged in these arenas because of the content. They find satisfaction in applying their skills in communications to subjects of interest.

Museums have a particular fascination as they have become so much a part of our culture, and Patrick Gallagher of Gallagher & Associates is a specialist in this area. Patrick says about his current work:

> We are currently in design of the New African American Museum in Baltimore that is based on the personal stories of the African American community along the eastern shore and is supported by the collections of artifacts and documents. The museum experience will be very emotional and very theatrical in the way the physical environment lays out. In New York at the Museum of Jewish Heritage the storytelling process is based on testimonials of Holocaust survivors and is again given context by the artifacts. Both experiences are emotionally much more dynamic and engaging than the traditional museum.
>
> The forces of change are directly related to the impact of connecting the visitor to the content. How to more completely engage them with the stories being told, focus on the concept or the magnitude of the collection. Museum educators today believe that by placing the visitor in 'the place and time' he or she will be more involved and more likely to experience the learning embedded within the space.
>
> This, in the broadest of terms, has been defined as immersion and the museum industry is being influenced by the world of theater and stage design. Families today have many choices of how to spend their free time. The entertainment and attraction industry has put great pressure on the museum world. The challenge has, in fact, awakened museums to explore how they can make their environments more dynamic and communications more clear. I anticipate continual changes as they meet the demands of educational goals and visitor expectations. The constant that remains is the basic idea that all great museum and exhibit experiences are based on rich and contextual stories that give resonance to artifacts and collections. The other major challenge to museums today is the ability to show visitors something different each time they come back to visit.

## WAYFINDING

This is a specialist term within environmental graphic design for the signs and system that keep a visitor from getting lost. It is most needed in any large complex such as a city, an airport, a theme park, a hospital, a convention center, or parking lots. Wayfinding systems are usually noticed only when they aren't working properly. Primary issues in successful wayfinding are hierarchical organization, consistency, and legibility; analytical thinking is an important skill. Mapmaking, color sense, and typography at forty paces are critical.

A project begins with planning and programming, understanding the architecture, deciding what signs are necessary and sufficient, and where to put them. Design involves choosing type, colors, and forms to insure clarity, as well as appropriate materials—remember, these are generally intended to be permanent, inside and outdoors. Everyday examples are the codes in parking lots where sections have different numbers and colors, or shopping centers where entrances and adjacent courts each have a different theme, re-iterated in nearby parking, so visitors can find their way out again. More serious is the design of signage for hospitals, transportation centers like airports, campus centers, or cities. Designers have to understand the architectural plans and the functional circulation patterns, and accommodate the level of knowledge and stress of the visitors.

In the best situations, architectural graphics are developed by designers in partnership with the architects or planners. EGD specialists work one phase behind in programming and planning, often contributing through their knowledge of how visitors read spaces, as well as the local regulations. It is also important that the signing is compatible with the architecture and the identity of the company or environment.

## DESIGN SEMANTICS AND OPTIONS

The distinction between environmental graphics and environments or experiences should be noted. Environmental design and experience design are activities that require a team comprised of people with a range of disciplines as appropriate to the situation: architecture, brand strategy, decoration, engineering, furniture, graphics, information design, interface design, lighting design, merchandising, planning, product design, programming, project management, storytelling, sound design, traffic management, wayfinding, and more. The expertise of an environmental graphic designer is one component, more or less critical, of success in designing either an "environment" or an "experience." Unfortunately, most schools do not provide opportunities for interdisciplinary exploration. There are few complete curricula in environmental graphics or retail or exhibit design, although there seem to be increasing numbers of classes taught by professionals in the field.

Designing for a store or a park or a trade show is not a matter of taking great print and making it bigger or turning it sideways. There are technical questions of materials and aesthetic ones of scale. Designers interested in dimensional projects have to start working with the "other half"—that is, industrial designers or architects need to strengthen type and color skills, and graphic specialists need to learn more about materials and how space works.

Good brand strategists may even find themselves involved in the design of corporate office environments. Increasingly, these are understood as reflective of the corporate culture and are designed to accommodate management structures and communications goals.

The idea of experience design is most obvious when talking about "leisure activities" like shopping or entertainment, but it can be applied globally. The broadening influence of trained designers in vast cross-disciplinary endeavors is being felt as businesses identify the need to create impressions on employees as well as customers. We see corporate offices being planned to accommodate the organizational models and demands of workers. Bull pens are out, corner offices are out; mobile cubicles, customizable "pods," flexible spaces, main streets, and lounges are in.

In looking at the scope of environmental design, we approached M. Arthur Gensler, Jr., FAIA, FIIDA, RIBA, and chairman of Gensler. With more than 2,000 employees focused on this very issue he has had ample opportunity to reflect on the evolving situation: "People today ask a great deal from the built environment. They're looking for 'consonance,' which means that they expect settings not just to provide shelter and comfort, but to express a philosophy of living or working that aligns with their own. Organizations, too, expect these settings to express their 'brand' and support their plans and strategies. As values and strategies change, the settings change, too."

We asked him what changes did he anticipate and what are the constants that will remain. "We're leaving a period of 'irrational exuberance,' to use Alan Greenspan's memorable phrase. The last time we made this transition, work settings were relentlessly pared back in the name of efficiency—to the point of excess, finally. Then the focus shifted and workplace design underwent a revolution. As the floodwaters of exuberance recede again, the bedrock of this transformation will be revealed. Rather than arriving at 'constants,' we've reached new and higher ground."

And what would he recommend to a person entering this field? "Design is a rich and wonderful field, one that embraces the broadest spectrum of talents. As every good client knows, you don't necessarily have to be a designer yourself to make remarkable contributions to it. Design's focus is humanity—its goal is to make a better world. As this implies, its scope is endless. As you launch your career, remember that there are no trivial projects—no matter how small, each embodies this goal in microcosm, with all of its implicit opportunity."

# Advertising and Design

## 7

There are different facets of the world of advertising, although the use of "advertising" as a descriptive term is fairly ubiquitous. Advertising consists of work for print media, broadcast and direct mail, and/or direct response, among other things. Within the broadcast area it can be broken down into categories for radio, television, and interactive media. Promotional advertising and design have their own sets of parameters as well. This business, like most, has experienced enormous change and speed of execution due to technology. This constantly changing work environment can be heard in the accurate assessments as summed up by Sylvia Laniado, RGA's recruiter for advertising, and Myrna Davis, director of the Art Director's Club of New York.

Myrna Davis comments:

> Now that business in general has become more technical and everything is happening faster, there is not only no time for lunch, there is no time for meetings. The mystery of the design process is seemingly gone because the computer has made design more transparent. At the same time it has changed client expectations by reducing the amount of development time to create a project from "sketch" to finished art. Advertising suffers from this as well. Traditionally, graphic designers have been responsible for making things look good, while art directors

have had to develop a strategy because of the desire to create an identifiable brand.

"Many of the recent changes have been good," she continues. "The convergence of design firms merging with advertising agencies has formed powerful, multidisciplinary organizations, and globalization has raised the stakes as well as expectations. Advertising has become a multimillion-dollar business with a worldwide audience and market."

Sylvia Laniado comments:

The business has changed enormously in the past five years—primarily because of the computer. You can expect some clients to give an agency an assignment and ask to see ideas the very same day — depending on the account. In the past, creatives were given a number of days or even weeks to solve a problem. Not many people have the luxury of time anymore.

Another aspect of change is found in the agencies which are becoming more and more integrated. General, sales promotion, direct response, graphic design, and interactive now work much closer in hand, and we will see more and more of that in the future.

Since this book is focused on the work of designers, the following is a brief discussion with the view towards differentiating advertising from design and offering a viewpoint which might offer career options to designers. Its applications in interactive media are covered in chapter 9.

## GENERAL ADVERTISING

General advertising is categorized as the advertising that is found in print and television. This form of advertising is the one that most people will associate with advertising, and the work of the advertising agency covers all advertising found in magazines, newspapers, billboards, radio, and television. Large advertising agencies tend to have many divisions which will encompass the subcategories of advertising mentioned below. The agencies present themselves to their clients as a group of companies able to solve all communications problems and have in turn acquired many design firms as part of the host of services. A typical example of this structure would be to survey the structure of Ogilvy & Mather in the United States, which is owned by WPP. The Ogilvy group of companies consists of O&M Worldwide, O&M Advertising, O&M Interactive, OgilvyOne Dataservices, OgilvyOne Directory Advertising, OgilvyOne Interactive, OgilvyOne Worldwide, OgilvyOne Design Direct, Ogilvy Public Relations Worldwide. These divisions are replicated on a global basis in many cities.

# DIRECT MARKETING/DIRECT RESPONSE

Direct marketing refers to the type of advertising used to initiate a consumer response by contacting the consumer directly, usually through a mailed letter, packet, or brochure. Catalogs are a form of direct marketing, as are bill-stuffers, solicitations for travel, charities, etc. Ads on Web sites are a very direct form of advertising. Direct response has the subtle difference of controlling how that response will be made, such as offering a coupon to be mailed in or an 800 telephone number to call.

# PROMOTIONAL ADVERTISING AND DESIGN

Promotion represents an exceptionally broad area, one probably least known to most young designers, and yet offers the largest number of employment opportunities. Sales promotion is also the place where design and advertising meet. Therefore, an understanding of marketing strategies, copywriting, and marketing communications is necessary. The promotional designer has to connect these elements to produce a printed piece that will cry out for attention and sell an idea, service, or product.

# INTEGRATED ADVERTISING AND DESIGN

We have touched on many of the differences between design and advertising. It must be noted, however, that there are many firms that are true hybrids of these two disciplines. This is a new breed of agency that is generally smaller and stresses a type of problem solving that breaks down barriers and stereotypes. These companies are also common in smaller cities where they are required to multitask for their clients. However, while their work will utilize and emphasize a strong design element, in many cases it is still conceptual advertising. Other similar groups are the divisions within many large advertising agencies that are devoted to sales promotion or marketing communications. These groups require the talent of designers who can think of marketing strategies. It is an opportunity for the designer who wants the challenge of thinking on a different scale.

Some of these firms are philosophically wed to the concept of integrated marketing. Integrated marketing is a method of approaching a communications problem from the most sensible point of view. The strategy may combine a package of various media for the client to promote his goods or services in a variety of ways. These packages may include promotional design, traditional advertising, packaging design, direct marketing, or special events.

# SALES PROMOTION

Although the premise is similar to advertising, it must be remembered that promotion is not print advertising. Sales promotion is printed matter that can be in the form of brochures, sales kits, sell sheets, rate cards, point-of-sale displays, banners, and posters (POS—or sometimes called point of purchase, POP—as seen in supermarkets, drugstores, banks, or any other retail establishment). Special promotional gifts can come in the form of kits, boxes, special events marketing and sales giveaways (such as kits, T-shirts, buttons, matchbooks, hats, and menus), or contests, sweepstakes, and other incentive offerings (which are also found in direct marketing and can be in the form of special mailers, posters, and displays). Within the publishing field we can find special inserts in magazines (for subscriptions, mail-aways), magazine advertorials (editorial inserts sponsored by an advertiser). Many package goods companies will offer freestanding inserts ( FSIs are coupons, often part of an ad, inserted in newspapers and magazines). Outdoor promotions include billboards and posters on mass transit or bus shelters. The cosmetic and fragrance market has made special promotions of gift-with-purchase and purchase-with-purchase (GWP and PWP, as they are prevalently known) a way of life in department stores. They also utilize special mailers distinct from, but sometimes similar to, direct marketing advertising.

# PROMOTIONAL FIRMS

As you can see, promotion covers a vast area. The products promoted can include anything that is marketed throughout the world. This accounts for its huge diversity. To understand how broad-based promotion is, apply these items (all of which have to be designed) to the diversity of companies needing these services. Think about all the sales promotion generated by an IBM: the product categories; sales tools for sales personnel; giveaway information for the consumer; trade shows for marketers and retailers with their trinkets of balloons, pens, and discs; the retail outlets' need for display cards, posters, signage; the promotions for a charity or cause (fund-raising, ecology, etc.); the awards given to distinguished personnel (gift and travel incentives, as well as trophies and awards); and materials for corporate sales conventions (programs, name tags, and menus). Now consider what it might be like handling the promotion for a television network: developing sales kits to promote sponsorship of specific programs (promoting the time buying); attracting affiliate stations to airing specific shows (which are "leased" from the network); or creating consumer awareness (on-air promotional spots). If you were working for a fragrance/cosmetic company you would develop many of these same products but with a completely different image and point of view.

The diversity is enormous and underrated as an avenue for career opportunities. I've often felt sales promotion is an unknown field in the minds of young designers, for it certainly has a very low recognition factor. It may not be the most glamorous design work, but it can be a lot of fun and does offer a significant number of employment opportunities.

## LICENSING

This area of design has expanded greatly in the past few years and offers a whimsical, fun side to graphics. Its essence is close to the thinking behind sales promotion. Producing products with images to promote a personality or idea dates back to ancient times. While the Romans sold souvenirs at gladiator fights, no one could foresee the ubiquitous effect of sports and entertainment marketing in this century. Today, the team identifying logos and mascots for the National Football League or National Basketball Association, for example, have generated a complex and multibillion-dollar industry. The marketing gurus have discovered that almost anything can be sold with a famous character or slogan such as Garfield, Batman, the Simpsons, or "I Love New York" (which has spawned an industry of copied promotions). I often think of Mel Brooks using his annihilating humor to nail this subject on the head in his movie *Meatballs*. While not as well known as *The Producers*, it is a wonderful caustic view of promotional advertising as applied to the entertainment industry. In a scene discussing how the movie they are making can be merchandised before it's even made, Brooks unveils a table filled with samples of merchandising products such as Meatballs the Sweatshirt, Meatballs the Towel, and Meatballs the Toilet Paper. They will guarantee the movie's success. Unfortunately, he didn't think of including a Meatballs Pavilion at a Meatballs Theme Park.

Theme parks and the expansion of this entertainment related environment into restaurants, fast food chains, and shopping malls have developed a further outreach of the licensing program into the creation of a total fantasy environment. The surroundings are a complete escapist world in which the consumer enters a habitat offering experiences which foster the desire to buy some object in order to retain the memory of the experience. It's fun, expensive, and big business. These enterprises are a source of employment to graphic and industrial designers as well as architects, illustrators, and planners. Every facet of these parks requires graphics, products, and environmental design. The Disney Imagineering group is famous for developing this work genre, but there are several others.

The phenomenon of licensing promotion exploded in the 1980s and has produced an expanding industry mainly catering to team sports and cartoon characters. It has also spawned a new category in retail of entertainment-driven stores, sports bars, and restaurants (see chapter 6). Licensing can also include fashion designers lending their names to fragrances and accessories. In fact, any famous personage, brand, city, country, or entertainment vehicle is ripe for exploration or exploitation, depending upon your viewpoint. Nonetheless, all these products and their accompanying logos need to be designed, and so offer interesting avenues of employment. The significant factor in all this activity is the growing demand for a sophisticated product. Quality of design is an integral part of much that is produced. The graphic designer's input and imagination has moved this industry to the higher ground.

The branding of these images is the motivating strategy, so that Mickey Mouse, the Muppets, Peanuts, and NFL (National Football League) teams, to name a few, are becoming marketable brands. The branding phenomenon moves the images or characters far beyond their sometimes humble origins and the branding produces a perception of the consumer that they are "buying into" the essence of what the character represents. The branding function creates products and merchandising systems every bit as sophisticated as merchandising a designer fragrance. The image (i.e. design) of the product must be appropriate to the marketplace. Accessories, home furnishings, and clothing are sold to all ages and economic groups. Again using Disney as the preeminent pioneer of this genre, the 1990 Disney Consumer Product catalog included over 14,000 items. Today the *www.disneystore.com* menu offers "Disney Grams," "Clothing and Accessories," "Home and Gifts," "Toys," "Video, Games and More," and a "Collectables Corner." As always, items can span all price points, for a watch can cost $12.95 or thousands of dollars.

Licensing has also expanded to the corporations, who are applying their image to incentive or consumer products, in a desire to proliferate the branding of their corporate identity. It is an interesting mixture of image and marketing when catalogs are offered with company logos adhered to mugs, jewelry, luggage, etc. It seems no company is immune from this form of promotional marketing and it can be a modest baseball hat or a full catalog of offerings. Caterpillar, the heavy machinery company, has merchandised their yellow triangle logo and applied it to "rugged—durable—genuine" clothing and other articles, which can be found at *http://merchandise.cat.com/caterpillar*. The August 8, 2001 edition of the *Wall Street Journal* reported on how this trend has captivated the European marketplace with a story about the popularity of the Caterpillar brand. the *Journal* headlined, "The $500 Jacket, $80 Jeans in Caterpillar's 'Cat' Line Borrow Bulldozers' Allure." The *Journal* commented, "Caterpillar says it is branching out into casual wear mainly to boost its image among people who drive its trucks and tractors 'In order to expand our share in the work shoe market'. . . In Europe the situation is reversed. Cat gets a high reading on the hip meter but wants more people to wear its construction gear at work to buttress its industrial image . . . Next year Cat plans to expand its line into 'fashion forward'." Apple computers, Aetna Insurance, and American Airlines also offer a broad range of products to consumers and employees. The inherent differing nature of these corporations also offers insight as to how divergent the corporate image can be and still adapt itself to this marketing arena.

It is important to be observant and to analyze all that you see as you are a member in our society. Consider what development and design is behind these products the next time you see them on the marketplace. Remember their purpose and that graphic designers are employed for the creation of the design impact.

## WHERE ARE THE PROMOTION JOBS?

Promotion can be produced by design studios as well as in-house corporate groups. Most publishing firms devise a large sales promotion effort. The balance between design done within a company and the amount given to outside studios or agencies is a pendulum whose swings are dependent on the economic times and mood. Many advertising agencies have traditionally had sales promotion groups within the agency. When they are part of the internal structure of the agency they work for the same clients as the agency. The agency does the print advertising, radio, and television. The promotion group does anything else required by the client, from packaging design to cookbooks. Many of these groups have been spun off as separate profit centers, perhaps with different names that may or may not be directly associated with the agency name. These spin-offs occur to allow the promotional group to seek clients different from the parent company without causing a conflict of client interests. For example, an agency might have a banking client, which would prevent them from working for another financial institution. However, a separate promotional design group could pitch other financial services clients, promoting their expertise in that area. Advertising agency promotional groups are, in many cases, the "diversified studios" that many designers desire. The downside is that often the quality of design produced by many agencies is mediocre. While some agency sales promotion divisions do exceedingly fine work, the general level is below that of design firms. Perhaps this is explained by the general agency business focus on producing work for television spots. Promotion has traditionally been a "stepchild" department. As these groups now are becoming more attractive profit centers and the focus shifts, the quality should improve. The key to quality is determined by the quality of the client and what the client demands, regardless of where the work is done.

# ADVERTISING: ROLES AND PEOPLE

Advertising is made by a group of people who work in teams, sometimes dedicated to specific clients. These teams are comprised of different talents, each contributing a strategy and specific point of view or responsible for a specific role. Classically, a team will include the creative director (who could have an art or copy background), the art director, the copywriter, the account manager, and maybe an account planner (strategist). Penny Burrow, an associate at RGA writes, "These people conceive of and implement the positioning of a product and its brand image. Think of a funnel where all the ideas and input are put into the top and at the bottom a campaign emerges which will appear throughout the sales initiative." Titles can vary depending on seniority. Here are some comments identifying the personality, characteristics, and training necessary for success by our RGA advertising team, who deals with these issues on a daily basis.

# THE ADVERTISING ART DIRECTOR

*Connie Wolf and Sylvia Laniado, RGA*

Connie Wolf:

A good art director has to be a good designer, but this job also requires the ability to think conceptually... a combination of hand skills and brains. An art director should know how to work as a team with a copywriter... the writer should develop visual skills and the designer needs verbal and written skills. It goes without saying that knowledge of the latest computer programs is essential as well as an understanding of integrated Web design, plus print, TV, collateral, promotion, and direct marketing. How do you learn all this, especially when there are so few, if any, entry level jobs in advertising now? I tell young designers just starting out in advertising, "Don't talk too much and keep your eyes and ears wide open!" If you are lucky enough to get good advice and direction from senior people in the business you can pick up a lot. Temperament and personality are particularly important in this business; an art director needs a strong sense of self and the ability to accept rejection of his work.

Sylvia Laniado:

An art director needs to be conceptual as well as a good designer. He or she must be able to communicate an idea in an exciting, memorable way and to sell a product. He or she should also be able to write. "The best candidates for these jobs are those people who are confident, articulate, personable, resilient, and flexible—with a certain amount of maturity. You will constantly be asked to make changes to your work, often your ideas will be rejected; and you'll be competing with other creatives. You'll need to keep revising your work until everyone in the process—including the client, of course—is satisfied. One needs a healthy ego to handle the process.

Both Sylvia and Connie recommend going back to school at night, suggesting in New York the School of Visual Arts or Ad House,which as Connie says,"gives students instruction from the best in the business and the opportunity to brainstorm with their contemporaries. Read about the history of the advertising business, learn about the profession you have chosen, study the greats.

## COPYWRITING
*Penny Burrow and Sylvia Laniado, RGA*

We cannot exclude the copywriter who is the partner and soulmate to the art director. Many times they seem to be indistinguishable from each other. As Sylvia puts it,"The best work is a collaboration between art director and copywriter that is a big idea, simple and clear. A copywriter also needs to be conceptual as well as a wordsmith. He or she must be able to communicate an idea in a captivating, interesting way, sell a product, and have a good visual sense." Penny adds, "A copywriter usually graduates from college with a BA in English, creative writing, or journalism. However some of the greatest writers have come out of a theatre background, sometimes film. Being a writer takes devotion to the business, an ability to dig deep into an intelligent mind and bring forth an advertising concept that will translate visually and verbally to the consumer.

## ACCOUNT MANAGEMENT IN ADVERTISING AND DESIGN
*Frank Dahill, RGA*

The focus today has shifted away from creative concept and execution to client service and strategy. There is an increase in the number of design companies that consider themselves primarily consultants, with the majority of the company consisting of account managers, product managers, and strategists. Account management and strategic planning in either advertising or design present excellent opportunities for non-creatives who want to work in a creative environment.

The people who are great candidates for this job are those who are personable, very outgoing, sure of themselves but don't have a big ego.

Those who do best as account managers are flexible, get along easily with others, and are able to make compromises. Although an M.B.A. is sometimes important, I look for people who are strong strategic thinkers with experience in doing research, comparative analyses, and marketing skills.

The advice I would give to someone interested in this job is to get an internship in a well-known agency while still in college. This guarantees an entry level position after graduation, because all big agencies hire entry level people. Target large, established firms right away to get the traditional training; later you can always move to smaller, more exciting shops.

## ADVERTISING TIPS FOR A CHANGING MARKET
*Sylvia Laniado*

What's different, what's new in the advertising business? Everything. The computer has changed advertising completely. Clients give an assignment in the morning and expect to see ideas in that afternoon, the day after or in a couple of days. In the past creative people would have had a week or two to think about the strategy, conceptualize with their partners, and fine-tune the execution. This makes working on a few assignments simultaneously even harder than before. The most important part of the process, solving the problem, is given the least amount of time.

Here are some tips for those entering the field:

*Portfolio*: Put together four or five books so you won't lose time waiting for each agency to review and get it back to you. Don't send your book out until you feel it's the very best it can be. Keep your books up to date and when you are employed, get copies of everything you produce. Your portfolio should show your versatility, intelligence, and humor.

*Organization*: Keep good records of everyone you talk to or meet with, including dates, their titles, agency, phone numbers, and e-mail address.

*The Interview*: During the interview be a good listener, show enthusiasm, and know about the agency and their product before you meet. Agencies look for shining personalities as well as breakthrough books. Your ability to communicate is as important as your art direction and copywriting skills. If you can't sell yourself to an agency, you won't be able to sell your ideas to a client. You must be able to interface and interact with many different kinds of people. Agencies want confident candidates who will work well with their peers as well as management and clients.

*Be patient.* Very often the agency you start with will determine your future path. If you begin at one of the more creative shops, you have a much better chance of continuing with award-winning agencies throughout your career.

*On finding that 'right' position*: Where you start your career often determines your career path. If you start out at a very creative boutique, you will be able to attract the more prestigious agencies when searching for your next position. You will also be working with the best creatives and learning more than you would in a more account-driven agency. Keep in mind not only which agency is significant—but also which accounts you will be working on. Obviously, the more creative the client, the more opportunity there will be for you. That can prove to be just as important—sometimes more so—than the specific agency. Both factors should be considered.

Try to get an internship during your summers off. It's not only a good way to learn, but it's also a great way to start networking. Join the One Club and/or Art Directors Club. That's another excellent way to network. Read as many books about the industry as you can. They can be both informative and fun. Stay in tune with art, film, theatre, music, and television. Read the annuals, go to the award shows, and study magazine advertising as well as TV. Identify ads and commercials you don't like—and change them. Identify the client's work you do like and find out what agencies they're at. There's a *Redbook of Advertisers* (at the Public library as well as ad agency libraries) that tells you which agencies advertise their products. This is valuable information to have before you even start your search.

Once you land your first job, there are things you should be aware of. While the work you do is key, it is also important to get along well with all the people you interact with. You need to understand the protocol and learn about the personalities you're working with. Their liking you is just as important as their liking your work. This applies to your clients, as well. Getting the job is the first step; keeping it is the second.

Myrna Davis added, "My advice to a young person interested in working in this business is to try to get an internship or an apprentice position or take one of the high school workshops available. See what's going on, watch someone practice advertising. Look at other people's portfolios, save ads that you like, read art directors' annuals and learn the names of the best agencies. You must keep being inspired, excited, and interested—it never ends."

# Industrial Design

## 8

**T**his survey of industrial design (ID) is directed toward its relationship with graphic design. While industrial design is a discipline unto itself, no discussion of graphic design would be complete without considering the alliance of the two.

## ID: A CORNERSTONE IN THE EVOLUTION OF GRAPHIC DESIGN

The origin of industrial design in the 1920s has been glamorized by larger-than-life figures that gained much media attention. Raymond Loewy, Donald Deskey, and Henry Dreyfuss were true renaissance men who integrated many facets of two-dimensional and three-dimensional design. Loewy, somewhat like Frank Lloyd Wright, was famous for his personal charisma, was something of a media star, and through his fame he was able to communicate his vision of design's role in our culture, and thus was able to attract a broad range of projects. His fame defined the classical American designer. He was responsible for the design of locomotives, automobiles (the Studebaker), corporate identity (Exxon), packaging (Lucky Strike cigarettes), housewares, and china dishes. Loewy's designs had a profound effect in shaping the look of modern-day life at the middle of the twentieth century. Industrial design took on an aura similar to architecture (often considered the mother of all the arts) and certainly was instrumental in developing the concept of graphic design as a profession.

# CURRENT ID PRACTICES

Today ID has developed into a business dominated by small-scale design firms that can still control an unusual array of diversified assignments. These firms work for manufacturing corporations, usually under the direction of and in tandem with the corporation's internal design group and design managers. These design consultancies function as developmental think tanks to the corporation. While ID's focus is primarily three-dimensional as opposed to graphic design's two-dimensional base, the industrial designer can still have a significant graphic involvement. Sometimes the firm or individual will do it all, or sometimes they opt to work in tandem with graphic designers.

In fact, ID most often encompasses product design and new product development. The graphic component is utilized in relation to the product and is often applied graphics. New product development can, because of its intrinsic nature, require or spin off into full-blown identity programs. The products naturally can be anything and everything consumers use, from disposable to durable products. This includes the design (but not engineering) of transportation vehicles (cars, planes, bikes, motorcycles); consumer products (bottles, jars, containers); durable and "white" products (refrigerators, coffeemakers, small electrical products, household products, etc.), as well as scientific equipment and instruments (computers, medical and surgical products, instrumentation panels, testing devices), housewares and tabletop (dishes and giftware, cookware, eating utensils, and furniture.

All design work of this nature relies heavily on training, the ability to understand human factors, and the designer's proactive role in research and development. Henry Dreyfuss pioneered the original guidelines for products being used by the human body and the products' ergonomic requirements. Industrial designers are often charged by their clients with the developmental problem solving required to establish a new product, or they may initiate and create new product ideas based on their own observations. The research and development aspect to ID is truly innovative design not experienced in many other design disciplines. Today's industrial design has many new challenges, some of which are articulated by Tucker Viemeister: "The most recent changes in industrial design have been in the amount of technology that can be imbedded in a product; what I learned from my teachers at Pratt still applies—you have to design in context. In the future, industrial design and interactive design will be connected. Traditional ID will stay the same, but there will also be another kind of designer.

The applied graphics on ID projects are an inherent part of the complete design program. Often the industrial designer will create all the two- and three-dimensional design. The two-dimensional components of three-dimensional projects are most often realized in identifying or decorative graphics, signage, and exhibition design. It is common practice for industrial design or exhibition design firms to hire graphic designers to work as part of the design team or form co-op ventures with graphic design firms.

A survey of industrial design projects, which would incorporate graphic design, would include the following:

## PRODUCT DESIGN

Products frequently need graphics. Sometimes graphics are instructional or informational. Sometimes they are purely decorative. Computer, medical, or telecommunications instruments require labels, numbers, buttons, instructions, and general typographic information. Sporting equipment, clothing, and accessories have become graphically decorative. For example, consider the dynamic graphics on sportswear pioneered by aerodynamic designs for swim or ski teams in the Olympic games or the variety of graphics applied to snowboards. These purely graphic expressions of speed or emotion contributed an altogether new dimension to visual impression of the sporting event. And the revolution was started by Swatch in watch design, which challenged a whole industry to seek new graphic dimensions for product design. Often when these graphic solutions unite with the name of the product, we enter the world of licensing as well (e.g., the Nike swoosh, the Movado watch dot, NFL teams applied to clothing and accessories, Mickey Mouse on everything).

## ENVIRONMENTAL DESIGN/
## EXHIBITION DESIGN

Retail environments, public spaces, trade shows, museums, special exhibitions, and corporate shows are the venue for this work. The three-dimensional planning and graphics cannot be separated. The graphics in exhibitions often require an editorial feel or point of view, for they tell a story. Museums devoted to history encompass time lines (Ellis Island, the Rock 'n' Roll Museum, the Johnstown Flood, for example). While environmental design is covered more fully in chapter 6, many industrial designers find employment and a career direction in this specialty.

## SIGNAGE

The development of sign systems found in airports, shopping malls, hospitals, office buildings, zoos, mass transportation, and the like require a special group of skills. (This subject correlates to the work of environmental designers; see chapter 6.) The designer needs to be highly organized with a strong ability to analyze and structure information while having a love and commitment to typographic and graphic systems (graphic design). The designer also needs to know manufacturing materials and three-dimensional structural elements (usually stemming from an ID education). Lastly, the designer has to be able to draw and read drafting plans (architectural drawings). The recognition of these unique skill combinations clears the path to understanding why signage designers can, and do, develop from all three disciplines.

Signage designers are special folk who derive much pleasure from their ability to work within a fully integrated design environment. These projects, by their nature, require the collaboration of architects, store planners, industrial designers, and graphic designers. It is an interesting milieu.

## THE INDUSTRIAL DESIGNER'S ROLE

The beginning of the twenty-first century finds the industrial designer in a pivotal role in a society that seems to have an insatiable need for new products. For example, the explosion of telecommunications in an expanding wireless world, sporting goods for an increasing leisure class, hi-tech products of every type, and a multitude of vehicles have created a demand for innovative design. Design has become marketing's darling, as it is the vehicle to create the all-important differentiation of similar products. Design sells. Design can be elegant (Apple), funky (Visor,) or amusing (Graves teapots).

Industrial design departments in corporations have gained a new focus of importance. Michael Gerke, vice president of industrial design at Black & Decker, expresses his perspective from the manufacturing side:

> As always, the unpredictable end user is the predominant driver of change throughout the retail landscape, and the design professions at large. Industrial design—almost by definition—requires a keen sense (possibly even a sixth sense) of trends. We are dragged along with some, and we do the dragging with others. Yet we are all tightly woven into the fabric of consumer taste, and are expected to give it shape. The shape we choose, whether ordinary and derivative, or fresh and inspired, will either attract or repel the end user—their money and their loyalty.
>
> Anyone entering the design professions must be inflicted with chronic curiosity and an obsession for observation. Making difficult connections between things—man and machine, money and materials, or motivation and the mind—is the inescapable obligation of every designer. Those who embrace that obligation are often rewarded.

Industrial designers' catholic design training has allowed them to transcend narrow definitions and to take on a variety of roles. A view of this training as espoused by Tucker Viemeister: "An industrial design education gives people training in ergonomics and what I call 'physionomics.' The trick is to take what you learn in school and apply it to real situations. It's important to know how to read people, including employers and clients, and be able to tell a good, coherent story."

Eric Chan, partner at ECCO Design, sees the role of the designer taking on greater importance beyond the creation and recreation of products

Today's industrial designer is evolving into more of a production, marketing, and general business consultant. This requires the ability to think strategically, to understand the latest technologies, and have a deep knowledge of the lifestyle changes that affect purchasing. An engineering-driven, today design is driving technology. There is a new structure, a new mandate to create a meaningful product. Young designers must obviously have the necessary computer skills, for this powerful machine designer must possess a diverse background and sensitivity to life outside of design.

When we begin a new project we conduct an internal workshop as part of our research. By inviting different kinds of people to contribute their ideas, we arrive at a reason for designing the project. Ideas are evolving so fast that the future and present have become very close. In many fundamental areas the actual quality of the products has not improved. In the kitchen, for example, there are more options but is the quality better? As consumers become more educated, "new" is no longer enough; there must also be value and quality. In the past product design was, but they also need basic artistic skills like drawing, which is becoming scarce. The computer screen is limited and without three-dimensional, tactile qualities. You need skills to be creative, to support the vision, but your work has to have a playful, emotional quality… it has to be something you love.

At Razorfish, design director, Jean-Michael Ekeblad finds the ID profession more democratic, inclusive, and collaborative.

Industrial design has changed from being a narrow world of formally trained product designers and is now beginning to welcome people from a variety of disciplines. I have been deeply disappointed in the past by people who are without any visual language, and now I might prefer, for example, to hire a jewelry designer. At Razorfish we look for people who have different sets of skills. The results are unpredictable, exciting, and may often involve a certain amount of risk. It takes a brave organization to understand the value of this fresh source of energy and this involves a great openness on both sides, often working with difficult people or circumstances. Our profession needs to be more challenged and willing to learn. Industrial design is finally becoming more humble, farsighted, and nurturing.

## THE GRAPHIC DESIGN CONNECTION

To recap this short survey of industrial design, I should point out how industrial design functions as an occupation with interconnecting bonds to graphic design. The relationship between the two disciplines has had several developments beneficial to graphic design. Initially ID pointed the way for graphic design to be recognized as a discipline unto itself. The development of ID as a profession has also provided a guide and model toward establishing graphic design as a recognized profession. However, at this writing, graphic design has not achieved that status. It is a complex question of accreditation and licensing. Architects must be licensed by the state in which they practice. Industrial designers are not licensed, but through their membership in the Industrial Design Society of America, attach IDSA after their name. This signifier denotes a level of professional acceptance and elevates the individual in the public and client's eye, much the way architects will attach AIA (The American Institute of Architects) after their names. Graphic design has no equivalent practice.

In presenting the alliance between these two disciplines it is interesting to observe how these design careers can merge. Quite often industrial designers find their life's work ends up as graphic design. Some of the motivating forces are the sheer quantity of graphic design projects available compared to the much smaller industrial design business arena. While ID represents an important, integral discipline in the large scope of design, there are fewer industrial designers, fewer firms, and, naturally, fewer positions. And, of course, the transition from ID work to graphic design is fairly simple because of the breadth of ID education. It is far harder for the graphic designer to function as an industrial designer. To do so usually requires an intense involvement with design in the third dimension, an intimate knowledge of structural materials and CAD computer systems, or enrolling in an ID program.

# Interactive Media

## 9

The interactive industry has always been known for its breakneck pace. In so-called Internet time companies have launched and gone public in a modicum of the time that companies have traditionally taken. And, as the market has changed, they experienced layoffs or closed shop just as quickly.

Simultaneously, the technologies these companies were founded on or used as tools change equally fast. Whenever one software, device, platform, or protocol becomes established, you can be sure an improved version is moments behind. There has been no choice but to upgrade, upgrade, upgrade. It leaves one dizzy. For those who try to gain the skills necessary to be successful in this arena, the challenge has always been how to keep up with the pace.

At the time of the original edition of this book in 1992, this chapter was entitled, "Computer Graphics," and the opening stated: "Anything written about the latest innovations is obsolete possibly at the time of writing and certainly by the time of publication." At the time of the last edition, in the later half of 1996, it was noted that the caveat was still necessary and that "staying 'current' in this fascinating and complex field, dependent upon the latest technological progresses, is dismaying as the continuous chain of advancements show no sign of slowing . . . . The speed of change challenges everyone's imagination, as well as energy and dexterity in keeping abreast of the innovations." Today, in 2001, the challenge remains. And, in the interim, an entire industry has grown.

# A SHORT HISTORY OF A SHORT HISTORY

*Jessica Goldfarb, Chief Operating Officer, RGA*

While our concern is so much with the present, what is the newest and the latest, we should not forget to keep a perspective of our past. The digitalization of our workplace is still a comparatively recent thing, and hence, a short history. The utilization of computers in design firms began shortly after the Macintosh and the PC were introduced in the early 1980s. In 1985 computerized multimedia was limited to on-screen PowerPoint-style slide shows, with bulleted text on a small range of colored backgrounds, but no sound and no video. More often, the term "multimedia" still meant on-screen video with a separate, but complementary, sound track and lighting. Hypertext allowed for the first interactive computer experience, enabling the user to jump from a reference in one document to related references located elsewhere. In the early 1990s, interactive digital technologies fully emerged, allowing for touch screen kiosks and consumer titles on CD-ROMs. By 1994 Mosaic added graphic capabilities to the Internet, paving the way for uses with more mass appeal, the explosion of the World Wide Web, and the so-called New Media industry was born. In the last couple of years, even the concept of New Media has changed, moving more away from the Internet. Increasingly it encompasses other areas of connectivity, including broadband interactive television and wireless applications, such as GPS-based information systems used in cars, on cellphones, or on Personal Data Appliances (PDAs) like Palm Pilots.

The introduction of such digital and interactive technologies with significant graphics capabilities rapidly attracted the attention of design firms and brought graphic designers to the attention of a multitude of industries that struggled to integrate the Web into their strategies and daily operations. But it has also caused confusion. Many companies experienced periods of difficult decision-making to justify the expense of this innovation, determine whether it was even necessary, or identify the appropriate equipment or tools to purchase. Many costly investments were made in hardware or software that today are completely obsolete. And companies found themselves heavily invested in new marketing communication tools or products that ultimately proved to be neither revenue generating nor brand enhancing.

During the mid- to late-1980s our requests for skills needed for hiring would sometimes note that computer experience was a plus factor in the decision-making process. In other words, if a designer had some

Macintosh literacy they were way ahead of the pack and most often knew more than the person doing the hiring. By 1990 the tables had completely turned, with Mac literacy more-often-than-not a necessity. Today complete digital fluency is a standard, with Mac still dominant, but with PCs increasingly in use. Variations of software and platforms have become the deciding factor in hiring.

At its inception, the so-called New Media industry was a conglomeration of a large number of companies within diverse industries—from software to marketing communications to entertainment to publishing to broadcast media to advertising and to graphic design—which were situated to take advantage of the developing technologies. Today, it's solidly it's own industry, which has become a permanent aspect of all other industries. In 1994 the New York New Media Association (NYNMA) was founded to support and promote that industry in New York; in 2001, it has a membership of approximately 10,000 individuals representing nearly 2,500 companies.

As it continues to develop, New Media is more and more becoming simply "Media." The continued convergence of different media will crystallize this trend, bringing together the tools and capabilities currently limited to separate industries. More video, animation, and motion graphics will come to the Internet and will be commonplace in Broadband interactive TV as faster and faster connection speeds are made possible, as consumers have DSL lines or cable modems at home. Graphic designers will have to develop these additional skills and sensibilities. The onset of the wireless explosion will surely add demand for user interface designers and information architects, who will help guide users through the myriad of information and services available to them. And branding, which has become a mainstay of marketing techniques (see chapter 3) only increases the demand for all of these new tools throughout the business landscape, as companies seek to keep customers aware and loyal by establishing direct marketing products or special deals online.

The one irreversible change is that computers have become the indispensable tool for designers and marketing communications strategists, a presence moving from the single unit at a shared table to their ubiquitous presence at each desk, connected by extensive networks. The drop in initial costs (as with most new electronic equipment) has greatly contributed to this proliferation. Another aspect to these transformations is that young designers will not take jobs with firms that are not technologically current. These designers feel that lack of access to up-to-date equipment will limit their creativity and hamper their careers in the long term. And they are right! Therefore, many of the questions raised in the past regarding technology's viability in design are long dead and buried.

The creative studio is digital, interactive, and online. At this point a fully-equipped studio requires a team of technologists, who not only keep the computers, networks, and open pipes for Internet connectivity operating, but also work with designers to create databases and applications that integrate with their designs to implement the goals of the client. The ongoing challenge to obtain, maintain, and purchase the most innovative equipment and software tools available for this is the dominant technological force in graphic, architectural, and product design studios. We obviously must be creatively dominant, but many echo the fear that the seduction of instant gratification is changing the way we think and design—but not for the better. As we shall see, traditional skills have not been lost and need to be retained if the integrity of the work is to be maintained.

## A VIEWPOINT FROM A PRO

In keeping with our methods of tracking change and trying to determine what it means for those working within the business, we turned to Hans Neubert, executive creative director for Interactive Red Sky.

> The biggest change in our business is that design isn't dominated by designers anymore. Especially interactive design, where no specific breed of talent is in charge. . . there are architects, videographers, filmmakers, animators, illustrators, character designers, cartoonists, some traditional graphic designers, product designers; interestingly enough, this comes closest to the generalist approach to communication that was preached in some schools fifteen years ago. The good news is that although we are celebrating style more than ever, design is about content, contex, and relevant innovation.

> Before interactive design—that just began about five or six years ago—I did graphic design, package design, branding, and print design. interactive design has become global, making style and trends so much more accessible, ideas become immediately available. In fact, today there is access to too much information. Every media vehicle, television, newspapers, magazines, online, and e-mail, compete for our attention. What influences today's trends? Video games have outsold Hollywood box office numbers, and are the most influential source of style and content. The variety of entertainment is incredible, including TV, video games, Web sites, wireless, plus the traditional radio, CDs and

movies. The field of digital design is now dominated by entertainment and being able to captivate an audience with a compelling story.

In interactive, and other media as well, we have become globalized by the way information and influences are exchanged. The ability in interactive design to combine different skills is not as important as the potential applications: broadband, TV, computer, CD-ROM, kiosks, etc. Designers now have to design for many different delivery forms.

The big news today is that a huge amount of designers are going into business for themselves right out of school. Young creatives under 30 with marketing and strategic savvy can now be independent. In London there are many design co-ops. Design and creative people have filled spaces in the present culture. In New York design co-ops are already contributing to New York culture and design. Small offices are nimble and flexible and are influencing design at a higher rate of speed. I advise young designers to start with a small company where they will get to hear directly what the client has to say about their work; this is real world experience.

## A DIFFERENT WORKPLACE IN INTERACTIVE

*Rita Armstrong, Recruiter for Interactive and Digital Design, RGA*

What is different about today's workplace? When it comes to interactive talent teams, a lot has changed over the past three years. Work hours have become more palatable due to the addition of more experienced managers of both creative and production. A clearer understanding of the site architectural strategy as a part of the creative process has also come into play. Where "content is king," writers/copywriters are now an important part of the site creative team. (Some graphic design studios are not too sure about how to work with them, but they now know they need them.) Lastly, those who are looking for a job within the interactive creative community are better informed. They go into job interviews knowing what they want, and whether they are in a position to ask for it.

When I first started placing within the interactive arena, I found the breathtakingly disorganized, exciting world of Web agencies and design firms extremely frustrating. My candidates, which is what we call those designers we present to companies, felt the same way. Offices were in disarray. Designers were either working in a bunker-like atmosphere, or cubicles that made Dilbert's environment look like a castle. Companies were growing so fast that the real estate market couldn't keep up, so designers sometimes accepted a job without knowing where they would be working—Silicon Alley or the Wall Street wired valley. Worst of all, they might be working with little or no supervision. The growth rate of these firms could not keep up with the demand for creative managerial talent. Everyone thought the best flavor of the day was young, hot, and sassy. The combination of these three elements—young, hot, and not very experienced in the area of management—created total chaos for very busy interactive firms. It really wasn't until the year 2000 that articles relating that 'Grey is ok' seemed to appear. Our clients at this point in time seem much more interested in finding 'conceptual mentors,' and those experienced in design management, than bringing in the latest hot design jockey. All of these developments mean that now young designers in technology aren't left out to dry. It is so important to the beginning of a career to find a true mentor as a manager. One may have the raw talent and the technology to get a job, but that job is rather worthless if it does not allow you to continue learning. Several companies offer formal mentoring programs, where young designers to art directors are assigned a senior partner to whom they report once a week to discuss their work and career direction. Not only is this approach important to the designer, it inspires and instills a sense of loyalty to the company, which makes an employee stick around. So I'd say one of the biggest changes in the workplace within interactive is the sense that it has matured, and therefore must provide a more stable and nurturing environment in order to stay creatively viable.

The other area of growth is site architecture and strategy. Your Web site can't leave your client's customers stranded, or frustrated. A site is mapped out and dissected now before it goes live. We will go into some of the new and improved job titles that go along with this expertise later. The development of this area has caused some real challenges for many firms. Should architecture be a part of the creative process, and if so, at what point do we add these people to the process? How much should the design be driven by the site mapping? How should the staffing be structured for the best effect and synergy of talents? Where do these people come from? Should they have a cognitive science background, or should they just be designers who have a knack for dissecting and assigning data? How technical should this person be? How do we train someone to grow this expertise? Whether it is an agency or design shop these companies are all struggling with how to include this expertise into their process. That means that those who have architectural skills and are interested in joining a company need to do their research on how a company works before agreeing to come on board.

Copywriters and art directors have always been teams within ad agencies, but many interactive groups have not adapted the same model for their groups, at least in the beginning. The exploration of content and communities tied to commerce has made the need for wordsmiths a necessity. More detail on the role of copywriters is below and can be found in chapter 7 on advertising, but the addition of the copywriter to the interactive team is an interesting one. Within advertising agencies, copywriters grow into creative directors, just as their art director counterparts do. They have all the conceptual skills that art directors do; it is just that they come from the idea with copy in hand, not visuals. interactive agencies still seem to be struggling with how to bring these people on board and to grow them into managerial slots. Several have devised content design director titles as an entrée into management.

With these experiences it's important to note how much more we all know now. People now know that at a certain level they should no longer be doing HTML. They now know a bit more about salaries and just how much is that stock worth? We are better informed as to what makes an interactive company great, and what just makes it news. Companies now know how to ask seniors about their ability to direct others and do they want to present work to clients, or are they accustomed to handing that off to the account guys? The workplace is different when all parties involved are informed parties. Some of the excitement is gone, but now we can get back to creating beautiful things that work and will be used. We can even make deadlines.

## PRESENTING CREATIVE WORK

*Rita Armstrong*

How do you show your work if it is mostly Web based? 75 percent of my candidates have their own Web site. My clients have come to expect work to be shown this way. It is also a great way to archive and keep a portfolio alive. Too often you may design a lovely site, hand it over to a client, and then watch the site slowly disintegrate as their in-house graphic group adds content. What you put up so proudly in March is a disgrace by June. Quite often candidates come to me at the beginning of their search, not quite ready to present their work. They have a list of URLs they want me to send my clients as a stopgap until they have their personal site up. This rarely works to the candidate's advantage. Many of the sites have been changed and no longer reflect the design structure that made them work and be beautiful. This puts the designer at a disadvantage, limiting the effectiveness of the portfolio. Archiving work on zips, which can be posted later, makes a lot of sense if it's not possible to keep a site fresh. As backup, always keep two to three screen grab portfolios. These portfolios should consist of fifteen to twenty-five pages of Web site printouts. It is also a good way to show a work in progress. The screen grab portfolios have two uses. They are backup, if during an interview it's not possible to get to a site that is crucial to showing one's appropriateness for a job opening. These mini-portfolios also act as a good introduction to a company. These mini-books can be dropped off along with a resume, including fresh URLs, and hopefully lead to an interview. It is much more effective than just a resume. People are also much more willing to peruse a book than to pop a CD in or quit what they are in the middle of doing to surf the Web. It is not the final presentation, but the visual foot in the door.

A personal Web site should be very much like a traditional portfolio, and if you have bypassed the sections on print portfolio presentation in chapters 11 and 12, it would be worth going back for a look. The site should reveal something about your personal taste, but it should not push only a specific look. The tone of the site is very important. Don't put your picture or the picture of your dog on a professional portfolio site. Don't get so steeped in presenting your design philosophy that the meat of the site is lost on the audience. Don't get so hyped on your flash skills that the viewer decides that the work is not worth the wait. Abuse a friend in the process. Make someone within the design community look at the finished product and offer a review. Make someone who knows nothing about the Web or what you do look at it and critique the architecture. Remember that this site will be viewed by the well versed, and the not so well versed, in technology. Human resources people may be viewing your site, as well as your design peers, so it is not just tech knowledge, but the design experience of the user, that will run the gamut.

A portfolio has always had a sense of architecture. How are you arranging your pieces, does that arrangement reflect your interests and, therefore, interest the people you want to work with? The best online books are presented as quick downloads of your work arranged in a clean, pleasant manner. Arranging the work by print, moving images, and Web works well. The viewer can go to the area that interests them most and then proceed to the other specialties. Make your resume section versatile. The resume should be able to do gymnastics if possible. I should be able to print it out, download it, and it should be easy to attach to documents. I send many of my clients PDFs and MS Word documents at the same time, so I'm sure they can read it, and forward it. Human resources groups utilize MS Word documents. Creative directors want to see PDFs. If you are more comfortable with a bio format, provide that as well, but don't limit yourself to only that format. If possible, offer an automatic e-mail link. You will get responses faster.

## DESIGN JOBS, DESCRIPTIONS, AND TITLES

*Rita Armstrong*

So what do you call yourself and what responsibilities go along for the ride? Several of our clients have given up on knowing what to call their creatives. Some had even come up with rather ridiculous titles just to poke fun at the process. (Thankfully, we are seeing fewer of these made-up job titles, such as "evangelist" or "cyberguy.") The old design models for titles hold up rather well in most instances. Of course, we do have other areas of expertise, which exist primarily in only interactive.

The creative director title within interactive covers a lot of ground. Creative directors may be directing as little a group as five or upwards to forty. They may be hands-on if they choose to be, if the group is small enough. In a large creative department the primary focus is on driving the brand and site concept, looking over the shoulders, so to speak, of art directors, leading the presentations to the client, and leading conceptual think tank meetings. Many creative directors get frustrated with the lack of hands-on design at this level. They find themselves traveling about to clients and pushing papers instead of ideas. Realize that, in most cases, this is a natural progression in a career. Executives and VPs of creative have even less contact with the process. In this market they are often asked to drum up interest in the company by speaking at quite a few conferences. They try to catch the eye of the star designers so they can build up their bull pen. They may present work to clients, but they are not the ones building the sites.

Many interactive companies have beefed up their creative departments with associate creative directors. These are the people between the creative director and the art directors. They are mentors and organizers, really creative-directors-in-training. They make a lot of the day-to-day decisions on where the concept work will be headed and who will work on it. The recent trend to hire quite a few assistant creative directors came from the dearth of talented ADs who could step up to fill creative director positions. They lacked the experience of juggling a large group of people's assignments and needed to have a bit more supervision before they were granted the full responsibilities of a CD. Many companies found themselves caught up short by the number of Indians to chiefs; ACDs were a way to get the work under control.

Art directors are the real guts behind the Web work. They may be called senior designers if the art director title is not in play. Normally an art director supervises designers, and production designers, may also have a partner who is a copywriter, and will take direction from either an ACD or a CD. It is the art director who presents the ideas of the team to senior management. In most cases the art director is still hands-on, and very responsible for those who report to him or her. The ACD or CD may hire and fire people, but the art director is usually the person behind those decisions.

Designers are the ones who are coming up with the concepts that are utilized or rejected by the art directors. Their computer skills need to be top-notch in order to produce the most varied options for design. They need to know programs like flash, in order to design for optimal utilization. Designers can be a major influence on how technically deep a site will be. They are also usually younger and closer to the investigative environment of their education, so technical and design experimentation is a large part of their process. They are coming from a world of all spec work to working within the confines of a client's brand perception. At this point having an AD who will invest time into a designer's growth is critical.

## PRODUCTION DESIGN

Rita Armstrong continues, "Production for interactive media has been separated into its own chapter because of its importance as an integral facet of design. Production relates to all activities from Web production through producers." A detailed description written by Joanne Kivlahan, associate for interactive media at RGA can be found in chapter 10. From the design point of view, Rita adds, "Being a production designer puts one into a rather tenuous position. In some companies you are strictly following the marching orders of your assigned designer or art director. In other companies you are really a junior designer, who will be given opportunities to create your own work. What you must determine before accepting a job is what percentage of the work that you will be doing is design, and how much is production? Realize also that some production is actually design-driven. Icon designs, illustrations, and PhotoShop imaging can all be design and not just follow-through. If you can, freelance at the job first to find out what you are getting into."

## JOB OPPORTUNITIES/WRITERS
*Penny Burrow*

Although interactive media is visual discipline, Web sites, too, are dependent on copywriters to generate headlines, or banners, which is traditionally an advertising copywriter's skill. Also, if the site is in support of an advertising campaign, the copywriter must ensure that the branding of the product is integrated with other advertising media. It is interesting that the growth of Internet sites has really opened up the market for writers who don't come from traditional ad copy backgrounds. More informational sites usually hire writers from an editorial or journalism background. But copywriters also have been given an opportunity to expand into these longer format projects and to provide content for the site. Copy- and other writers are also involved in the navigation of a site to assure that the words are flowing in a way that makes sense.

Additional information on copywriters and their role in advertising can be found in chapter 7, "Advertising and Design."

## CLIENT SERVICES
*Amy Fried, Associate for Interactive's Business Side, RGA*

Client services people handhold the client and interface day to day and at higher levels. They are primarily responsible for the initial strategy of the project and for its ongoing management. Like their counterparts in the traditional advertising agency structure, their titles are: account manager, account director, group account director. These members of the client services department work on teams with creatives as the liaison to the client. They report back to the creative team on the objectives of the client and present the deliverables to the client. As the go-between, they must deal with both the client's complaints and satisfactions.

Inside a corporation, or in-house, the responsibility for marketing the company to consumers (so-called B2C marketing) or to other businesses (so-called B2B marketing) is the work of the marketing manager, director, VP, or CMO. These marketers can act as the client to in-house or agency creative team when asking those teams to develop new products, campaigns, or areas of Web sites, or sales presentations.

The duties of selling the company's services or doing deals like revenue sharing, custom product or various types of arrangements with other Internet companies is the principal work of the business development manager, director, or VP. In some cases, the in-house client function for business development people is the same as marketing, but they are less likely to deal directly with creative.

Skills needed in this industry are the same as any other business. M.B.A.s are now a standard requirement and a credential that can always help. An M.B.A. is particularly useful for general management skills, as well as for higher level, more strategic positions

A fundamental skill that is advantageous to all business side staff is the ability to work in teams, either with other business staff or with creatives. Each company or type of business has its own culture and these skills can vary tremendously, so sensitivity to these nuances is also important. Many marketers need writing skills for putting together proposals or for writing solicitation letters.

Management skills are helpful to nearly all business side personnel, who are generally involved with operating in and with teams. These skills become a must, for any businessperson who succeeds will ultimately graduate to higher level positions which require the supervision of others.

Marketers working in interactive media must have knowledge of both online (Internet, e-mail and wireless-based) and off-line (traditional print, broadcast, and outdoor media). Neither one stands alone and in the Internet world, off-line guerilla marketing techniques have proven themselves to be an effective source for driving people to Internet sites and services, helping companies that are first to market become first to get name recognition and be first to IPO.

Those in sales must understand how to sell, including how to network through current contacts, cold-call potential customers or clients, and understand the intricacies of setting up sales teams. Interpersonal and communication skills can also benefit a salesperson.

Business development specialists who focus on deal-making for either revenue streams (such as licensing deals) or for strategic partnerships will also benefit from cultivating negotiation skills. These deals are always detailed and most often very specific to the market segment that one is operating within, resulting in some cases to significant specialization.

## MAKING A JOB TRANSITION/DESIGN
*Rita Armstrong*

Initially everyone wanted to design for the Internet, but for those who kept their print roots and would like to become involved with the

Web, and if you would like at least one-third of your work to be in interactive, there are ways to make the switch. First of all, take a look at your print portfolio again. Are there pieces in there that would translate well into Web work? I remember looking at a lovely print book and pulling out some CD cases and thinking, each of these could be a Web site. The designs were all architecturally sound. The cover set the tone and the interior work was clearly laid out in a manner that made all the information about the songs and the lyrics easy to find. Even the graphics looked like they would download quickly.

If your work has this kind of flow, making the change to designing online projects should not be all that difficult. It is getting others to see your potential in this arena that may prove to be a challenge.

There are several ways to improve your skills in this area. Go to a night class for the technical aspects. You already know Quark, Illustrator, and PhotoShop. Learn Web page layout skills. After working on several school projects, post your own site showing past print work. Even better, volunteer to work on that school's Web site or a nonprofit organization's site. Your goal is to provide some URLs that you can show prospective employers or your current boss. Taking a night course or just hunkering down and teaching yourself will also let you know if you like the work. Much like editorial design, Web design has its limitations. The brand for the product, company, or service may already exist, and you are applying that brand to the Web. If you have access to strong programmers, and clients with deep pockets, you can really get to play, but most of the time the work is bread-and-butter information design.

## THE BUSINESS SIDE
*Amy Fried and Jessica Goldfarb*

On the business side, the interactive industry has always been a rollercoaster ride. Job transitions into interactive from other industries was once very easy because there really was no industry expertise. Then the financial and career opportunities afforded by the extreme growth of the interactive industry meant that these jobs were very popular and everyone wanted to get in. As the industry recognized its own skill requirements, it became more difficult to transfer into interactive, and those who possessed these skills found themselves in great demand. As a result, salaries and perks skyrocketed and the pace of job switching quickened. And companies fought to keep those with these skills.

As the industry matured, companies began to understand that traditional business and marketing skills were in many ways more important than industry expertise. This opened again the gates for those who looked to transfer into the interactive industry. And as the industry expanded, the sheer numbers of people needed who had these skills kept the demand high. Throughout this time, just finding bodies was a challenge; finding truly talented businesspeople was really hard.

Today, the pace of changing jobs is much slower as the industry has slowed down and companies are looking at more long-term, slower growth. Less demand means that jobs—new or a transfer—are harder to come by than two years ago. And today more traffic flows both ways, in and out of interactive. Skills remain transferable, with the focus on the skill and not the media. So, if you were an account executive at an interactive services shop like Organic and want to go to be an account executive at a traditional advertising agency such as Deutsch, it is easiest to stay within the same kind of position. Much more difficult is to try to move from traditional to interactive while also trying to get an entirely new kind of position, such as going from traditional account executive to an interactive brand planner.

In any event, if you want to work in a mid-level or higher position at an Internet company, you must have some experience in the space. For those looking to get first foot in the door, the best way is through networking and through local Internet industry organizations.

## WHERE IS ALL OF THIS GOING?
*Rita Armstrong*

Think Global . . . In more ways than one this is all headed toward globalization. What does that mean? It means that the most successful Web sites are those that ride the worldwide wave. The trend for global awareness is happening on several levels. If you have worked elbow to elbow with someone with European design school training, you have probably experienced the differences in their approach to a project. They may specialize early, but their areas of study cover more ground. As our product develops more of a technological bent, the lines between product, architecture, and graphic design blur. If we become too comfortable in our specialties we may miss being a part of design's evolution.

One of the most interesting developments over the last few years that will affect the future of design in interactive is the blend of skills required to service technological developments. The Web designers I've worked with may come from broadcast, product, architectural, or traditional graphic design backgrounds. Many of these people would never have been given a chance in traditional print to apply their skills.

Interactive, especially in the beginning, provided a think tank atmosphere of anything goes, or if you have some kind of design degree, and some good ideas, come on in.

The growth of broadband and handheld or wireless technology further bridges the gap between design specialties and design markets. Product designers will know more about interface design, and graphic or Web designers will know more about product design. In the same fashion there will be a more even exchange of design specialists abroad. Americans will be in demand for their Web knowledge and Europeans will be in demand here for their wireless experience. Making mistakes with new technology is very expensive. Hiring people who have had the experience of making those mistakes and correcting them is wise. Therefore, the exchange of specialists is probably the most efficient way to attack new product development. We've already seen how design has changed with the introduction of those granted visas during our Internet boom years. The technology has broadened our sense of what design is, but so has working with those who have different design educations and cultures to draw upon.

## THE FUTURE FROM THE BUSINESS SIDE PERSPECTIVE
*Amy Fried and Jessica Goldfarb*

The ever-changing marketplace in the interactive and Internet industries means that the rollercoaster continues. For at least the short-term, companies must again focus on traditional business issues, keeping marketing and salespeople in high demand. Any business development position that focuses on non-revenue generating dealmaking will become a much less important role as companies need to make money to stay alive. There will be more long-term, strategic marketing and less splashy, expensive consumer marketing as companies tighten their belts and prepare for the long haul, rather than having to be first to market, first to IPO, first to get name recognition. But what lay around the corner is anybody's guess.

Globalization in the interactive industry means that the business side is already focused on international markets and cross-market expansion. Right now, American companies are spreading their Internet expertise with those in Europe and Asia. And Scandinavian wireless companies are transferring their lessons in real-time, wireless interactive connectivity to companies in the U.S. and U.K. that are just catching on. Those with telecommunications marketing expertise in Japan are helping European companies determine how to take advantage of the proliferation of cellphones. And those in the U.S. with expertise in direct marketing are helping to transplant businesses into the strongly e-mail based Asian market. And those with broadband experience are quickly being deployed across the globe.

And as convergence continues, all of these skills will further overlap. Whether an individual has broadband, Internet, interactive, wireless, or software business experience, opportunities will open up. new media will move one more step to being just media.

## INTO THE UNKNOWN

This is all good news, but how does it affect you? Rita Armstrong's last word of advice is: "Don't get too comfortable. You may be making a really lovely salary in interactive, but interactive is all about change. The push and pull of the very stuff you design requires you to change as the technology develops. Stay on top of motion graphics and take courses in interface design, or human factors. Get a handle on what is hot in Europe. Attend conferences that may seem a bit outside your specialty. Start picking up magazines that cover product and architectural design. In other words, feed your brain. More is going to be demanded of you. You just need to be up to the challenge."

# A Guide to Production Jobs:
# Print and Interactive

## 10

**P**roduction departments, and the people who comprise their staff, are some of the most important people in the creative process. Simply put, no creative group could exist without them. They are key players in a team effort and often the unsung hero whose job it is to make things happen. They are the "glue" in the creative process. It is very important to remember that all production decisions require design knowledge, ability, and taste. If God is in the details, it is the production artist who is often making the last decisions. Designers need to recognize how important and how essential the production and project management roles are, how much this is a part of the entire process of producing a creative product, and how employment in this area can mean a fulfilling and lucrative career choice. Any well run organization places the proper emphasis on the production department and fully recognizes the influence and formidable role the production group plays to achieve quality creative solutions. For designers entering this field the best recommendation is to make sure you enjoy the working environment and the finished product. You want to be in a position in which the quality of the work continues to stimulate and challenge you. As in all creative choices the variety of firms to choose from is the same and the working environment is very important, as this is the place where you will spend most of your time. The satisfaction level stems from the realization that it is the production artist who is often making the last decisions.

I have asked the recruiters in my firm that know the most about production, Tara DeConigilio and Joanne Kivlahan, to contribute their expertise and thoughts on this important subject. In the following, Tara DeConigilio, who specializes in print production, vigorously defends the importance and necessity of the production artist.

# PRINT PRODUCTION
*Tara DeConigilio, Recruiter, RGA*

### Are you a Designer or a Production Professional?

For some people production can seem to be a secondary world in design, and some don't want to do it, but let's face it: designers can't do without you. Doesn't this make the production artist just as important as the designer? When I interview people they often say to me, "Well, I've just done the layout," or "I've just done the retouching." I advise them, "Drop the 'justs,' production is not just a 'just.'" Production plays an important, integral role in the design process because if the work can't be produced, then it doesn't exist. Some designers take great pride in their role, their professional recognition, and the contribution, and there are those who may feel production artists are like "failed designers," but it's not possible for everyone to be an exceptional designer. A good production artist is a partner to the designer, a guru, and computer wizard. The best production artists understand how to make designs come to life by interpreting and enhancing the vision of a designer and taking it to the next level.

### Print Portfolios

Know your own strengths and weaknesses and start arranging your portfolio accordingly. Portfolios should be arranged best work first. Not every piece you ever worked on needs to be included. Show only pieces that reflect your skills, the more printed pieces, the better. Your book should be current and up to date and should reflect who you are, and should be clean, organized, and interesting. The principals of constructing a print production portfolio are the same as for a design portfolio and you should refer to chapter 12.

### Roles and Titles

There are many great job opportunities for production artists that offer various levels of creativity as well as mobility. Often, as in all creative choices, it depends on where your personal interests lie and what kind of creative environment you wish to work in. The skill set requirements can be different. In corporate identity firms, for example, production artists have to have fully developed skills in Illustrator and PhotoShop. They are traditionally asked to produce mechanicals for media ranging from credit card plastic to store signage, and it is not unusual for them to also supervise the printing. In advertising agencies, positions require Quark and PhotoShop capabilities. Production artists work with many different kinds of creative teams and often service prestigious accounts. In packaging design, the production people are responsible for all line extensions as well as a great deal of Illustrator work. This requires a full knowledge of the design process and the ability to design these panels. One look at consumer packaging will confirm how many important design decisions are required and how important it is to have a creative person handling these responsibilities. No matter what your niche, there are interesting jobs at all levels.

Print production managers play an integral role in the creative process. By thoroughly understanding paper stock, printing, estimating, and budgets you can separate yourself from the rest. Super production managers can save the company bundles of money by using their knowledge of printing to cut costs in the design process. Creative production managers usually develop contacts in the business to call on to find obscure promotional details for a fraction of the price. Production managers that are resourceful and creative will find design teams depending on their invaluable knowledge and abilities much more than the standard production manager. Good production managers will find themselves called in, during concepting stages, to offer new and innovative ideas.

## Career Opportunities

Advancing your career while still staying on the computer can be difficult but is highly recommended. The personality traits required to accomplish these transitions are being a very good communicator and total dedication to detail. Production artists should continue to be hands-on while taking the leap to studio manager; balancing the two is the key to a successful career as a department head. By positioning yourself as a troubleshooter, creative thinker, and an effective communicator, you can move your career to an entirely new level.

Studio managers, creative service managers, or production directors are the most lucrative, high-powered jobs available in production.

Once you have become part of senior management it is important to stay "fresh," on top of your game. Always research better equipment, streamline and refine the process, paying attention to the companies' bottom line, and saving money by bringing costly vender services in-house. You will also have greater control over the entire creative process. All of these important positions originate from a production background; great opportunities are always available to those with skill, discipline, and ambition.

# PRODUCTION FOR INTERACTIVE MEDIA
*Joanne Kivlahan, Recruiter, RGA*

## Titles and Responsibilities

Titles and responsibilities vary greatly from company to company. The responsibilities for members of a Web production team depend on the size of the company and how well established the company's processes are. The makeup of a Web production team also differs between online content providers, e-commerce retailers, large corporations, and the agencies that service these companies. Some common titles in Web production teams are:

- Production artist
- HTML coder
- Project manager
- Producer
- Web production manager
- Executive producer
- Director of production

*Production artist:* The activities may include preparation of images for the Web, updating pre-designed sites, and modifying already-designed banners for different sizes or requirements. A production artist ensures that the design of the site or banner looks and functions by checking for color palate issues, capabilities of browsers, and general design constraints on the Web. Many production artists have graphic arts degrees. Companies require production artists to have expertise in design software like PhotoShop, Freehand, and Illustrator. Many companies find knowledge of Quark, Director, JavaScript, and Flash helpful. In addition to design responsibilities, sometimes production artists are called upon to hand code HTML. A production artist might report to a production manager, a producer, or an art director, and may move on to become a producer or designer.

*Design technologists, or creative producers:* Company hiring requirements usually mean they are seeking a combination skill set, including graphic design and technology experience. A design technologist has, as one of our clients stated, the "technical expertise to help make creative ideas online realities." He or she may develop and build HTML pages, make graphic enhancements to existing sites, and sometimes create conceptual designs for clients. Hiring managers look for a proficiency in Flash, Photoshop, QuarkXPress, ImageReady, FrontPage (or other HTML editors), and knowledge of coding and scripting languages, including HTML, dHTML, and JavaScript. A design technologist reports to an art director or a production director. Communication and organization skills are always appreciated and can mean a more timely promotion to the next level in a company.

*A Web producer or project manager* is a person who has their hands in a wide variety of a company's business. A producer/project manager creates project schedules and budget estimates and tracks these through the life of the project. Frequent written correspondence with the client, including project specifications, and technical documents require strong business and technical writing skills. A producer/project manager is expected to understand the capabilities of specific Web technologies, which may include HTML, JavaScript, Flash, ASP, and server-side technologies (databases, CGI, and Perl). He needs to understand the practical applications of these technologies and may be called upon to tweak or edit code, but would not be relied upon as a programmer. He also needs a general knowledge of the graphic tools used in production, including PhotoShop, Image Ready, and, Illustrator. One producer/project manager told me that he is the "#2 person" during meetings with existing clients. A producer/project manager may accompany an account executive who has a strong relationship with the client to a meeting, and contributes by discussing the feasibility of a project and a time line estimate.

*An executive producer or a production director* is similar to a producer/project manager, but is involved in projects at a higher and more strategic level. He or she may oversee producers, project managers, graphics Production people, and HTML coders. Often, an executive producer works hand in hand with an account director and a creative director to plan projects. An executive producer can be the key person on new business pitches, accompanying the account director to discuss the scope and breadth of the agency's experience in particular areas. Usually he or she will participate in proposal generation and pitch strategies. This person will need to maintain a keen viewpoint of the business objectives and will have to defend the creative vision. An executive producer can be asked to mentor and support junior members of the department, thus providing vision and expertise in executing Web strategies. Additionally, these people are usually responsible for hiring and structuring departmental staff. And, when necessary, this person must be flexible enough to pitch in, providing hands-on management of projects. As one can expect, exceptional communication and organizational skills are required of an executive producer, including articulate writing and presentation skills. He or she needs to be up-to-date on current design and technologies as well as industry happenings.

## What Makes a Good Web Production Person?

One thing that makes a Web production team member's job tough is that people or whole teams of people who Web producers need to get their jobs done don't report directly to them. A producer needs the co-operation of a designer who reports to the creative director or a Java programmer who reports to the chief technology officer. They need to be able to motivate people to work on their projects even when these people may have other priorities.

Generally, people don't go to school planning on becoming a Web producer or project manager. A person may start out as a production artist or an account executive and then discover that they have a knack for pulling together people, rounding up resources, and understanding what it takes to make an idea become a reality. Many people come to me who started at a small company as an account executive or a production artist and then became "titleless" or never found the perfect title for what they do. They became the person that other account executives could go to when they didn't know how long a large Intranet project would take to complete, and they knew what agencies or freelancers to call when the creative department needed 1,000 images retouched by Wednesday.

## Hot Companies for Web Producers

What companies have the best opportunities for a Web producer? A branding consultancy or a sports content site, a business-to-business e-commerce company, or a company that builds sites for other companies? It depends on a person's interests and background. Some producers say they love to be around creatives and choose work at creative shops. Others say that they want to be behind "the next big thing" and choose to work at start-up ventures. Still others enjoy playing with the latest software and having many resources to work with and find a large corporation the place to be.

## Interviewing for Web Production

When a company is hiring a producer, they will ask the candidates questions about the scope of their work and their style of management. They may ask, How do you determine the cost of projects? What is your methodology for managing and tracking a project's progress? How do you handle changes in project requirements? Tell me about how you provide documentation of their projects? What is a typical budget size that you work with? Hiring managers are usually looking for well-balanced candidates. When a company sees that a Web producer candidate understands Web technology, has a sense for the creative, can talk comfortably with clients, and has an eye for budgets and time lines, they've found a winner.

## Portfolios for Web Producers

Sometimes a prospective employer will request a URL list with a blurb about the candidate's contribution to each URL. A Web producer will not necessarily be expected to show sites they have designed or coded. He just needs to list sites he has made significant contributions to. The highest profile, best work, and most recent work should be listed first. For some items on the URL list, it may be impossible to show a link to an active site. If the site is not yet complete (though possibly months have been spent on the project), if it contains proprietary information, or if it is an intranet that is not accessible from outside a Firewall, a URL cannot be listed. In these cases, it is sometimes possible to take one or more screen shots of the project and house them on a password protected portfolio site. Earthlink, AOL, or HomeStead.com are some of the companies that will host portfolio sites for free or for a nominal cost.

## Education and Networking

In New York City, people in Web production have many options when they decide to take classes or attend seminars to expand their professional knowledge. They might attend New York New Media special interest groups, *www.NYNMA.org*, or the Edgewise Conference, *www.Edgewise.com*.

One of the most comprehensive graduate programs and certificate programs in Digital Production is New York University's interactive Telecommunications Program. United Digital Artists *(www.UDA.com)* is another great place to attend classes. (See chapter 16.)

# Getting Started: How Do You Get There?

11

Starting a job search can be a daunting and sometimes intimidating process. It should be comforting for the novice to know that the experienced professional faces the same challenges and, while for the seasoned designer the ground rules may be familiar, the process is rarely a comfortable one.

Although few people enjoy a job search, the guidelines in this book will point the way not only to a goal but also to a process in which the collateral benefits are educational, informative, and enriching.

Seeking a job or changing jobs means embarking on a process of introspection and exploration. You need to define priorities and goals as well as research opportunities to learn "what's out there." Done properly, such a search gives you an opportunity to study market conditions, take the temperature of firms, and learn more about what's current. It also gives you the chance to interview, allowing entree to the inside of firms not otherwise accessible. How many times do you get a chance to visit competitive companies? Often, you only know them by reputation, grapevine gossip, or by seeing work published. And then add to your list the companies referred to you through your networking activities which you never considered. This affords a more objective view of one's worth in the marketplace as well as an evaluation of the marketplace itself.

The ability to go "inside" is all too rare. It affords a very special kind of education to those who are observant. You can learn a lot about the company image as manifested in the ambiance of the work environment. By just observing the art on the walls, the clothing people wear, their manner of speech, and how you are treated, a comfort level may or may not be established. All this tells you more than any written company profile or job description and ultimately presents the opportunity for eye-to-eye contact, which is the best gauge of all. We will, as often as time permits, visit a client to observe the work environment for all these reasons. Often, the tie a man wears, the accessories worn by a woman, their method of communication, the noise level, the existence or lack of interruptions, and the attitude of the receptionist—all send very important messages. These messages are the most telling. They establish the "culture" of the firm and intuitive feelings which overcome the initial objective view of a company, making your opinion subjective and attitudinal.

Many times the people I interview request I refer them on as many interviews as possible. This request stems from a sophisticated knowledge of the benefits of interviews. These people are not seeking an easy way out of the job search process. They are not less concerned about the time or effort in interviewing, nor are they concerned about exposing themselves to rejection. They want the experience and recognize the advantage of exposure. Unfortunately, I can't send people to my clients without excellent reasons, for that is just what my clients seek our services for—to save them money and the time of unnecessary interviews. However, there are other methods, as we will see, to get an inside peek at the inner workings of companies.

It should be obvious now why a job hunt can be a learning process. The exposure to a variety of personalities, different evaluations, feedback, and critiques, as well as the exposure to the atmosphere of a company, can be an eye-opener. It also tells you a great deal about how to make comparisons. The "corporate culture" (a overused term) is evident the minute you walk through the door. This process allows you to form opinions independently, based upon contact and not hearsay.

However, before you get through the door, there is a lot of work to be done. Above all, you want to convince people it is necessary to meet you and you want to make sure you are approaching the right people. You also want the confidence of knowing you are on the best possible trajectory, the best possible strategy for your talent and your goals. One thing is for sure: You are going to face rejection. It is a fact of life, so you might as well get used to it. It is a necessary part of the learning process.

Rejection in itself need only be painful if too much emotion is riding on the nature of the contact. Since it is to some degree always inevitable, it's best to recognize it as a fact of life, deal with it, and get on with the rest of your business. So don't let it stop you. You just cannot be all things to all people. Don't let it dim your aspirations or your determination. Never, never take a rejection as evidence of your self-worth. Often the ability to sustain repeated rejection is simply a matter of personal courage—and you'll definitely need a lot of courage. We all do. Too many people I know allow their fear of rejection to influence their decision-making. Sometimes it can stop them cold in their tracks. Sometimes it prevents them from trying the "impossible." Trying—always trying, taking a risk—is one of the most important characteristics for success. Measured risk-taking (not being foolhardy) is a key ingredient in the ability to move forward, so rejection or failure can be the by-product of risk. However, nothing is achieved without risk. In many ways, a certain amount of fear is a healthy self-regulating emotion—it keeps you on edge and prevents you from becoming "cocky" or, worse, arrogant. Therefore, it's necessary to take a deep breath and "go for it." And, most importantly, keep moving on. Never let setbacks or failures cloud your sight on your goals. I used to work for a firm that had a little neon sign that said "moving right along." I greatly appreciated that message glowing at me in vivid color on days that were black for me. Maybe we all need something like that to keep us moving. However, move you must—or you'll be stopped.

## WHO ARE YOU?

When presenting yourself to anybody, in a social or business context, the introduction process sends many messages. When embarking on a job search, you need to determine where you want to go and how to introduce yourself into a defined milieu. In order to do that successfully, you must first ask some self-searching questions.

- What am I best at?
- Is what I'm best at what I think I want to do?
- Am I sure about what kind of work I want to do?
- Where do I want to do it?
- Who do I want to do it for?
- What kind of position do I eventually want to hold, or do I want my own firm?

Until you can fairly deal with most of these questions, you're not in a position to accurately introduce yourself to a future employer. It is critical to know yourself and at least your short-term goals in order to make a focused presentation. With the right self-knowledge you can "package" yourself as an identifiable asset for hire. Our experience has proven that when a person is not clearly focused on their abilities and goals, the message sent to the interviewing individual is confused and the resulting outcome is, at best, indecision. Your goal in any interview or presentation is to present yourself as a clearly focused talent with distinct goals (even if you are not sure and are just testing the water).

So let us go over these key questions that will help establish personal priorities.

**1 and 2.** *What are you best at? Is what you are best at what you think you want to do?* What comes easily? Do you sometimes mistrust that which is easily attainable? Do you place too much value on projects that have been a struggle? Is it because you had to sweat over a project that you cannot give it up? I don't want to assume that laboring over a project means it doesn't have value, or has not met with success. It is just that very often we lose our objectivity when our effort becomes labored. Too often, what comes easy is really because it's more natural to who we are. I remember when I was an undergraduate struggling with the classical empty canvas. I was studying with Robert Motherwell, who was a great influence. I had learned that painting was a metaphor and that the visual poetry was something for which I strived. However, while I loved painting, I had a great deal of trouble painting spontaneously. Everything was such a big decision, so I would stand in front of the canvas—seemingly forever. I painted slowly, although with skill. Ultimately I took a course in sculpture and found working in three dimensions a snap. But in my mind's eye I considered myself a painter. I didn't take the "sculpture thing" seriously. I mistrusted my natural talents because they were so inherently an extension of myself. I thought it was "healthier" to suffer the angst of creativity.

As a faculty member at Pratt Institute I found students doing the same thing. Perhaps they were intrigued with editorial design. But they really shone in packaging design. Or perhaps there was a fixation with creating logotypes but the person had a natural promotional bent and responded to copy concepts with strong imagery. I'm sure you see the parallels. Think about what it is that you really do best and trust in it—because that is where you will be successful. Uphill battles are not much fun after a while.

**3.** *Are you sure about what kind of work you want to do?* Does this question make you particularly nervous? Do you feel something is wrong if you are unsure of yourself and what it is you want to do? You probably feel the ideal is to be totally self-assured with a clear goal in sight and I'm sure you know people who seem to have all the answers. Your may find yourself envious of people who seem to be completely in control. For sure, having that clear vision makes it easier. Nonetheless, the majority of both students and people beginning their careers are not sure about what they want to concentrate on. In fact, most people really want to have the most diversified experiences possible. Most designers prefer to be generalists. However, as we have discussed in our survey of graphic design, the marketing or geographical impositions on the field can make it difficult.

So what does this "average" person do? This question leads to the next part of our inquiry.

**4. and 5.** Where do you want to do it? Who do you want to do it for? First, you have analyzed what it is that you do best. Now you must research the field. Read all the trade periodicals, see the annuals, study the awards given, learn what current work is being done, and learn who's doing it. Analyze what you see. What do you like? Where does your aesthetic focus seem to lead and what is a logical fit with your philosophical point of view? What companies are on the same critical wavelength as the work you do best? Researching Web sites has to be the easiest way of looking at companies. Prior to Web sites, one had only trade publications and industry awards annuals as a way of seeing the work that firms were producing. Additionally, one could not access information about the structure of the firm and their clients. Now most of that is readily available, helping designers make decisions on which firms may offer the opportunities they seek.

This is the basic methodology we use with candidates who approach us for work. We look for the visual connections. We try to detect the common threads of an aesthetic approach as exemplified through the presentation portfolio and try to match that to our clients. We think about what would "work" with various firms. We are always seeking a "fit." Fit means the best possible match in all factors of creativity and personality. On the creative side, in the last analysis, when people review portfolios and need to hire, they really want to see what they want to see, meaning that while they may value and appreciate something other than the way they solve their visual problems, ultimately they will hire because they feel there is a strong relationship between what their firm does and your past experience or what they see in your portfolio. It is the rare person who will hire in order to establish a dramatically different design point of view. From the personality point, these people have to be able to get along in the workplace. The "chemistry" has to be there. The ultimate question is could you work with this person at two a.m.?

This is how to start creating the logical links, looking for the connections, and making a "hit list" of companies you'd like to work for. Don't worry if there is some variety in the output of these firms. What is important is that you feel attracted to their output and you feel your own work is compatible. For those working in an area which is dissimilar—for example, you've got a job in a promotional agency, but you want to work on a magazine—an adjustment will have to be made within your portfolio samples. (See chapter 12, "Your Portfolio.") But for now, know that you are now developing a strategy for your future and a methodology for dealing with those goals.

**6.** *What kind of position do you eventually want to hold, or do you want your own firm?* This is obviously a question about your long-term goals. However, it is important for you to start thinking about the differences between short-term and long-term goals. So often the short-term becomes so all-encompassing with its pressures that anything that smacks of long-term isn't given any serious thought. Long-term goals are easily eclipsed by the reality of the daily struggle. Objectivity is lost and the subject doesn't even come up. This question is a memory jogger. You should start thinking about what you may eventually want to do and give serious consideration to the level of responsibility you are comfortable with. Not everyone should be a creative director or president of a firm and take on the responsibility of running a company. Nor should everyone be a freelancer. As you take on jobs and new experiences, look for your role models. Think about what makes you happy. Think about the correlations between title, salary, work hours, and lifestyle as well as the differences between full-time employment and freelancing.

## NETWORKING AND PORTFOLIO SUBMISSIONS

Your next step is to develop your personal "hit list" similar to the way we work described. This will be your target list of companies for whom you would like to work. At this point you should have:

- A sense of what you want to do.
- Researched the firms to which you feel attracted and feel compatible: your "hit list."
- In other words, set priorities and goals.

You have your portfolio ready to go (again, see chapter 12). You are ready.

The first step is to augment your list through personal contacts. If you are a student or a recent graduate, show it to your faculty. Find out who they may know at these firms and if there are other similar firms they might recommend. Go to your placement office and talk it over with a counselor. Think back to summer employment or internship contacts whom you could approach. If you are working, it is time to pull out every business card you have collected to analyze where these people are now and who might be a valuable and interesting contact. If you know people who are printers, paper salespeople, or other trades contacts you feel are trustworthy, ask them what they know about hiring opportunities. These service tradespeople are favorite industry couriers of all kinds of information as they travel from firm to firm. They are often asked for referrals by companies who want to hire. They represent a great way to "get the word out."

## SHOWING YOUR PORTFOLIO AND DROP-OFFS

Start by checking the Web site and telephoning the companies on your list if they are geographically accessible to you. Start at the very top and work your way down. Don't be intimidated by the fame of the firm. The worst that can happen is that you'll be rejected and that is not the worst thing that can happen. We have discussed the relative unimportance of that act. However, who knows, you may be surprised! Who reviews portfolios may not be the person you would anticipate, so ask for the art department or ask who reviews portfolios. Most Web sites will refer you to a human resources representative. Most importantly, you want it to be seen by the right person. Therefore, ask your questions carefully. Find out what their policy is for portfolio reviews. If you can get to the most appropriate person, you can e-mail a URL, send files, or drop off your book. If there is genuine interest in you and your work you would meet with the HR person at some point. Many firms will have some kind of structure regarding reviews. It might be on a particular day of the week, or it might be only between certain hours. Ask how long you need to leave your book (in whatever format it is). And before you pick it up, make sure it's been seen! Too often, someone may be called out of town or just be busy and not able to see your book. For entry-level positions or for people who are not concerned about protecting their confidentiality, the portfolio drop-off is probably the quickest route to get your work seen, even in this digital environment.

While many people object to the drop-off system as being too impersonal, it has become almost an industry standard, a necessary evil. It is the most direct, timesaving way for a busy, often overworked manager to find the people he or she wants to interview in the first place. You need to remember that while your personality, motivation, and goals are every bit as important as your talent, without the talent the rest isn't necessary. And when someone interviews you, to be even moderately polite, the interview must take at least half an hour. However, it probably takes no more than two minutes at best (and probably much less) to know if a portfolio is interesting. That is a difficult fact for most people to accept, but it's true. The pressure this puts on you to create the best possible portfolio is enormous and we will discuss that in the next chapter. Suffice it to say that the prevalent system caters to our 24/7 world, and allows the person who doesn't have a moment to spare the ability to look through portfolios in a flexible period of time, perhaps stolen moments between meetings, and determine whether a book belongs to someone they would want to meet. It is also important for young people to know that this system exists for the very experienced, too. In my firm, on a daily basis, we have to send portfolios first, even when we are submitting people for highly-paid positions. I don't want you to think that all job applications are necessarily handled this way. However, the vast majority are.

When someone has seen your work, and hopefully liked it, they will have some method of letting you know. It may be personally, through an assistant, e-mail, or perhaps a note. What they usually will not tell you is that they didn't like your book. People are always asking for feedback—but they rarely get it—for few want to take the time for a constructive review. The answer most often is a simple "no interest" or "not a fit." Any favorable response should, therefore, be viewed as an opportunity to create a larger network. If they were positive but didn't have an opening, could they possibly recommend other people or firms to you? Most people are really happy to try and help someone, and likely, one contact may bring you several others. And so it goes on. A domino effect. The true meaning of networking. Don't be timid about asking secretaries, administrative assistants, creative directors—anybody who could help and seems friendly. Don't be shy and feel guilty, as if you are "using" someone. While there are negative implications to people who are indeed "users," these methods are just basic, good business practices.

## DIARIES FOR BUSINESS CONTACTS AND TAXES

A diary or log of your activities is a necessity at this time. You should keep a record of everyone you contact, the nature of the contact, and, of course, the date. This information can prove to be very important as time moves on. For example, people often change jobs, and the person who indicated an interest in you and didn't have an opening may offer another kind of opportunity for you in another firm. When you are showing your portfolio over a period of many months (yes, it can take many months), it's easy to get confused as to where you've been, or perhaps who asked you to try again in two months. This information also will prove to be an important resource the next time you seek employment.

Did you know there is a tax benefit in conducting a job search? Keeping a complete record of your activities can provide tax deductions on your next return. The key is maintaining a diary or log of everything you do and everybody with whom you have contact.

The IRS is on your side when you are looking for a job within the same field of employment. This means as long as it's a graphic design or advertising position, and you don't want to do something else with your life, the costs incurred in the job search process can be a legitimate tax deduction. You must keep accurate, complete records of all your costs applicable to your search. Any directly connected expenses to your work and search, including transportation, lunches, faxes, printing of resumes, and any supplies, including your computer, must be tracked for tax purposes. Besides keeping your diary of portfolio drop-offs and interviews, keep all your receipts by either attaching them to the appropriate diary pages or start a chronological receipt file, separating your costs into travel and entertainment in one category and supplies in another. If you itemize your deductions, all costs that exceed two percent of your adjusted gross income can be deducted on your tax return.

## HEADHUNTERS

Developing a personal affiliation with an excellent headhunter can result in one of the most important and enduring business relationships. And it's free! It is the recruiter's client (the firm that wants to hire) who pays the recruiter's fee. Our firm only asks the candidate for undying loyalty (and sometimes a thank you) as recognition of our contributions to his or her future. Of course, this is the moment when I should proudly proclaim the unquestionably high ethical standards of our work as well as the caliber and quality of my firm. However, putting the self-serving part of it aside, the quality and nature of the relationships we have developed over a period of many years have had a profound affect on many people's lives.

Your headhunter can become your confidant, your career counselor. You can be introduced to opportunities you would never be able to access on your own. We have been most successful when we have met people who we have believed in, who have had a talent we could focus on and, therefore, introduce to a sector of our client base. We have been able to not only find them a job but track their career over many years and, in some cases, place them in several positions throughout their careers. In other words, we were fundamentally proactive in molding and guiding their careers, finding jobs, business opportunities and, ultimately, partnerships, acquisitions, and mergers. These people recognize the value of our relationship, often coming to us for ad hoc career advice or for advice in helping them structure job descriptions and salary/compensation packages with their firms.

The first duty of a recruiter is to service his or her client, i.e., the firm who wishes to hire, who has asked the recruiter for help in solving a hiring need, and who pays the recruiter's fee. The recruiter can only properly refer candidates to the client when the recruiter fully understands the candidate's personal and professional capabilities and goals. So the recruiter walks a fine line between servicing the clients in the best way possible and helping the candidate almost as a "rep," i.e., representative. That is why, so often, our candidates become our clients. Recruiters can become a networking resource for the young, for while we do not normally place entry-level candidates, we are always on the lookout for new talent and have the ability to catch our client's ear when there is someone special we feel would be appropriate. However, it should also be remembered what a recruiter cannot do. A recruiter cannot be your only source, for no one has access to every possibility. And a recruiter cannot be successful for everybody, so recruitment firms may not be able to solve your immediate problems. They may, however, turn out to be an excellent resource the next time around. The best advice is to try to get access to more than one recruiter and see how the relationship develops. The quality of communication between the two of you will determine the quality of your future association.

## A SIMPLE "THANK YOU"

It's a simple maxim: The more successful your networking strategy is, the more expanded your contact list will become. The sheer number of diverse people you'll meet will be an education in itself. You are utilizing many resources: faculty, mentors, friends, business associates, tradespeople, online job search sources, and recruiters/headhunters. And many of those resources are recommending other contacts. Along the way many people will show an interest in your future and take time from their busy day to avail you of their expertise. It's time then to say a formal thank you with a simple note, and show you not only have good manners but a good business sense. It has often been the finishing cap to an interview for a highly competitive position! I often tell students who have spent a great deal of time and money on their education that the best business move can be achieved for the cost of a stamp. As previously noted, people move around a lot in this business and you never know when you'll meet up with someone again. The platitude, "it's a very round world," is amazingly true! So remember your manners and say "thank you."

## RÉSUMÉS

There are an infinite number of methods to produce a satisfying résumé, and many firms offer professional résumé writing services. I do not recommend résumé services for creative people. My experience has proven that the résumé that accompanies a portfolio has special requirements. Most often, this résumé is not viewed separately, but serves as a companion to a visual presentation. However, when submitted by itself, it must still be able to stand alone, if only as an introduction to the portfolio and/or interview that follows.

The résumé that accompanies a portfolio has to have the following characteristics: it must be clear, concise, clean (no folded corners, creases, or smudges) and without errors. Résumés must be typographically legible and stand up to the formatting requirements of various software. I am ambivalent about using a résumé to make an unusual design statement. The bottom line is when the design works well, it's great. However, I have seen too many overdesigned résumés create a negative impact. Your safest bet is a simple, clearly laid out (that's design), highly legible résumé. In e-mailing a résumé, be aware that most designers work within Mac platforms and many companies use PC based computers for data. Résumés are best sent as attachments, and make sure your résumé can convert to these operating systems and be an easily opened document.

With digitization, multiple résumés are a flexible and easy option. Having more than one résumé is often an excellent idea. One of the most applicable uses would be to change the "objectives" when necessary. It is an appropriate choice for the person who can have different directions to pursue. Just as you can manipulate the structure of your portfolio (see chapter 12), you can have two résumés with two separate objectives. For example, you might like to alternately stress their management experience or your creative experience. This could be accomplished by the manner in which your current job responsibilities are emphasized, by focusing on one more than the other.

Some do's and don'ts regarding paper choice: Do not use dark-colored paper, as it cannot be photocopied. Paper that is too heavy cannot be faxed. Some papers do not accept ink well, cracking the type when the sheet is folded. Be sure to test for all these possibilities. For the sake of good taste, do not use pastels that are best left for cosmetic packaging. Some people choose to have their résumé on two kinds of paper, one for reproduction and one as a statement of taste values. Paper choices are an important part of the designer's toolbox, so naturally the selection for a résumé is a statement in itself.

Be sure that whatever format you use, your layout is clean, logical, and easy to read. Lastly, remember to write succinctly, with clarity. Make sure your résumé honestly represents your experience without misrepresenting, and be careful neither to omit nor exaggerate important responsibilities. Always, always proofread for typos and spelling. Have someone else proof for you as well. Two or three pairs of eyes are best. It can be a killer factor on an otherwise terrific résumé (and can lose you an opportunity).

The following is a sample résumé that offers one of many possible solutions. It is clearly meant as a suggested format for a résumé to accompany a portfolio. It will, nonetheless, have enough information to "stand alone," or work independently, if submitted by itself. The format is set up to give you instructions within the form of a sample résumé. It is, with a few exceptions, the form we give to applicants in my office when we feel it is needed.

## SAMPLE RÉSUMÉ
(Two pages at most with your last name in the upper right corner of the second page and "Page 2" added, and no pictures, please!)

**Name**

**Address**

**City, State, Zip Code**

**Home phone number**

**Work (or message) phone number**

**e-mail address and URL**

**OBJECTIVE:** Only if goals are very specific, the danger being it can cut you out of an unforeseen opportunity if the objective does not match the job description or title currently available at a firm. The objective should be two sentences at most. Consider two résumés, one with and one without objectives. Consider multiple résumés with different objectives.

**PROFILE:** A profile can be used instead of an "objective." A profile should be no more than three sentences. The advantage of a profile over an "objective" is that it gives the individual an opportunity to express how they feel about their strengths and attributes. It also immediately focuses the reader on how you would wish them to consider you as they read the rest of your résumé.

**EXPERIENCE:** List your last position first. (See example below.) If you are currently employed, show date as "to present." Job titles must be included. Describe the level of your responsibilities (what you really do). Include a client list (who you do it for). If you have worked for many years, you need to keep the chronology of your employment history but you need not detail the responsibility or job description on positions more than six to eight years prior. A listing of the firm, dates, and title is sufficient. Assume you will get your next position based on your experiences from the last five to six years. Be sure to include a description of your recent work experience: who you reported to, the quality and level of client contact (middle management, upper management), budgetary or fiscal responsibility, supervision of vendors, support staff freelancers, art direction of illustration and/or photography, and interfacing with copywriters or marketing, relationship with technology, knowledge of production, and any other applicable points that show responsibility and accountability. You want to make clear distinctions between creative and management responsibilities and how much of either you are involved in.

## Sample

1998 - present  THE AMERICAN CORPORATION:
Art Director/Designer

Responsibilities include design ideation and presentation to clients and management; staff supervision—full-time, freelance, production; selection and art direction of photographers and illustrators; budget estimates and proposals, and on-press supervision. Projects include all required corporate communications, including company magazines, quarterly reports, online promotion, press kits, and newsletters.

**ENTRY-LEVEL APPLICANTS:**  List all work experience using the same principles as above. Be sure to list first any career-related experiences, such as internships, summer work, and workshops. Stress experiences that included interpersonal skills (selling, working as a waiter, etc.) or those that required problem-solving, computers, or detail-intensive work.

**EDUCATION:**  College and postgraduate work only. Omit high school. Include special classes or training programs. Be sure to include date of graduation, degree, and major.

**EDUCATION SAMPLE:**  Pratt Institute: B.F.A., Graphic Design; May 1999.

**SPECIAL SKILLS:**  A very important factor for junior and mid-level positions that rely on a high degree of technical expertise. List knowledge of operating systems, software, special equipment, and any other applicable programs.

**SPECIAL INTERESTS:**  Include only if applicable to your job search. Omit hobbies such as traveling and gourmet cooking. (Everybody is interested in these.) However, if you are applying for a position on a magazine stressing travel or skiing, your personal interests are important.

**PERSONAL:** It is completely optional to put in any personal information and there are legal restrictions under the Equal Opportunity Law to request information on age, race, religion, health, or citizenship in any interview or application. It is preferable to omit personal details and if you are seeking a relocation, citizenship, marital status, and children can become a factor and volunteering this information is at your discretion.

**AWARDS AND PROFESSIONAL RECOGNITION:** Always a plus to include if they are recognized industry awards pertinent to your professional life. However, do not include the actual awards in your portfolio. For example, include awards from higher educational institution and professional design or advertising organizations, and omit an award for painting in a local show.

**GRADE POINT AVERAGES:** Do not indicate unless they are exceptional.

**REFERENCES:** Always state, "Available upon request."

**SALARY REQUIREMENTS:** Never indicate a salary history or a salary requirement on a résumé. This information can be included in a cover letter, if requested.

As always, when dealing with résumés or interviews or life in general, what can go wrong will go wrong. I thought it would be amusing, and possibly educational, to tell you of some résumés that would have been better left in a drawer. We collect them under a file called "Résumés I have known but not forgotten."

- Under "Skills:" "I can do the Rubic's Cube in 60 seconds."
- The Asian designer who, under "Foreign Languages," listed "English."
- The recent graduate whose résumé took four pages.
- The "Special Skill:" "Left Handed"
- Under "Organizations:" The National Association of Floor Covering Women
- Résumés which have a picture covering a least one quarter of the page
- The person who had a sex change operation and noted: "born August 23,1949—born again June 12, 1984."

- The proofreader who wrote ". . . support teamwork ethic, illicting enthusiastic participation. . ."! This same person went on to say, "Hired two new proofers to replace one unreliable one." (Some proofreading, and what a budget!)
- And under the file, "Illiteracies We Have Known," is the person who went to Fairleigh Dickinson University and spelled it "Fairlegh" on our application.

## CHOOSING A JOB

Now your job search is becoming effective and you have received an offer from a firm. Once you have gotten over the immediate rush of excitement at a job offer, you need to ask yourself if this position is really the one you want. This is not necessarily an easy question. You will have to consider many conflicting issues. How much do you need to work (it's called paying the rent)? How much do you want to keep your other options open? How much do you like or trust your future employer? But the most important question should be: Do you want the work produced by that company in your portfolio? While we'll discuss career building in greater detail in chapter 12, it is important for you to consider some of these issues now, for they cross-reference. The overriding issue should be the knowledge that the quality of work in your portfolio will always determine your next job. It's as simple as that! Therefore, you must always consider that the work you see in the portfolio of a possible employer will be the quality of work entering your portfolio once you work for them. It's not that you won't have some creative freedom, or contribute your talents. It's what the firm's client base is and requires, what the firm's reputation is based on, and how they attract new clients. It is a rare time that you can expect to work on projects which are significantly different than the firm's previous work.

## NONCREATIVE POSITIONS: ACCOUNT SERVICES, NEW BUSINESS, AND STUDIO MANAGEMENT

While these areas are covered in detail in chapters 4 and 10, it is useful to cross-reference them here, if only briefly. A consideration of career paths towards these areas offers wonderful and important opportunities for the designer who learns about business, or who has the managerial or technical acumen that is superior to their creative capabilities. It is not uncommon for individuals to experience a reassessment of their skills after a few years in the field. The person who is attracted to account services is the individual who enjoys problem solving and contact with clients more than the actual hands-on process of design. Business development is a highly compensated area for the entrepreneur who can successfully market a sales effort for creative services. Studio managers operate from a knowledge base of production methods and strong organizational skills. All these directions provide key positions in firms with significantly less competition in the hiring process than creative positions. Employers perceive these areas and skills as invaluable components in their organizations and the person who enters these positions with a creative background adds the substantial element of design sensitivity to the position's qualifications. If this seems a viable career option, please review chapter 4.

*Studio managers/production managers:* These positions represent a valued component in the design office, for it is these individuals who often represent the "glue" that connects the design processes and makes everything happen. These managers must have a strong sense of design, computer technology, printing, and materials. They must have excellent organizational skills, and are generally detail oriented. Their management of internal personnel, outside vendors, purchasing, budgets, and scheduling makes them ultimately the point-persons to insure a project is delivered on time and on budget. Excellent people skills and an equal capacity for verbal and written communication are a must. A firm's profit or loss status can hinge on the skills of the studio or production manager. Salary compensation packages for studio and production managers are usually equivalent to middle management design positions, but this does not mean they cannot rise above that level. Some of these managers eventually become partners in design firms. (See chapter 10.)

*Account services/account executives:* These are the individuals who hone their strategic skills beyond their creative ones. Account services personnel or project managers are middle management or senior management positions, and, therefore, their compensation falls within those ranges. By the nature of their positions, account people are exposed to the new business development process as practiced by different design consultancies. They are sometimes brought into that process, asked to assist new business efforts, or, perhaps, to expand business by developing additional components to existing projects. Thus, they enter the sales arena.

*New business development/marketing:* For some, the sales process is totally intimidating. For others, it is perceived without fear of rejection and almost as a sport. Since it is apparent how critical these individuals are to a firm's success, it should be no surprise to know that their compensation would be tied to their effectiveness. They are usually paid a salary plus performance-based incentives, most often in the form of commissions. This career track can easily result in an equity position or firm partnership.

# FREELANCING

What do you do if you don't have too many other options and need to work? Try to consider working on a freelance basis instead of on a staff. The downside is that you won't get health and vacation benefits, but you will be able to continue looking for a better job. What if the employer doesn't want a freelance arrangement? Take the job—but try not to stay too long. Most likely, you shouldn't stay more than six months to a year. You'll probably get some good studio experience and be a little more seasoned for the next job search.

Freelancing is an excellent way of sampling a variety of work environments. Although you'll be paid more on an hourly basis than you would on staff, you won't receive benefits, you won't have economic security, and the number of hours you work will be irregular. As it is impossible to live without medical coverage in today's society, be sure you are covered, either by yourself or through a family member. Many people like to freelance because of the sheer diversity of experience in the work environment, the flexible hours, and the tax benefits they receive from the IRS as an "independent." This is a good time to get some expert advice from an accountant who can instruct you on the proper forms of record-keeping. When you are freelancing, you are self-employed and, therefore, entitled to the business expenses attached with being self-employed. It can be an excellent way of life for the more independent soul. It also means going without the security of a full-time position and not feeling a part of a team. Freelancing on a temporary basis serves well for the person who is holding out for the "perfect" job or for the person who wants a break from moving from one permanent position to another. It also represents an excellent solution to bad economic periods. When jobs are scarce, there is always an increase of freelance opportunities. Freelancing can serve an additional purpose when it allows both company and employee to get used to each other. Some possibilities are the trial testing period before a full-time offer is extended or the proverbial "foot in the door" opportunity at a highly desirable firm. From the employer's viewpoint, it's often used as a method of "try before you buy."

Individuals with their own electronic setups have established an important niche market by offering a new range of choices to employers with flexible staffing needs. This is the bedrock of the "virtual office" in which talent can be accessed on an as-needed basis. A cottage industry has developed for these individuals, many of whom are parents who can take full advantage of working at home. The flexibility of these arrangements services everyone's requirements, work is often sent by modem, and the result is a win-win situation.

A negative aspect to freelancing, however, is the consideration that the process rarely contributes anything substantial to a person's portfolio. Most often you will be asked to work on the implementation of assignments, instead of seeing them from beginning to end. There is hardly any opportunity to put work into your portfolio that shows any real personal contribution or impact. If you freelance for too long (more than a year or eighteen months), the results could be damaging to your portfolio. After a time your work would become dated and you could have difficulty showing what you did for that period of time. There are, of course, people who are permanent freelancers. In this instance we need to make distinctions between freelancing and being self-employed. The subtle nuance is the assumption that after a prolonged period the individual is really self-employed (although there may be no other employees working for the individual) and truly committed to independent status. If, for economic or other reasons, work dries up and the designer wants a staff position, we have great difficulty placing people. While the foremost reason may be the structure of their portfolio, there is always a latent suspicion in the employer's mind that the candidate will return to a freelance or independent status as soon as it's viable. This is a realistic acknowledgment of the different goals of independent designers who are very content with the lifestyle and income afforded through their freelance business. Certainly it is an option to consider as one of the many paths available.

# Your Portfolio

## 12

**Y**our portfolio is your most important expression of everything you are and want to be. It is a unique display of your talent and an exhibit of your experience. While it is a visual expression, it demonstrates a psychological shorthand that must tell your special story. And since life experiences or personal histories are never alike, it follows that no two portfolios are alike. The consistent individuality of portfolios remains a constant fascination to all those who are in a position to review many "books" (in the jargon of our business). They are analogous to human faces, who have some similar characteristics, but are never actually the same. And it is this individuality, in content but not necessarily in presentation, the creative person must strive for. The structure of portfolios must always be flexible and always subject to the needs of the individual, but should express in the best possible way what you have done, what you can do, and what you want to do. It is, therefore, the visual embodiment of your past, present, and future.

Accepting this portentous pronouncement, is it any wonder that the content and presentation of a portfolio is, without question, the single most anxiety-producing element and the most critical part in the entire job search process? While I have gone to great lengths to show how important every other element of your persona is, and that your ability to be successful is not totally dependent upon your visual talent, it is nonetheless your portfolio that makes it all possible. It will get you in the door, after which your other skills must take charge. Remember, in the vast majority of application processes, your work will precede your persona as an introduction. Often, you will drop off your portfolio or send digital files of your work (see chapter 11). Without the talent and its proper presentation the rest is simply not possible. And to compound the pressure placed on this visual introduction, the number of people who lose opportunities not due to their talent but because of the condition of their portfolio is simply astonishing. It is not only astonishing but sometimes cruel, for without a knowledgeable person pointing the way, many get lost. We have been effective in creating conditions conducive for individuals to be hired because we insisted on an interview after the portfolio had been rejected. We accomplish this difficult task only because of the level of confidence we command as recruiters. Lack of information or (more seriously) misinformation can eliminate years of valuable study and training. Obviously, this chapter will not only point towards a direction, but will give you some important insights into how people evaluate the look of portfolios when they need to hire.

## TRADITIONAL PORTFOLIOS

Many people like to be rather dogmatic about the construction of a portfolio. Examples would include dictums as to how one should only use boards or perhaps certain kinds of folios. Others advise that your portfolio should stand out from the crowded masses of black books and make a statement! They advise that you should construct a unique personalized statement.

While we have reviewed many unique, wonderful books, our experience has shown that attempts at these unusual constructions have proven to be a disaster in most cases. A trip to any fully-stocked art supply store will quickly confirm the selection available is so large that the number of choices and the decision of what to select is difficult enough. The critical decisions regarding your portfolio format should relate to content and ability to avail you with a flexible system. You need to analyze the essence of your work. Is it primarily two- or three-dimensional or is it interactive? Is the two-dimensional work flat or does it include pamphlets and brochures? Would the three-dimensional work be best served through photography? Maybe there will be times that you need a combination of formats to adequately show phases of a project. You need to approach your portfolio with an attitude of what is logical for the specific problem and not feel locked into a format. There are no rules as to right or wrong. The only rule is what "works" makes for success. And you must give clear consideration to size.

## SIZE

Somehow the size factor is often the last to be considered. However, size also affects weight. Therefore, you should think about how you will feel carrying your book, looking for work for perhaps days, weeks, or months. How will it hold up on buses, trains, subways, and planes? How will it fare in bad weather? Is it waterproof? Since the use of a messenger service may sometimes be necessary, would you want the service to refuse to carry it because it's too heavy? Would you want to see your portfolio have to be checked in at an airport? Will it fit into an overhead compartment on a plane? Would you ever have to ship your portfolio? In that case, size will affect cost.

There seems to be an equation that the more experienced the designer, the smaller the book, and for some reason, students very often have the largest portfolios. Since size has important practical considerations, imaginative solutions are required. I liked one designers' solution to reduce his presentation to a 4 x 5 box of transparencies, presented like a deck of cards. The wiro (wire) bound brochure of color printouts has become popular and very practical for initial presentation purposes, but does not fully equate or satisfy as a final portfolio. These examples demonstrate the logical desire to individualize a presentation and a move away from the "black book" standard. The success in these solutions is achieved by realizing the objective to condense as well as personalize. The message is, size bears no relation to content. Size also seems to bear no relation to the person carrying it. We often are amazed to see the smallest individuals bringing in books that we can't lift!

## LOSS PROTECTION

Will you want multiple portfolios? It often helps to have either a duplicate or books that serve different purposes. Duplicate portfolios can have a variety of purposes, not the least being the safety factor of not ever losing everything that is the key to your future. You must protect yourself by documenting your work through photography or digitally. Never, never send original work. Never send anything that cannot be replaced. Create a lasting archive of your work and think of it as a document of your creativity. Do not discard work. You will view it differently in years to come.

Unfortunately, every once in a while someone loses a portfolio with original material, and the results are heartbreaking. One recent graduate lost her portfolio in a subway. She simply forgot to take it with her when she got off the train. Another person left his portfolio in the taxi that dropped him off in front of our office. He was, however, able to get it back through the New York Taxi and Limousine Commission. And it can happen to experienced travelers, too. Several years ago, a call was placed to me from a baggage handler in Chicago's O'Hare Airport saying that he had a small case with slides, and an address book in German with my business card as the only identification in English. I was able to identify it as belonging to a head of a German design firm who I happened to know was on the way to a major conference presentation! This, of course, also makes a case for properly identifying your belongings. Portfolios have been lost through moving, accidents, and fire. Don't let it ever happen to you. I must add that only once in over ten years did we ever have a client lose a book. It happened at a large advertising agency. Most firms, ours included, have tightly controlled systems for logging books in and out. While you must protect yourself from accidents, do not let the fear of losing your portfolio prevent you from dropping your work off to be seen. Occasionally, we encounter someone who refuses to leave his or her book, insisting on an interview. The net result of that attitude is to be cut off from opportunities.

## CHOOSING A FORMAT FOR A TRADITIONAL PORTFOLIO

So, what works? Boards are heavy. Acetate scratches. Transparencies can be expensive. And what about a group of samples that greatly vary in size? While there are no absolute answers, the following are some suggestions based on current modes. When deciding on size, consider the average of most of your pieces and work within that framework. Oversized pieces such as posters should be reduced by utilizing 4 x 5 transparencies.

When having your work photographed, get it done as professionally as possible. If you are in school, seek out in-school photo services or photography majors. Most working designers know someone who can do them a favor. Obviously, the quality of the photography means everything. It is awkward to have to apologize for poorly photographed work during an interview. It also sends a negative message.

Transparencies work nicely when mounted in black board frames and have become, if costs permit, the preferred method of presentation. Three-dimensional work, packaging, exhibition, and industrial design should all be photographed. You can combine 35mm slides and 4 x 5 transparencies—sometimes even on the same mounting board, if it makes sense. And you should combine photographed work with the actual pieces or sketches when appropriate. At least a sampling of actual printed material should always be included, for most professionals want to have the opportunity to deal with the "real thing" and the touch and smell of the finished product, the paper, the quality of the printing, color, photo, and illustration resolutions are all very important to them. Slides most often lose much of the impact of the typography as well as any sense of the paper and quality of printing. However, slides do have the advantage of hiding the rough edges. The digital portfolio or laptop presentation has almost completely replaced the use of slides and, while a slide presentation is useful for presentations by job applicants, companies presenting their work to prospective clients, or in conference presentations, laptop software is the preferred method.

## INTERACTIVE PORTFOLIOS

The majority of digital portfolios can be viewed online through a Web site, sent by e-mail, or downloaded onto a zip-drive or CD-ROM. These methods have become the common currency of communication. Most work is now viewed on a Web site or by attachments. Sometimes, the designer has a greater sense of control when using a CD or zip. Either way, the designer must place great significance on and give a lot of forethought to the structure, interactivity, and architecture of the presentation. The digital portfolio has great advantages of speed and dexterity when several or many viewers are desired. The clarity of image keeps improving but anyone serious about typography will still want to see the real thing if the original medium is print. In today's market the digital solution is the most common method of introduction. It is, however, only an introduction and does not replace a traditional portfolio unless the designer is only working within interactive media. (See chapter 9.) Another option for the in-person presentation is to use a laptop.

The lack of uniformity of software and operating platforms still requires a few words of caution when e-mailing files. RGA's Rita Armstrong writes,

> Be aware when showing your work in an interactive format, if the viewer is MAC or PC based. Some programs will not load or will crash if not prepared properly for the particular operating system. Always have a friend view the work on their computer first; don't trust that just because it works on yours that it will work on all. Also, it's really important to make sure the CD or zip is virus free. Check it between presentations, too. Viruses can be a two-way street. I also have a few candidates who swear that their work is damaged by certain security viewing devices . . . so they mark their packages appropriately if they are being overnight delivered to other cities.

## SKETCHES

It is impossible to overstate the importance of including sketches in your portfolio, even in this age of digitized production. The bottom line is that no software, no matter how fascinating and dexterous, can accomplish the capability and creativity of the human imagination. One creative director said to me, "I don't want to see designs dictated by a pull-down menu." Many people do not sketch and work directly on the computer. Perhaps they should consider the power of the thumbnail sketch? Whichever way you work, it is important to save your ideas. The critical significance of sketches is often underrated by the designer who doesn't understand or appreciate the integral value of sketchbooks. Therefore, they should definitely be included in the back of your book and must be saved from the wastepaper basket at work. Many people cringe when asked to include what are often messy sketches or printouts. Don't worry. (I had one creative director say, "I don't care if they're torn and full of coffee stains. I have to see how he works and thinks!") They should be placed in a neat folder and labeled appropriately. They are a key ingredient in your presentation, for they indicate the process of your thoughts, your act of problem-solving, the variety of scope of your thinking, and often exhibit a more preferable realization of a solution than the finished product shown in your book (if they have been killed by a client or proven too impractical). Your sketches show the breadth of your imagination. They are the key to the essence of your fundamental creative personality. While I may risk redundancy, I feel I cannot stress sufficiently the importance of not being computer dependent and the importance of demonstrating your drawing, typographic, and conceptual abilities through these sketches. No person that I truly respect would view a book and not expect to see these drawings.

## FINISHED ART

Flat print work editorial, identity programs, packaging design, and labels are most often displayed in a spiral or bound acetate book in which the pages can be moved or replaced. The quality of acetate has improved and scratching is not as much of a problem as in the past, but it still exists. No one has yet seemed to develop ring binders that close so tightly that they will not catch the pages as you turn them. Just remember, no matter what format you choose, your presentation should be immaculate. If necessary, you must replace the acetate as needed. Never show anything that's dirty or dog-eared. When including a sample that has multiple pages, such as a brochure or annual report, freestanding acetate sleeves both protect your work and make the entire project accessible to the viewer. If you want to include a publication in which you were responsible for only certain pages, tabbing or clipping the work becomes an acceptable method. Since you will most likely be asked to drop off your portfolio, you may want to include a written description, index of the portfolio's contents, or labels on certain items if it makes sense. Remember, though, the résumé accompanying your work will indicate your level of responsibility. Please also remember to label everything that could possibly be separated. Your name must be on anything that could be taken out or fall out.

## PRESENTATION

Everything you include in your book says something to the viewer about your personality, talent, and attitudes toward work. How you treat your work tells the viewer not only how you respect your own work but how you will respect your future employer's projects. Needless to say, your presentation must be of the highest caliber. It sounds obvious and simple, but you can't imagine how many portfolios we see that do not fulfill these requirements. Some people literally throw work into a portfolio and just zip it up. Whatever format you choose for presentation, traditional or digital, it has to be clean, logical, and flexible in order to reflect your interests. Digital portfolios have to give special consideration to how they navigate. As for flexibility, digital solution has some obvious advantages. As to its flexibility and order of presentation, you must consider everything discussed in this passage along with the suggestions made in chapter 11, for the two are completely interrelated. One relates to the inner self, the other to the outward manifestation of that self. In order to tailor your presentation to the firms you approach, you need the physical capability to communicate the inner reality.

I always suggest that the first project exposed to the viewer when they open your presentation is your best. It is your initial introduction. You really do have a few important seconds to create a first impression. Your "hello," appearance, and handshake set the tone for all that follows. So, too, does the first piece in your portfolio. The tone should be one of excitement and anticipation for all that is to follow. It sets the stage. It dictates the psychological atmosphere that will predispose the viewer's thinking to your other work. This is the very important psychological "shorthand" mentioned in the first paragraph of this chapter. You must create an anticipation that your book is going to be a wonderful experience for the viewer. After that, you must follow with the most appropriate work for the particular situation and end with a piece almost as good as the piece with which you started.

Everyone always wants to know how many pieces to include in a portfolio. As usual, there are no magic formulas, but a portfolio shouldn't have fewer than ten to twelve samples of projects and probably no more than fifteen to eighteen. If you have twenty, you probably have gone too far. This is clearly a case of quality and not quantity. The old adage that your portfolio is as strong as the weakest piece in it is absolutely true! It is amazing how often a person is refused an interview because one or two pieces were included that should have been left in the drawer. Try to include as many projects as possible that show implementation of an idea or a campaign. The implementation of a project should be considered as part of the whole project and, therefore, not as additional samples in your book. Ideas that show many components and applications are better than a single solution with a single purpose. Consistency is a tremendous characteristic of a well-composed book. Inconsistency is perceived as lack of taste or lack of focus. Both characteristics are frowned upon and have a negative effect. The concept of consistency in showing a body of creative work is a subjective and abstract process. Any critique of work is by its nature totally subjective. However, developing consistency in the level or quality of the work is a separate issue from consistency in the type of projects shown.

We are all familiar with the question of style. Most well-known fine artists or graphic design icons of this century have a style that is easily recognized. We can spot a Rauschenberg or Warhol in a minute. We all know Paul Rand's work (or should). But could we recognize all the stylistic changes in Milton Glaser's work over the years? It is a question of consistency of approach versus a personal style.

The strongest portfolios show a consistency of approach toward design. But we need to consider what to show a prospective employer. The book also needs to address specific business directions. Therefore, the difficult balance must include a consistency of projects specific to a business direction. To this end, how does your book address the prospective firm's business focus? What do they do and how do they do it? Therefore, what do you show? I have always believed in the philosophy that people see what they want to see. So I recommend establishing a (marketplace) consistency of business direction in the portfolio. It is the reality of the marketplace that creates these demands. We discussed why one needs a flexible format. This is the optimum moment to utilize that flexibility. Some of our tricks of the trade are to rearrange work often, delete, or add if the missing links are available to produce a whole response which:

- reflects your individual goals
- reflects your level of talent and experience
- functions logically to the needs of the marketplace

When we hear of a job opening, we will ask a person whether they are interested in submitting their work. We will describe the position in detail. If the designer wants to be considered as a candidate, we may, if we think it's necessary, ask them to show X, Y, and Z, delete S and T, and ask if they perhaps have some samples of R that would be appropriate in relation to the job. However, as a general modus operandi, we will not show any work if we feel it's not up to the client's standards.

Since a "tight" and objective sampling of your own work is extremely difficult to achieve, try to get private criticism from as many people as possible by showing your book to those whom you respect. While it is unlikely that they will all agree, you should get a general consensus to consider. Ultimately, it must be your decision as to what to include. However, beware of emotionally attaching yourself to projects that were very difficult or involved a great deal of work. They are hard to let go and exclude, but they may not be the best representation of your work. It's a similar syndrome to the decision-making process of choosing a field of endeavor. (See page 111, "Who Are You?") At the same time, you should always have the confidence to stick to those beliefs in which you have a strong conviction.

Tucker Viemiester, executive vice president of research and development at Razorfish, offered these thoughts when asked about what he looks for: "First it's the portfolio, the actual presentation of the work. Not only should the work look good, but the story that the designer tells, the why and how of the project, should give a clear idea of their process. Verbal and visual presentation skills are important. There are tons of people who have a good spiel but not a good portfolio and lots of good portfolios from designers who can't tell why they arrived at that solution. In addition to being talented and articulate, the best designers have ambition; for me this is the most revealing quality.

## CHANGING WORK GOALS

Often a person wants to diversify their experiences and change their goals or field of specialty. This is a wonderful way of staying fresh. An example would be a person who has spent several years working on magazines and decides he or she "wants out" of editorial design. The challenge presented by this type of shift is a portfolio which has become very specialized. As stated, most often people see what they want to see. This means that if they are seeking a packaging designer, they want to see packaging. For a designer to merely express an "interest" in working in that field is simply not enough to demonstrate the ability, nor will a passing knowledge or a few packaging projects do the trick. The only way I have seen a career segue possible is when:

- ☛ The designer makes a strong attempt to find freelance work in the area of choice and then include it in the book.
- ☛ The designer reworks existing projects into another format or includes "spec" work demonstrating his or her ability in the area of choice.

- There exists some logical connection within the essential character of the work. Examples would include utilizing the art direction of fashion photography toward another direction or perhaps an editorial designer moving into annual reports.

- A person is somehow able to convince another to give the designer a chance.

In any case, the common denominator is to put "other" work into your book that will clearly demonstrate your flexibility as a designer. It is difficult and takes enormous effort to develop "new" work or samples, especially when you have a full-time job. However, it is a way to make change possible for you.

Although I often make these recommendations, few people have the energy to follow them. However, if one is committed to change and recognizes that it is truly harder to convince someone of talent rather than demonstrating that talent, it should be clear that the effort of creating new samples is the most viable method of creating change. It is unfortunate that creative people are not always creative when contemplating another individual's talents.

## SHARED PROJECTS AND WORK ETHICS

The content guidelines outlined here obviously apply to samples from either work experience or from school projects. In any discussion of portfolio content, the question of shared projects or projects that have had a strong collaborative input must be addressed. As a young designer you may find yourself working on a project in which the concept or art direction has been set. You may be asked to do the type specifications, crop photos, work within an established grid or pagination, and so forth. Yet, that contribution is important and the work deserves to be included. Ethically, your résumé should indicate the level of your responsibility, and in an interview, you should indicate what your role was on a given project.

Our clients sometimes complain about "duplicate" portfolios. Perhaps they are seeing more than one person from the same firm or same school. This becomes a sticky wicket when the individuals work on the same level and there is no clear reporting structure. An example would be two or three art directors leaving a firm who worked for the same client. If the same projects appear in each portfolio, it's natural to raise questions of conflict. As long as you clearly represent your role in a project there shouldn't be any inquiries requiring you to validate your contribution. When you don't clearly represent your role, the fallout can be quite destructive. Any misrepresentation weakens everyone's position. The worst condemnation is the phrase, "I don't think the work is his." The word "think" casts a long shadow. Once you are questioned, it is hard to get into the clear light again.

This subject is appropriate, on a more complicated level, to senior-level staff leaving a firm, sometimes as a key player in another company, sometimes to start their own business. Their ability to present their past work is key to establishing their credentials to new clients. It is within the same guidelines and principles for any designer to have the freedom to demonstrate experience and creativity and it is general industry practice to do so as long as the work shown is accurately described. The bottom line is to be completely honest and fully describe the conditions under which any work was done, crediting the appropriate firms or individuals. If there is a dispute, legal action will often follow (see chapter 13).

Today, we perceive a renewed emphasis on business ethics as having significance and value. The designer, whose career is built on individual creativity, must always recognize the need to protect that individuality in a business world that often structures work through team efforts. The designer needs to establish a delicate balance between being a "team player" and a creative "individualist." At the end of the day, your talent and personal reputation are all you have.

Recently, there seems to be a renewed emphasis on ethics and the evaluation of what is ethical. We see it in the media and in the workplace. Fortunately, for some, these values have never changed. To cut corners for expediency's sake is ultimately to cut off opportunities. It's an old platitude, but true, that the world is very round. I have witnessed business opportunities lost because of word of mouth on the "street" about "indiscretions" made many years before. The individuals losing the opportunities are never told why and probably would never associate it with a long gone past history. The dangers of using innuendo are clear and can be frightening. Perhaps the information is true, or perhaps not—but the power of a bad "rep" is formidable.

There is another dimension to the negative fallout of questionable business ethics. Many designers will not take a job with a firm whose reputation is in doubt. The industry "grapevine" is very powerful. Often, the telling points are how much turnover a firm may be experiencing. We have often been exposed to expressions of this syndrome when designers leave jobs because of disapproval of the owner's methods of doing business. Since our subject is creatively-driven businesses, those firms are, in the last analysis, significantly hurt by a cutoff of their prime resource, creative talent.

In short, mistakes made in your twenties or thirties can follow you into your forties and fifties. Value yourself, value your reputation, and others will hold the same opinion. It's not being a Pollyanna; it's good business. Ultimately, in any discussion of business ethics, the issue of degree of personal "comfort" within a given situation is paramount; but even for the most pragmatic of businesspeople, the bottom line is the ability to maintain the "critical mass" of the business. In short, no one wants to diminish their business because of incorrect ethical decisions.

## PRODUCTION WORK IN A CREATIVE BOOK

Sometimes the designer, especially in a first job, will be asked to do mundane, noncreative work. Perhaps you may have taken a job doing production on work you don't like, but the job at that time was necessary. In other words, you may have worked on projects you won't want to include as part of your portfolio, but, nonetheless, you have spent significant time at that job. It shows on your résumé and you don't want it to represent your level of creativity. The solution to this quandary is to put the work into your portfolio, but into a rear pocket or a separate folder. It should be marked "production" and may be next to another similar folder marked "sketches." It still represents a quality of experience that should positively add to the body of your work. By separating it out, it will not conflict with your creative persona.

## STILL CAN'T MAKE THE FINAL CONTENT DECISIONS?

When all else fails in trying to decide which samples to delete, I suggest the following: Take six or seven pieces, lay them out for comparison, and delete the weakest one. Now do the same with five or six other pieces. Shuffle the remaining samples together and repeat the process. In this manner you will constantly cut down the number of samples as you increase the quality.

## WHY YOUR PORTFOLIO WILL NEVER BE FINISHED

I'm sure you can understand the rationale behind this statement. You may not realize that some designers do consider their portfolio finished. It is a mistake to do so. Just as there are designers who can never quite deliver a completed book because they are so enthusiastic about their "latest" project just coming off press that must be included, there are those who are perfectly content to present the same book to everyone for all purposes and for a long time. Clearly, it is this person who is "stuck" in time, never growing or being able to demonstrate something new.

Your portfolio should always be considered a work in progress representing the last five years or so of your work experiences. You should always be thinking about updating it and wrestling with the process of addition and deletion. As you grow professionally, your attitudes, point of view, and creative style will grow as well. New jobs, new interests, and new perspectives will all flavor the content of your portfolio. Your portfolio is a current and demanding diary of your work and personality. It always requires your care and attention. And while you must keep it current, never discard the past. Keep it filed. It will become a valuable personal history. I hope you'll enjoy these souvenirs as much as you'll enjoy your future.

# Hiring Practices

## 13

Looking for work with a realistic expectation means recognizing the full scope of the dynamics at play. It means having a "big picture" viewpoint and thinking beyond your own objectives. Otherwise, you will get lost in the trap of a consuming subjective experience in which your agenda seems to be the only issue. Most individuals are so wrapped up with their own priorities, they do not focus on what may be the primary need of the employer (the very person with whom they desire to develop a relationship). For that matter, many employers can only focus on their immediate dilemma of finding someone to fill a specific spot and solve their pressing problems. Rarely do they relate to how they felt when they looked for a job.

## ESTABLISHING BUSINESS RELATIONSHIPS

The key ingredient for a successful relationship is the synergy that develops between employer and employee. The only way that can be accomplished is for the employer and prospective employee to recognize and understand each other's points of view. For the candidate looking for work, understanding the employer's needs is the first step toward creating that relationship. Often, it will also spell success in the job search. The employer's recognition of the candidate's goals completes this equation.

It is my belief that the quality of these employee/employer relationships defines both of their futures. Their relationship also defines the quality of the product they produce. The quality of the end product will determine the success of the firm and the future career paths of the individuals involved. Employer and employee should recognize the essential fact that, in a creatively-driven business, people are the inventory and they walk out the door every night. Therefore, the level of talent and commitment possessed by employee or demanded by the employer establishes the internal synergy of the relationship and the profound power one has over the other. This synergy controls the essential give-and-take in a creative business relationship. The possible issues of personality, office politics, ambition, work environment, sex, culture, title, money, work ownership, the quality of the work and clients, and many other more subtle elements create the dynamics of successful or unsuccessful relationships. These components are key guideposts in making decisions when questions of hiring, firing, leaving, or taking a position need to be acted on. Most people erroneously discount the role of personality and emotionalism in the decision-making process, and both employer and employee may assume that position and money are the usual motivating ingredients. The extent and variety of these issues should always be factored into your thinking and you will approach situations with a far more pragmatic and sophisticated outlook.

If there is an inability for both sides to maintain this strategic business relationship, their lack of synchronization can contribute to the decline of the company. There are dramatic examples of how firms have been crippled by the loss of key talent who left for greener pastures. The issues at work are more often creative freedom and recognition than title and money. While we understand the concept of maintaining a standard of lifestyle, maintaining a standard of "work-style" is just as important. Happiness and comfort in the workplace can take precedence over other forms of compensation. Individuals have left key, senior level positions because they traveled too much, leaving young families; because they were promoted to positions in which they lost touch with the fun of the business, where they were now involved with running the business rather than making the business; or because they had philosophical differences about what constituted a good creative solution or as to how clients should properly be serviced. A hallmark history lesson of a creative defection dates from 1987, when much of the creative staff of an entire advertising agency walked out claiming lack of creative freedom. They got into a taxi and started another agency, taking the client with them. That was when Lord Geller Frederico Einstein, a New York agency of major reputation, which was part of the J. Walter Thompson (WPP) creative group, felt the management was too controlling. It resulted in a major lawsuit, which took years, everybody lost the client (IBM), and the suit was won by WPP. The WPP Group is the communications powerhouse who additionally owns, among their many holdings, the Enterprise Group,

Ogilvy & Mather, and recently acquired Young & Rubicam, of which Landor is a division.

## IN THE BEGINNING: THE HIRING

The creative relationship between employer and employee begins in the hiring process. This can be fragile, dependent on a special synergy and ending when one of the two breaks away for another goal. Both parties participate in an important *pas de deux*: joining together in a creative effort in which the quality of the choreography determines the success of the business as well as their careers.

The beginning is the formation of hiring policies and procedures that combine these talents into successful business partnerships (and sometimes the development of important mentor relationships). The dynamics of this subject are often discussed only behind closed doors and rarely in print. Nonetheless, these difficult questions are critical to anyone developing a career:

- How do the decisions get made on both sides of the fence?
- What are the priorities and criteria that determine hiring policies and the acceptance of the employee?
- What are the underlying agendas?
- Just what is the "chemistry" of a successful interview?

Critical honesty is as rare a response as it is a painful process. Furthermore, it can be a dangerous course, as it can make the individual vulnerable to all sorts of retaliatory actions. Due to the subjectivity of many decisions and the general unwillingness of employers to say anything negative about an individual, the focus is shifted elsewhere during interviews or in conversations with recruiters. The true concerns don't surface and the person only experiences rejection without constructive feedback. Although this dynamic can be very subtle, in the role of the "headhunter" I see many examples every day pointing out how crucial (and sometimes damaging) these factors can be to both parties. Therefore, I'd like to point out the following:

- Anyone interviewing should always consider and respect the other's point of view and agenda.
- Anyone who has ever been in a position to hire staff knows the choices that are made affect the reputation and creative work of the entire group.
- Anyone looking for work should recognize how important that next job is toward their career development and future employment.

Tables can turn rapidly in business. Everyone should recognize and remember what it means to be in the other's place. Too often, we find that our most cooperative applicant becomes the most unnecessarily demanding client, or the difficult, inaccessible client turns suddenly into the vulnerable job seeker. Therefore, we should remember what it is to walk in another's shoes. Anyone who makes hiring decisions should recognize that the decision-making seat can quickly be turned into the applicant's chair.

- Hiring is about choices, priorities, and decisions—and what drives people to make them. It's also about how important these decisions are.
- How the structuring and hiring policies of an office can be the key to its growth.
- How the relationships can be maintained and nurtured for the sharing of success.
- How careers can be nurtured.
- How not to blow an important interview.
- What people in positions of power really want from an employee.
- How reputations can be made or broken.
- How the players commence their dance and, sometimes, why it ends.

## THE EMPLOYER'S VIEWPOINT

Candidates under consideration for a position always ask us what the "feedback" was and often sincerely desire constructive criticism. Most employers do not want to take the time and make the effort to comment constructively. As discussed, if the criticism is negative it's especially distasteful to do so. However, the standard response we receive is: "It's just not right," or, perhaps, "It's not a fit." Understandably, designers find it hard to face these ambiguous responses. However, the word "fit" does tell a significant story. Fit means everything. Fit relates to attitude, intelligence, and talent. It relates to everything previously mentioned, from "tailoring" a portfolio to meeting client needs and expectations. It also tells more about certain expectations that sometimes are not accurately expressed in job descriptions. The firm is seeking appropriateness.

We turned to three experienced professionals and asked about their hiring priorities: creative directors Kenneth Cooke of Siegelgale and Marc Gobé of d/g★, and a CEO, Simon Williams of the Sterling Group. This is a special opportunity to hear the diversity of their thoughts.

*Kenneth Cooke:*

It doesn't really matter whether I'm looking for graphic designers, copywriters, art directors, or Web designers, I look for much the same skills, intelligence, and persuasiveness. I assume that someone who is interviewing with me has superb computer skills, knows the difference between something that looks good and something that doesn't, probably has a bias towards a certain type of expression (design, advertising, Web development, etc.), and understands the basics of human interaction (I've been wrong on this one) and business practices. Those characteristics just get you in the game. What I'm looking for is someone who knows how to bring an idea to life, who can persuade someone to consider a proposition, or even change their minds. Someone who can move people to action and stir the emotions. These are hard people to find, and when you do, all the other stuff (education, computer skills, etc.) take second place in why you want to hire this person. We're not here to simply make things look better; at least, we hope not. We want to actually make things better by having real impact on people's lives, to help them understand, to consider, and, hopefully, reconsider how they think and what they do.

*Marc Gobé:*

Young designers today must have the latest technical skills; they absolutely must be completely Web-savvy with all of the latest knowledge to make them appealing to any design company. They also need to be able to think broadly, to have well-developed conceptual skills. It is not sufficient to simply apply a logo on a stationery system or a package; you have to know how it will translate to the Web. For example, colors are chosen based on digital-friendly standards. There is a totally new set of challenges. However, some people will always be traditional package designers, and as long as there are consumer goods, they will be in business, but the fastest growth is in projects within the digital area. For us, a young person's portfolio is only exciting if he has digital experience. They also need to be articulate about their thoughts, how the design was arrived at. Designers in my company are now interfacing with clients directly all the time rather than through account people. Those who are able to discuss design strategies are at a great advantage over those who are too shy or inarticulate. I place a high value on people with the ability to express their thoughts in writing; this documents their skill in selling their rationale and I would welcome seeing this type of essay or article in a portfolio.

*Simon Williams:*

We definitely look for technical skills but you can't tell from a portfolio whether this person actually has this skill. The antiquated notion of assessing a candidate by a book of pictures is an archaic system. I would want people to undergo a half-day test for which we would pay them $1,000. My concerns about this industry are that it is too embedded in the past, with a love of craftsmanship and self-belief. I look for a brilliant solution-provider whose designs may range from close-in evolutionary solutions to those that are innovative and totally unorthodox. I look for someone to not be a designer. Design is a sub-segment of the creative process; one has work on a broader canvas, and is equally happy with art direction, copywriting, or typography. We want someone who is not just practiced in technical skills but is trained to think and act in a strategic way, which sees the commercial impact in the marketplace. The designer's real focus should be to build the client's business. In any creative environment, personalities play a disproportionate role in the culture of the business. Each member of the creative team has the added role of torchbearer, and these extroverted individuals have to be magnetic, to have the ability to be great, collegial team workers who inspire everyone they touch.

Let's step back and consider what happens when a company determines that it's time to hire. The first driving force will be the workload. Since 1995 there has been a tremendous demand for talent, and the explosion of interactive media in the late part of the decade created a shortage that cannot be overstated. Almost every firm was in desperate need of talented designers and business-side people. This may change with the downsizing and consolidation expected. However, the criteria and standards for intelligent, articulate, and talented individuals are always in demand. The comments quoted above give a glimpse of that issue. Still, no company can afford or tolerate individuals who do not have clear responsibility and a rational role. The body of the workforce is made up of people who are flexible team players, ready to assume a variety of functions. Job descriptions are written to articulate the need for people who are more knowledgeable of the "big picture" and generally more sophisticated.

The kind of person who will enter this workplace is, therefore, another key component in the newly augmented hiring criteria. The 1990s have produced a market for the educated talent who is not "just creative." There has been a general acceleration in the past few years for individuals who understand the broader scope of the job, department, or firm. Creative talent must understand the business of the business and recognize that design is only a tool for information in order to communicate a marketing strategy or image.

The question of who gets hired and why is often answered by the ability of creative people to verbally as well as visually articulate these principles.

In a very competitive marketplace how and why hiring decisions are made is the critical point of concern. What are employers looking for? What will make them choose one person over another? While we began to explore some of the answers in the preceding paragraph, that is not the whole story. The overriding common thread in job descriptions focuses on personality and the ability to be a team player. Time and again we are requested to find individuals who cannot only contribute on the highest level of creativity, but who can contribute to the group as a whole. It's a constant quest for the "perfect person" who can assume a leadership role (if senior) or have the potential for more responsibility than the position calls for, but can also function as a member of the team. That someone can grow within a company and be promoted is a factor. It is far more desirable to find the individual who can go the long course, stay and grow with the firm. Many companies only prefer to hire at lower levels, train, and "grow" their own. And absolutely no one wants a high-strung creative ego. I cannot stress how often these same words are repeated and by vastly different firms. Strong egos and temperaments are not welcome. No firm wants a disruptive personality within their work group. It is necessary to make clear, however, we are not diminishing the person who has a strong vision or opinions. The key is how opinions are communicated to others.

Demographics are not a hiring issue and it may be a surprise to some that minority considerations are only brought up in a desire for diversity. Many firms wish to create a creative community based on diversity, for they have learned it is very helpful to the creative process. And, of course, all employers are legally bound by state and federal laws. Graphic design is truly color-blind as the portfolio usually precedes the individual. There does seem to be an increase of Asians and women and a very small percentage of African Americans.

Another important criteria is the work ethic. Everyone who is successful (without exception) is highly dedicated to the quality of the product and willing to put in whatever effort is required to make the product as perfect as possible, on time, and within budget. This is not an easy objective but a necessary one. In this aspect the fundamental criteria are motivation and quality. The "good" people are manic about quality and are obsessively unrelenting. This all translates into a passion for one's work. While passion can be stimulated by challenge, it cannot be learned, and all too few have it. It's a characteristic not readily found but instantly recognized and appreciated.

These value-added characteristics and requirements are all in addition to the importance of individual creativity and various technical skills necessary for employment. They are the fundamental deal makers or deal breakers in hiring decisions. These attitudes cannot be communicated through the portfolio. Your portfolio, remember, is just your introduction to a firm. It is the first cut on screening out individuals. It moves you up to the shortlist. It is during the interview that your attitudes and personality traits must become evident. If the appropriate questions are not being asked, you must aggressively address these issues. You must be able to communicate your awareness of business issues, work priorities, and your personal dedication into any conversations about your work or portfolio.

To summarize what employers want, the following is a classical listing of skills and personality requirements made by employers, large and small, when giving my firm a hiring request. It is a time when they can, in candor and off the record, vent their frustrations. I use the word "frustrations" because, when looking for work, you rarely consider that the employer is often at his or her wit's end trying to find someone with the necessary skills! In any case, the following is a list of characteristic requests made by employers in a majority of current job descriptions for people at different levels of expertise:

- **Talent:** always first, but never enough by itself.
- **Business savvy:** innate understanding of the firm's objectives.
- **Intelligence:** not just I.Q., but street smarts, too.
- **Commitment:** to quality and the need for perfection.
- **Motivation:** toward the firm and getting the job done.
- **Verbal skills**: ability to articulate the design process to client and staff alike and participate in client presentations.
- **Appearance:** looking professional, representing the company. (We have observed many instances in which a candidate got the job because their appearance contributed to the nature of the job and the image of the firm. I need to make the distinction that these are legitimate factors and not those based on sexism.)
- **Organizational skills:** ablility to establish priorities, supervise others, and control budgets.
- **Technology:** hands-on or, if in a supervisory role, a significant understanding of current technology for printing, paper, alternative forms of digital media, and production as well as a commitment to remain current.
- **Writing skills**: the ability to contribute or originate written proposals.
- **Flexibility**: no job description can say it all. The ability to roll with the punches, wear whichever hat is necessary, pitch in, do the job, and fill the void.

- **Attitude:** do it all cheerfully, always working as a team player.
- **References**: and a general reputation for accountability on the job.

## THE CANDIDATE'S VIEWPOINT

Impossible requests? Not really. The above list of characteristics defines virtually every successful person I know. While you will not be expected to do it all on your first job, you will at least recognize the road ahead and aspire to those goals. However, you can perhaps understand how difficult it is to find "ideal" employees. As one of my clients stated with a sigh: "Good people are not difficult to find—they're impossible to find!"

Well, what about the other side of this equation? What do designers want when they are looking for work? Why do they want to leave a job? What's going wrong? Why are they frustrated, too? The following is a listing of motivating factors I've observed though the years:

- **Professional growth:** People will either not take a job or will leave if professional growth is blocked by others in the company.
- **Quality of clients:** Designers recognize that the level or nature of the work will affect their future work. They want to work for an organization that will defend good creative work and fight for the right decisions.
- **Need for diversity:** Most designers desire variety in their work experience. Sometimes they may leave a specialized job after a while to find diversity or move toward another goal.
- **Recognition:** A common frustration is the failure of employers to recognize effort. This recognition may be demonstrated in traditional ways with title and money, but often the lack stems from a very personal need for the "pat on the back."
- **Money:** What a job is worth is the crux of this issue. The financial realities of the marketplace and questions of employee value are the heart of the problem. Salaries differ substantially due to the size of the firm, the nature of the work, the geographical location, and the cost of living. Some firms pay what they think they can get away with, and some what they think they have to. Some corporate salaries are tightly scheduled by restrictive compensation scales often determined and evaluated by outside compen

sation consultants. These salaries are scheduled within a range allocated to the job description and do not allow for much flexibility or negotiation. Employees sometimes have erroneous ideas of their worth or perhaps no idea at all if they have been working at one place for a long time. However, this is of key importance when accepting a position or leaving one (see chapter 14).

- **Lifestyle:** There seems to be a newer outlook on the meaning and form a quality lifestyle can take today in contrast to five to ten years ago. Many individuals are focusing on family and the amount of leisure time available. Therefore, the relevant issues of length of commute, amount of overtime, holidays, vacation time, and relocation to other geographical environments arise. The need to put in unusual overtime is often a reason for leaving a job or not taking it.

- **Children and parental care:** Recent years have witnessed a significant increase in concerns for aging parents or the care for children (especially in the rising number of single parent families). These concerns become factors in employment decisions, especially relating to relocation, overtime, and full- or part-time employment issues. The Family Leave Act provides job security without pay should a family emergency arise.

- **Opportunity:** The best reason to take a job is opportunity and the best reason to leave a job is lack of opportunity. For the ambitious, nothing replaces the ability to realize one's goals. We have seen many individuals make a lateral move (accepting the same salary) as well as step back (take less) in title and salary because the new job was perceived as an opportunity to move forward.

- **Position:** Often, the way to move up is to move out. It is very common to leave a job because of a logical need to change responsibilities, title, and/or salary. The individual can feel blocked in his or her present job because of the structure of the firm (for example, it can be too small or too large to offer the next step up). Or, perhaps, there is someone in that coveted job who is not going to leave, or the employer does not recognize the need for promotion. The complaint is often, "There's just no place to go!"

- **Women's issues:** The demographics of design are heavily weighted towards women. For reasons not completely clear, graphic design is overwhelmingly female for those under forty years old. Employers will need to accommodate women who want a family and a career. While there is a slow movement toward flexible hours (flextime) and maternity leave (for men, too), at the time of this writing it is strictly token (see chapter 14). Talented women will not want to accept positions not offering maternity leave. Several have indicated the desire for four-day workweeks. This picture is a changing one and I feel, will play a stronger role in hiring issues as this workforce matures.

There are other hiring factors to consider in any discussion of women in graphic design.

- **Pay scales:** Women are not always paid as much as men. Sometimes the cause falls at the feet of women. They simply do not ask for as much money. This may be caused by a lack of security or lack of aggressive negotiation skills. I'm not sure. However, this condition will certainly change, since time is on the side of a maturing and growing female workforce. They will be assuming the senior positions of the future.

- **Travel:** As the world economy grows, many positions focus on extended travel. This can be difficult for those with young families.

- **Personal**: Many employers are in open admiration of and court the woman in the marketplace. If you refer back to our employers' wish list, you'll note the emphasis on flexibility and verbal skills. Women seem to excel in these areas. Perhaps it's because they are raised to assume so many roles and wear all those hats? In any case, savvy employers recognize these important traits.

- **Harassment:** Simply put, harassment exists and can take many forms. When possible, and when it's recognized, most people will change jobs rather than try to make a change in the workplace. Harassment can be physical (unusual workloads or extra-long hours), sexual, racial, or psychological (applying unnecessary pressure, destroying self-confidence). The protagonist is usually playing power politics or is simply a tyrant or bully. Some employers have been classified as "screamers" or "throwers" by people we have interviewed. A warning light would be an unusually high rate of turnover for employees in the firm. When too many employees come and go, some firms get reputations for being "revolving doors," and, while it can be for other reasons, subtle or overt harassment may be one cause.

## THE INTERVIEW

It's obvious, when considering the employer's and candidate's priorities as noted above, the interview is a critical session in which a great deal of substantive information needs to be communicated by both parties. Unfortunately, few people have extensive interviewing experience and personnel or human resource professionals can be jaded by doing too much interviewing. Often, what a person is saying and what they are thinking can vastly differ. However, the person who recognizes the variety of dynamics in play has an advantage and a better opportunity to get his or her message communicated as accurately as possible. Let's look at some methods to create the best platform of communication.

- ☞ **Be prepared**: Like the Boy Scout motto, always be prepared. Do "due diligence." In business jargon this means make the effort to properly research the project. Research as much as you can about the firm before your interview. Find out who their clients are. Find out what kind of work they specialize in (if any) and who is responsible for hiring. Find out who you will ultimately report to either before or during the interview. Recognize that the person interviewing you may only be able to make recommendations and not have the authority to hire you.

- ☞ **Additional portfolio material:** Based on your information, you may want to bring along additional material pertinent to their needs, perhaps additional sketches. You might also consider bringing personal artwork (illustration, photography, etc.) and ask if the interviewer would like to see it. Be sure to offer this work as an optional consideration. Do not be put off if the interviewer doesn't have time or isn't interested.

- ☞ **Timing:** Be punctual. Allow yourself some extra time if you're not sure how long it will take to get there. Check out your transportation options ahead of time, not at the last minute.

- ☞ **Attire:** Dress in a professional manner. Every company has its own "culture" which dictates what is customary attire. Even if dress is very casual, you won't make a mistake by dressing for the interview, and if you have only one interviewing suit, this is the time to wear it. When you are there you'll probably see how others dress and get a better idea of what it would be like for you inside the company. We knew one person who went to the office building a day or two before her interview and watched people leaving for lunch to see how they dressed. Another person we know took the subway on a hot New York day so as not to sit down and wrinkle her dress before an interview. She was meeting with a famous designer known for fashion and fragrance and knew her appearance was critical. This behavior is not silly or compulsive. It's smart.

The issue of "style" is the critical point. Style require ments can range from the high fashion image of a New York cosmetic firm to the conservative midwest corpora tion. Style can mean the trendy New York or Los Angeles design studio whose dress code is based on SoHo or Melrose Avenue. Style can also mean marketing communi cations firms and corporations that regard expensive, well-tailored suits with discreet accessories as the norm. Often, I feel life is one big costume party and you have to decide which party you wish to attend. However, to deny the impact of these factors would be naïve and, ultimately, close off opportunities. Lastly, the way you dress ends an impor tant message to others in the same way good manners do. It says something about how you feel about your own image, possibly about the future you crave, and how you perceive the needs of your future employer.

The bottom line of this subject is that people really do lose jobs and opportunities based on their appearance and personal presentation. Be aware and be careful.

- **Beginning**: The old adage is that you have thirty seconds to make an impression. The way you say hello and shake hands says a great deal. Look people in the eye. The inability to sustain eye contact reveals personal insecurities or hidden agendas. I know at least two people who lost opportunities directly because of this factor. The employers expressed a feeling of "being uncomfortable" with someone who didn't offer direct eye contact. Some people, aware of the need for a firm, positive handshake as a sign of character, can nearly break one's hand. I always feel they have read some self-help book and taken it too much to heart. On the other hand (no pun intended), it's also surprising how many limp, damp handshakes I get. The bottom line is: Be yourself, be as relaxed as possible, and know that nonetheless, someone is sizing you up instantly (and that person may be equally nervous). As an yoga practitioner, whenever I feel tense, I always try to breathe deeply, clear my mind of extraneous subjects as much as possible, and take heart in the fact that the person I'm going to meet is just another human being with many of the same insecurities as anyone. Be pleasant, respectful, and polite; ask where they would like you to sit, if it's not obvious. Try to think of this person as a professional friend. Think of yourself as being on the same side, as if you are already a part of their team and share the same objectives. Do not overstep your bounds.

- **Listening and responding**: Let the person interviewing you take the lead and direct the conversation, at least in the beginning. There are likely to be plenty of opportunities for you to ask questions, so practice the art of listening. The ability to listen to another person and concentrate on what he or she is really saying (and sometimes what they think they are saying) is a very important trait. This is true not only in the interview, but throughout your business activities. Too often, candidates are too intent on what they are going to say to listen to the interviewer. This may be because of nerves. If you listen carefully and address points the other person raises, your communication will be fcused to that individual's criteria. You'll be able to direct your answers in a germane manner. It's surprising how few people know how to listen. We even get this quality listed as part of a job description. The request, "I want someone who knows how to listen," is not uncommon. If you're worried about remembering all your questions, bring along a written list. It's perfectly acceptable.

- **Breaking appointments:** Obviously, this is something to avoid, as it complicates situations and may send a negative message. In the first place, scheduling interviews can be a difficult task when it involves people with busy schedules who perhaps travel a great deal. Sometimes interviews are with more than one person and those schedules have to be coordinated. Changing appointments is acceptable when there is an understandable and, therefore, acceptable reason. The risk is losing the "timing" or momentum of the op–portunity. However, if it becomes a pattern, it can mean a loss of interest (perhaps for both parties). If you are not feeling well and not "up" for an interview, the best course is to postpone. Many interviews have been "blown" because the person was not functioning at full speed. If you decide to go to the meeting be sure to tell them why you are not up to par, that you didn't want to cancel and request to come back at another time.

- **Confirming appointments: Do it.**

**Classic Interview Questions:** These are some common questions and topics you should be prepared to encounter. Every interviewer, natural-ly, has his or her own style of conducting an interview. Some are relaxed, some interrogatory. Remember, no matter how relaxed the atmosphere may be, it's a time for testing. It's also a time to remember that your interview is really a time to assess your presentation skills. No matter how relaxed the en-vironment may seem, you are still in a position of being judged. The yin and yang of the situation often hangs on the culture of the firm. People have not passed muster because they were too relaxed and informal (beware of break-fast meetings on this one) and their presentation was not deemed "profes-sional"enough or perhaps they were too "formal" in a firm that prides itself on its being "young and loose." The key to these experiences is that the per-son and firm were probably not a fit, but one can't help but wonder if errors in judgment are possible.

- **Why are you planning to leave your job and/or why are you interested in this firm?** We have discussed many logical and appropriate reasons. Now is the time for you to be prepared to articulate them. Never, however, say any–thing negative or damaging about your current employer.
- **Future goals:** Be prepared for questions about how you perceive your future. This can be a dangerous trap. If you view this job as a temporary stage in your life, do not say so. The employer wants to know that if you are hired you will be there for a considerable and fair period of time.

Understand that the first three to six months of your
employment is probably going to involve a learning curve.
The employer is investing in you and wants a reasonable
return. We had one memorable time when a corporation
flew a designer from coast to coast after initial interviews
in his home city. Early on in the interview at corporate
headquarters he was asked the famous and standard
"personnel" question, "What is your five-year goal?" His
response was to have his own business. He was out the
door soon after that answer, and the interviewer imme-
dately picked up the phone to call me.

- **Personal traits:** Be prepared to answer questions that
attempt to identify your personal tastes and beliefs. Who
do you most admire? What has been a motivating force in
your life? What books do you read? When was the last time
you were in a museum? Where do you like to vacation?
Questions that would be considered strictly personal
(for example, intimate family details, such as plans to get
married or have a baby, or about politics, sex, or age) are
illegal. Therefore, these questions are designed to learn
more about your personality and character. Employers are
usually seeking a well-rounded individual with a variety
of personal interests.

- **Motivation:** Your personal motivation toward this position
will be a key element in your interview. The entire manner
of your participation in the interviewing process points to
the level of your motivation, including your promptness,
dress, etc. You need to articulate the level of your interest in
the firm, job, and career opportunity, as well as the manner
in which you are accustomed to working and your energy
level. Basically, you want to communicate to your future
employer that you will welcome the opportunity to participate in the business, giving 110 percent of your talent,
skills, energy, and ability.

- **Lunch/dinner/drinks:** Part of your interviewing process
may include some time in a restaurant. There are several
objectives to this kind of activity that are very important.
They all relate to you as a thinking individual, to your
manners, and to how you conduct yourself publicly.

(1) While it is excellent to give both of you the chance

for a less formal, relaxed meeting and to get to know each other, remember, it is still part of the testing process. Knowing this, it is your task to show a relaxed, self-confident manner.

(2) Being in a restaurant gives your future employer the opportunity to observe you in the surroundings in which business is often conducted. Your deportment, table man-ners, and level of sophistication would all impact on your relationships with your clients. How you make "small talk" and how you move on to the business issues are part of the game. If you happen to be ordering first, try not to order a drink unless your host does. A majority of people don't drink at lunch. You want to keep your wits about you, anyway. Let your host be dominant, calling for the waiter, asking for the check. If you have checked your coats and are not paying for the meal, it is proper for you to tip the coatroom attendant.

☞ **Questions to ask:**
(1) Find out what is the organizational structure of the firm.

(2) Find out who you will report to and who will make the hiring decision. It may not be the same person who is conducting the interview.

(3) Ask if other interviews will be necessary and who you will be meeting with. Find out their title so you'll understand their position within the structure of the firm.

(4) Try to find out how long they have been looking for someone. If the job is open too long there may be a problem.

(5) Find out if it's a new position or a replacement. If it's a replacement it's always helpful to know why the person left; however, it may be a difficult question to ask. If it's a new position, carefully check out their expectation level regarding the job description. Often, descriptions change on new positions because the employers may not have thought everything out thoroughly. New positions can often mean a better opportunity. It's also easier not to follow in another's footsteps.

(6) Ask when they plan to make a hiring decision and

when they need someone to start. It is sometimes possible to find out how many people they are considering (giving you an idea of what the competition is like).

(7) Ask if you can see samples of their work. Remember what they do will go into your portfolio and affect your next position.

- **Freelance and projects:** Indicate you're available for freelance if it's possible for you to do so. Sometimes employers like to suggest a trial project as a test. If so, be sure to get as complete a briefing as possible of the nature of the project. You'll often be gauged against currently employed designers who may have the advantage of understanding the clients better. You should always be paid for any work you do. If you do work ask if a purchase order is required so that you don't fall into "accounting limbo" and not get paid. If you do a project, make sure you deliver it on time.

- **Salary:** Toward the end of the interview you should ask what the firm is planning to pay for the position. However, you will probably be asked first what your salary expectations are. This may even come as a response to your question. Remember, salary is only a base. It must be viewed in the context of a whole package with benefits. This will be discussed in greater detail in chapter 14, "The Money Question." For the purpose of this section, understand that it is an issue to be dealt with during the interview. This is always a difficult, sensitive moment if you don't have any prior information. Several options include:

(1) Telling your current salary and indicating you expect more (factors may include that you haven't been given an expected raise, the firm is having financial problems, you are up for a raise but you want to leave anyway for stated reasons).

(2) That money is not your reason for wanting this position and you'd feel better knowing how they evaluate your worth within their company.

(3) Indicating a range that you feel comfortable with, with out using specific numbers, such as high $40s, low to mid-$50s, etc.

(4) That this will be your first job and the opportunity is your foremost consideration (however, you still need to make a living). With regard to first jobs, please remember it's going to cost your employer to train you. You should always think of your first couple of positions as continuing education. Salaries are far less negotiable with corporations. You probably would be in discussion with a member of the human resources department who would be working with clear-cut schedules or guidelines.

☞ **Concluding the interview:** Make sure you understand the next phase of the interviewing process. Are you to get back in touch or will they contact you? Do they want any other materials from you? Do not fall into the trap of call-ing them too often. The ball will be in their court and you have to take their lead. Sometimes firms are too polite, don't know how to say no, and may lead a person on un-necessarily. When you leave, say, "Thank you." Get the per-son's business card if possible and send a thank you note if you're not coming back soon. Get the title and spelling correct on the note. If this is a position you are anxious to have, express that motivation in a note or letter. Tell the person responsible for hiring how much you want the job, why you believe you have much to offer, and how you would devote all your energies to the company. Strong mo-tivation is a major factor in hiring decisions and you have nothing to lose by assuming an aggressive stance.

## CONFIDENTIALITY AND NONCOMPETE AGREEMENTS

You may be asked to sign a letter or contract relating to the proprietary busi-ness of the firm. It could also involve nondisclosure agreements should you leave the firm. The purposes of most confidentiality and nondisclosure agree-ments are to prevent you from (1) discussing any proprietary information, (2) contacting or soliciting business from their clients, and (3) soliciting their employees for a defined period of time (a specific number of months or years) after your employment has been terminated (usually for any reason). Just understand that this is common practice among many design firms and the number of firms attempting to restrict departing employees is on the rise. While there are many terms of these agreements that are completely legal, it is not legal to restrict anyone from earning a living in their chosen profession. Therefore, the language of these agreements is critical, since the structure of these contracts can greatly vary and laws can vary from state to state. It is absolutely necessary not to sign anything without first showing it to an attorney, as signing the wrong agreement could hamper your future ability to be employed.

## PSYCHOLOGICAL TESTING

There are many types of tests to qualify different kinds of information. A small percentage of corporations use these devices. Your decision to accept taking the test is strictly voluntary, but may be a condition attached to getting the job.

## MEDICAL EXAMINATIONS

Passing a medical exam is a reasonably common practice among corporations but not consultant firms. It may also be necessary if there is an insurance policy attached to the benefits package. Drug testing has become prevalent in corporations. HIV testing is not legal and only done on a voluntary basis. It is possible you may be asked for a blood or urine sample. Several Wall Street firms we know will "spring" a urine test on an applicant during one of the interviewing appointments without forewarning. These tests can pick up traces of marijuana or a poppy seed bagel digested three days before the test. Needless to say, you won't be penalized for eating bagels, but we advise people to be aware of what they are ingesting if they know they're due for a test.

## REFERENCES

You should always be ready to offer references, if requested. If you have letters of reference, bring them to the interview. You can ask the interviewer if he or she would like to have a copy, but it may or may not be necessary. References are generally requested in the last stage of candidate selection just before an offer is extended. At that time it is common practice to present three references. Usually, if you are still employed, it is not possible to get a reference from your current employer. In that case, seek references from a confidant in your office or someone you reported to at another office. Other likely references would be people you supervised, those you dealt with as vendors (photographers, illustrators, suppliers), and anyone else who could speak about your ability to follow instructions, supervise others, meet deadlines, hold to budgets, and the like. References should be as recent as possible and no more than three to four years past. When your future employer is calling your references personally, be sure to allow time for you to alert them to expect the call (and, therefore, double-check that they are available).

# ACCEPTING OR REJECTING AN OFFER

Accepting an offer is a fairly uncomplicated affair. If you are not presently working, you need only find out when the firm wants you to start. Perhaps first, you'll need to fulfill a freelance obligation. Remember, though, if you have any work obligations, finishing them is professionally correct no matter how much pressure is placed on you by your new employer. Never walk away from a promise. Your future employer wouldn't want you to do it to him or her either, and perhaps she or he may need that as a reminder. For some reason, once employers have made up their minds to hire they often want the instant gratification of having the employee on premises immediately. If you have to leave a position, you'll have to do so in the same professional manner in which you conduct all your business dealings. We'll cover that subject in some detail in chapter 15, "Moving On: When and How to Leave a Job."

Rejecting an offer is a matter of diplomacy. Your reasons for rejecting a position can be many and show an exercise in sound judgment. However, it's important to remember that an employer faces your rejection with about the same aversion as you would feel being rejected by a firm you wanted to join. As always, it's important to consider how it is for the other person. The employer has made a decision based on the whole hiring procedure. Perhaps it was very time-consuming. He or she now has to start all over again. Significantly, you may want to "leave the door open" for future opportunities with that firm, or simply understand that as individuals who move about in an industry, you may meet again. The effect is the same. You need to reject the offer with grace and professionalism. Thank them for the opportunity the offer represents and give a reasonably clear understanding of why you are not accepting. Do not in any way insult them or their firm with your rejection. If you don't like their work, find another reason. Only raise the issue of insufficient salary if you would accept the job for more money, for they may come up with a better offer. Tell them the truth if you have another offer you feel is superior. The reason (such as working conditions, growth opportunity, benefit package) may be constructive. Just keep in mind that you may meet again.

In summary, let's consider the whole picture of the hiring process. Your portfolio is the access to the firm, the foot in the door to determine whether your creative point of view and talent are appropriate to the firm's business core. The next stage in this process centers around you as a person. All the criteria listed really focus on what you are about. Your personality, attitude, upbringing, and goals come into play as critical components. The last phase relates to whether you determine this position is the right direction for the long term. If the firm is of like mind, it will make an offer. I've referred to the synergistic relationship between employee and employer as a dance for two. It is a partnership of the first order of importance. Every combination of personalities is unique in every sense of the word. Situations never quite duplicate. (That is what makes my work so fascinating.) I always advise, when the decision to accept or reject is most difficult, to listen to that small internal voice within you. Sometimes it's just a "feeling" in the pit of your stomach. Contemplate, listen, but don't fear risk. Nothing is achieved without it.

# The Money Question

Salary requirements are probably the most difficult matter for the average person to negotiate. Compounding the issue is the perception that salary negotiations are essentially an extremely distasteful process to be avoided if at all possible. And because it's so subjective, most designers practice avoidance, diminishing their earning capability. The negotiating process with its resulting salary package is, of course, the essential ingredient of any employment contract. Negotiation is an art form not taught as part of any design curriculum. In addition, we are again confronted with the issue of choice. How can you negotiate if you don't know what the possibilities and choices are? Market factors are, of course, the wild card. When there was a glut of great designers in San Francisco, they were paid below market rate, and when the growth of interactive firms produced a shortage in the supply of talent, salaries skyrocketed. This can be very difficult for employers, who, when faced with defined profit margins, cannot keep up with rising markets. The influx of venture capital money into interactive media companies created havoc for traditional media firms who could not compete with what became inflated salaries. In 2001, there seems to be a normalization on the horizon. Talent is still the wildest card of all, for if you are truly special, everything is negotiable.

## SALARY VARIABLES: WHAT ARE YOU WORTH?

You are being interviewed for a position you really want, and you are asked what your salary requirements are. How do you respond? It is always easier to be passive and respond to a number offered, but the blatant act of firmly stating a number you want is often very difficult. Perhaps it's the whole issue of assigning a number as an indication of one's worth. It's putting a price on your head. Are you secure and forthright or do you hedge knowing that you'll take any reasonable offer?

How do you establish your worth as a creative person? How do you price creativity? The aspect of general financial ignorance plays an important role in this process because many designers simply don't know what they are worth in the marketplace or what the market will bear. This information is becoming easier to attain thanks to Web sites and the increasing number of surveys. The *www.rga-joblink.com* Web site is very specific, as it tracks prevalent salary ranges and is updated daily, giving job titles, brief job descriptions, and geographical salary ranges. The Web sites of individual companies list job openings and give descriptions but almost never give salary information. The *www.salary.com* Website is more than interesting and its current listings include advertising, architects, and graphic arts, which include Web designers and industrial designers but not specifically graphic designers. The site also links to a host of job boards. The salary surveys include those published by industry related organizations such as the AIGA (American Institute of Graphic Arts), and the Design Management Institute, for example. The best course of action is to check their Web sites, a selection of which is listed in our appendix.

Trade publications and newspaper ads are also a market-wise indication of current salary offerings. The online search has greatly diminished newspapers as a source but they are still viable, and most post the positions online as well as in print. However, many ads, as online listings, use the ambiguous phrase, "salary is competitive and commensurate with experience," and will request a salary history. It certainly leaves the person applying for specific jobs at a disadvantage. Salary information is most often achieved through grassroots information. Usually, the information is mostly hearsay of the classic "grapevine" variety, or the receiving of confidences from a trusted friend. Clearly it is not an accurate measurement. Within companies, there is often a "feeling" or underground knowledge by the staff of how much various employees earn. But more often, especially in a larger firm, individuals are operating in the dark with little knowledge of what their colleagues or counterparts earn. Friends are rarely of help, for few want to confide how much they earn.

Employers usually assume one of two opposing positions regarding releasing income information. One is to create parity between employees (probably recognizing as well that eventually, there are few secrets in firms); the other is that all financially related information is proprietary and strictly confidential.

Employees sometimes embark on job searches just to learn what they can earn by making a move, and use that information to negotiate an increase with their employer. I have always felt that is a form of blackmail and I wouldn't be happy staying with a firm who would only acknowledge my real worth at the equivalent of gunpoint. It's my opinion that the employee is never perceived the same way again, by the employer or by his or her colleagues in the workplace, who usually end up knowing the whole story. Counteroffers are reasonably common, however, and some feel it's a better course of action than making a move to another firm and, therefore, into the unknown. It becomes a matter of personal business philosophy and must be dealt with on a case-by-case basis. Also, there are many firms that will, on principle, never make a counteroffer.

What is the best way to overcome this lack of information and find a reasonable path toward salary equity? Once again, the responsibility for the research effort falls on the designer's shoulders. If you want a realistic picture, it is necessary to utilize the above-mentioned sources and try to make a personal survey. Professional recruiters, like those at my firm, are probably one of the best sources for this confidential information. In fact, our firm is such an excellent barometer of the marketplace and of salaries around the country that we are often asked to advise our clients on what they need to pay. In some instances, we work as consultants to design firms and corporations who need our expertise to resource comparative and equitable compensation scales. Some contributing factors in gauging salaries are:

- Regional: Questions of location are very important. The cost of living and cost of overhead will influence pay scales. There are distinct differences in salary levels in New York, Los Angeles, Atlanta, or Seattle. There are many online calculators, such as *http://verticals.yahoo.com/cities/salary.html,* which will give you comparisons from city to city.
- Economic: Salaries can reflect a buyer's or seller's market. Wages will be affected by recessions or what firms will be willing to pay for premium talent. Then there are regional factors. The booms and retrenchments of silicon valleys and alleys are an obvious but excellent example.
- Size: Small firms generally have smaller budgets. Size of the firm is only meaningful when considered in relation to their client base. There are many small firms (under twenty people) who have high-profile clients and, therefore, command parity in fees with large firms.
- Type of firm: Studios and marketing communications firms may not have the same budgets as large corporations.

But it is difficult to generalize because there are exceptions for every rule. One must consider that the major differences between corporate versus noncorporate positions are in the areas of benefits and freedom to negotiate. Corporate benefits are usually far more expansive (see benefits) than most private firms can offer. Corporate salaries are another matter. They are usually formulated on a sliding scale set to gauge levels of experience and the quality of responsibility defined in the job description. Corporate salaries will thus be graded and pegged to titles with a high and low range. Corporations like to hire at the low to medium range, leaving room for salary increases through the years of employment. Should the individual reach the top of the range, their only recourse to future salary growth would be a change in job description and title. With such firm guidelines, it is easy to understand that negotiating a salary with a corporation is far more restrictive than a group based on an entrepreneurial business mode.

☞ Specialization: Different areas of business command higher fees. Two extreme examples would be design for films and book design. The entertainment field offers much higher compensation than book publishing. Since creative people are often driven by what they enjoy doing in contrast to where the most money can be earned, this information will be more important to some than others. However, it is at least important to understand what the possibilities can be when making life choices. The salary survey at the end of this chapter points out some of the differentials.

## WHAT'S YOUR JOB WORTH?

A controlling element in setting salaries is the amount of business particular design projects can generate. The greater the financial impact of the product and its ability to persuade sales, the greater the financial rewards. With that principle clarified, it's easy to understand why an advertising creative director can realize a salary of perhaps a quarter to a half million dollars, which is far more than any designer would hope for. Consider the amount of money at stake in the placement of a television commercial scheduled to air during a Super Bowl broadcast. Consider the cost of airing the commercial, the cost of production in making it, and the financial and image risk to the corporate sponsor. With all that at stake, is anyone going to quibble about how much it will cost to hire the best talent?

The higher the stakes for image and sales, the larger the compensation for doing the job right. It's easy to understand. As we have discussed, within the design field we have companies which have various specialties. The associated expertise contributes to set the value of their services. They are experts who will be compensated more than generalists. A comparison to health care is not unfounded. A general practitioner will usually charge less for an office visit than a specialist. Design firms or agencies creating movie advertising, title treatments, and trailers find themselves in a particularly richly compensated, if volatile, area. Firms specializing in identity, whether corporate, branding, or retail, are at the higher end of the compensation scale. After all, how often is a corporation going to change its identity? Think of the impact of that new system. Packaging design can also hold great importance, as it directly contributes to sales at the point of sale. Book design, while hardly insignificant, has the least effect, as most people will buy a book for other reasons than its appearance (thus, they don't judge a book by its cover). Editorial designers have a direct impact on a magazine's image and sales. One look at a newsstand, with all those covers screaming for your attention, will confirm that the magazin's appearance contributes to the message, "buy me!" The interior spreads continue to reinforce the magazines' content, message, and legibility. The bottom line consideration is the bottom line. The profit margins of the company, large or small, are what matters in the long run.

## BENEFIT PACKAGES

Many benefits and perks are available, and can drastically change from one firm to another. The best option is to know what could possibly be available versus what the standard package is for a company. Then, see if there is any room to negotiate. A large corporation with a rather complete package may indeed offer most items while small design firms may offer just a few. The following is not a complete listing, but will give you an idea of some of the potential opportunities to add to compensation.

### Health Insurance

This has become the most costly area for employers. The explosion in health insurance costs has, in many cases, required employers to seek other methods of coverage. HMOs or organized health plans offering a selected group of physicians are the common offerings. Many firms have had to raise the deductible base and/or have made their plans contributory. This means that the employee must assume some of the costs. The percentages vary from firm to firm. While some form of medical insurance is standard practice for most offices, dental insurance is not as commonly available. Plans have to be compared, as the provisions for care can be so different. Many companies will offer the employee a choice of medical plans for that reason.

## Health Clubs
In recognition of the long-term benefits of a healthy employee, many large corporations will have on-site health clubs or gyms. Some firms will offer memberships in commercial health club facilities. For some senior level individuals, a country club membership is a negotiable point.

## Vacations, Holidays, Personal, and Sick Days
This category is self-explanatory and can vary from one firm to another to a great extent. The ability to "buy" an additional week of vacation is a newer option offered by some firms. "Buying" can mean approved leave without pay or earning "time credits" with unused sick day allowances. If seniority has earned longer vacation benefits and the individual wants to take a position in another company, it is most difficult to transfer that benefit without serious negotiation.

## Leave of Absence
This can be negotiated on a case-by-case basis. Most firms do not have specific policies in place. Leaves of absence have been achieved because of maternity leaves, elder-care needs, mental health issues, continuing educational requirements, sabbaticals, or other such personal issues. The negotiations would most likely be based on length of service in the firm and how significant a role the employee plays. Many firms appreciate the value in allowing the individual a temporary leave instead of trying to completely replace him or her and train a new employee.

## Life and Disability Insurance
Most major medical policies include a life insurance plan equal to one year's income. Senior level personnel can often negotiate an increased life insurance benefit as well as disability insurance.

## Expense Accounts
Travel and entertainment expenses that are directly related to the firm's business are paid directly or reimbursed by the company. It is possible to be given a guaranteed annual amount as a perk. However, all such expenditures have to be documented with receipts.

## Company Transportation

Many firms will offer a company car to senior level employees. Often, it is a negotiable item and the make of the car becomes a status symbol recognizing the seniority of the employee. Sometimes the negotiation surrounding the make of car can be tense, for the significance lies in the message sent to the rest of the firm regarding the person's status. Monthly auto rentals can also be part of the package when a firm needs an employee to travel as part of the job. It can also be a factor if the firm is in a fairly inaccessible location for the employee they wish to hire. Company vans, buses, and airplanes are occasionally available as necessary.

## Commutation

If the office location is considered a lengthy distance to a commute, the firm may offer to pay these expenses.

## Pension plans

There are several plans available, all of which operate on the same principle of placing money into holding accounts for retirement before paying taxes on those funds. Common plans are the 401k and SEP-IRA. These plans can be payroll deductions, employer's contributions, or a combination of contributions by the employees and employers. Most plans stipulate a period of time to become vested. This means you cannot be eligible to receive the funds unless you stay with the firm for a specific number of years. These vesting plans have a sliding scale of eligibility with common plans being over five years. For example, after three years of employment, a 60 percent vestment; after four years, 80 percent, etc. The advantage of all these plans, regardless of your age, is that they become a form of forced savings and/or additional monies to your base salary that are not taxable. They work as the common IRA. The money accrued in the plan is not taxable until you receive it.

## Education

Some firms offer continued education benefits, reimbursing you for all or part of your expenses. Most plans will only cover educational programs germane to your profession. Some plans will have coverage for family members.

## Seminars and Conferences

Since these are also considered to be educational, many firms, on request, will pay these expenses. They have added value as vehicles for making new contacts for the firm and as a general internal public relations effort.

## Company Stock

Stock or stock options are available on a case-by-case basis. Keep in mind there are many ways of offering stock and many grades of stock. Stock, as well as profit sharing, is used as a form of equity in the firm.

## Profit Sharing

Some firms distribute a percentage of their profits to employees as an incentive. The incentive is to have a vested interest in the general welfare of the company and contribute to its profitability. Obviously, the numbers will change from year to year but the system is an excellent method of insuring the employee's role within the company.

## Bonuses

Most bonuses are totally optional, with guaranteed bonuses as rare options. Signing bonuses are common when there is a need for an added incentive to the hiring process, and can be used to offset an expected year-end bonus when the hiring is done in the last third or fourth quarter of the year. For the firm it means a one-time additional charge without changing the salary base. Bonuses can be a year-end or semiannual disbursement and are usually based on performance and profitability. Remember, since it is a cash award, the money is completely taxable.

## Relocation

Relocation packages are rarely considered for junior level staff members unless the employer is a corporation and part of their recruitment program. Most corporations will include a relocation package for individuals who will move to the site of the company. This is most prevalent for firms located in cities where there is an insufficient talent pool. However, that does not mean a company in New York or San Francisco will not pay relocation expenses from one major city to another. The obvious fact is, no company wants to incur extra expenses, but if the individual has the unique requirements needed, the money will be there. For smaller firms, paying the price of a move is often out of the question. It should be clear that a smaller company will only pay these costs for experienced personnel and very often it is a flat rate that is negotiated. If a person of only a few years' experience wishes to be in a certain geographical region, the best strategy would be to research the firms in the area, perhaps by calling the local chapter of the AIGA or Art Directors Club. Get listings of member firms, contact them directly, and, ultimately, travel to seek the position and be prepared to move yourself. When visiting a new city give yourself enough time, perhaps even allowing time to freelance. It is always frustrating for me to see designers come to New York for a week or ten days and expect to return home with a job offer. Relocation costs most often include airfare (with, perhaps, a couple of visits to find a home), the cost of bringing a spouse to see the new city, and actual moving expenses for belongings. It can also include (but not always) temporary residence, expenses, furniture storage costs, help finding schools, day care, even a job for the spouse, help with mortgage points, and sometimes assuming the mortgage and sale of the previous home. Sometimes a flat package is offered to cover these costs and sometimes a smaller firm can offer to pay part of the expenses. Remember, in these cases, you must always be able to document your expenses with receipts.

## Child Care/Elder Care

Unfortunately, very few firms offer on-site child care or any allowance to pay for outside facilities for children or elders. The only firms that have moved in this direction are large corporations. The Family Medical Leave Act allows for employees to leave employment to care for a family member without jeopardizing their employment status, but they will do so without the employer being obligated to pay them.

## Flextime/Job Sharing

While very few firms are actively involved in flextime or job sharing, the concept of accommodating working parents has gained more attention in the media than in actuality. Flextime is defined as the right not to work the standard nine to five and to establish hours that are responsive to the desire of individuals or the needs of working parents. Solutions include working a shorter day or week on the condition that some work be done at home. Several firms have opted to support mommy track employees by telecommuting. Electronic networking capabilities are adding a new dimension to defining the workplace. Job sharing is another option. Two people share one job, usually overlapping one day to insure a communications flow. However, it is a concept rarely put into practice. Since graphic design is comprised of a vast female majority (and the numbers are growing every year), the ability to control work time individually will without doubt grow in response to the need. Conversely, the option for flextime in the consulting and account services areas are not supported by management.

## Employee Handbooks

Most large companies and many small ones have their benefits and policies spelled out in some form of printed material. You should always ask for it. It is a clear indication of what you can expect as the basis of the firm's offerings. However, many of the items listed above can become negotiable points in the hiring procedure. I have indicated the most common areas. It's always helpful to know what's possible. Keep in mind, however, that many perks are available on a seniority basis. There is a clear correlation between the perception of value associated with the employee and the amount of rewards a company will offer.

## NEGOTIATING A SALARY

Again, the advantage is with the person who can view the process in a holistic way, understanding the various economic forces at work. Taking a job and negotiating a salary is a complex endeavor and many facets of the opportunity must be weighed against the other. These considerations should include:

- The nature of the position
- The long or short-term goals of the designer
- The quality of the firm and its business agenda
- The areas of specialization (if any)
- Market factors
- Location
- Benefits

Benefit packages, as described above, are extremely important because they represent noncash or cash-deferred additions to your salary that have the equivalent of cash value based on after-tax dollars. This means that the cash value is more than its face value because it is nontaxable income.

It is important to remember that any negotiation is successful only when both parties are not completely happy with the results and there is a sense of compromise. Therefore, one always has to "leave room" for compromise when initiating a position to be negotiated. The actual negotiation can be informal, friendly, and brief. A scenario can be a casual, "This is what we feel we can offer you," and since the amount is not a surprise and is agreeable, you accept. Other offers can be far more formal and in a "testing" mode. The quality of the negotiation can establish the power relationships that will continue on the job. This is a time in which you want to be sure to conduct yourself in a cautious and professional manner. Be respectful and courteous, no matter what you may think. It is a general rule of thumb to ask for a little more than you expect to get. If you feel there is room to negotiate, on principal, don't accept a first offer.

A far more common scenario to the one above would be to not respond immediately after you receive an offer, but to defer your response a few days. Give yourself time to "sleep on it." This will give you the opportunity to ponder and gain some clarity. Make sure you know all the other factors in addition to base salary when you get the offer. If there is some part of the offer that is not satisfactory, bring it up. If you do not clear the air on issues of concern, the feeling of frustration may fester after you begin working.

The timing of salary reviews can become an important issue in discussions of this nature. The first stage is to have the firm specify their review policy and its definition. A review usually means an evaluation of work performance and a possible change in compensation based on the review. It can take place at year end or at the anniversary of the employee joining the firm. Sometimes it can take place much earlier. If the amount offered is deemed insufficient you may ask for an earlier review, perhaps within three or six months. We have found this a generally excellent method to negotiate a higher salary with a time limit for the lower salary. The amount of the future increase is usually not determined at the time of hiring, but the review agreement represents an understanding that an increase is possible at a specific time if performance matches expectation. It also affords the employer less risk if the quality of the employee's work and experience is in question.

The number of items to be negotiated can sometimes be a surprise. The belief that "everything in life is negotiable" may not be completely true, but is helpful to work on that assumption. As long as you do not have an arrogant attitude, your loss exposure in trying to change terms is negligible and you have everything to gain. However, I would caution you that in any negotiation, you must concentrate on realistic priorities. For example, it would be futile for a designer with two years' experience to negotiate a four-week vacation when the standard is two weeks.

Corporations and many firms may confirm the agreement with a written offer stating the terms. Smaller firms may consider a handshake sufficient. Nonetheless, make sure your offer is real and confirmed and not in an exploratory phase. Every now and then we find a designer who believes he or she has a job offer when the employer is really trying to determine if he or she is available at a certain salary. The confusion is easily understandable, but you would not want to quit a job based on an incomplete offer.

To sum it up, salary packages are always flexible, an ever-shifting set of priorities and goals. The possible combinations of all these components make for a tremendous variety of possibilities. The components of establishing a package that's fair and equitable to both parties rely heavily on what both perceive as fair. Designers are unique in that accepting positions often has little to do with the salary and a great deal to do with the quality of work, the quality of opportunity, and general lifestyle it offers. Perhaps the best advice is to always go with your basic instinct of what is comfortable for you. The bottom line is always an extremely subjective one.

# THE RGA 2001 SALARY SURVEY

This survey is based on the placement records at Roz Goldfarb Associates and experience of the RGA recruiters. These are starting salaries for base compensation on an annual basis. They do not include any benefits, bonuses, profit sharing, or other forms of compensation. It is important to note that titles vary tremendously and not all firms will utilize all titles. Therefore, these titles are in some ways generic. And while we have indicated basic years of experience required, this, too, can vary depending upon the individual. This survey is structured to core areas of specialization and do not indicate regional differences. These salaries are those prevalent in the large cities of the United States. Salaries can vary due to the cost of living index in geographical regions and to the size of the firm, with larger firms obviously being able to afford more than small ones.

## Corporate and Consumer Product Branding Firms, Environmental Designers

- Entry-level/junior designers: $30-40K
- Intermediate designers/3-5 years' experience: $45-60K
- Senior designers, project directors/5-10 years' experience: $60-75K
- Design directors/7 years' minimum: $75-100K
- Senior design directors/associate creative directors: $100–140K
- Creative directors: $100-175K+

## Graphic Designers, Print Design, Annuals, Corporate Literature, Collateral

- Junior designers/designers: $30-40K
- Intermediate designers/5 years' experience: $45-65K
- Senior designers/6-8 years' experience: $70-100K
- Art directors/7 years' minimum: $90-120K
- Creative directors: $110-160K+

## Editorial Design, Magazine Promotion Design

- Junior designers/entry-level–2 years' experience: $28-35K
- Senior designers/3-6 years' experience: $40-50K
- Associate art directors: $55-65K
- Art directors: $70-100K+
- Design directors: $100K+

## Environments-Retail, Entertainment, Exhibits

- Junior/intermediate designer: $35-50K
- Senior designer/project manager: $60-80K
- Project directors $70-90K
- Senior project managers/directors: $75-100K
- Studio mangers/design directors: $75-100K
- Executive level design directors/managers: $120-200K

## Environmental Graphics

- Junior/designer: $30-50K
- Senior designer: $45-60K
- Senior designer/project manager: $50-80K
- Design director: $75-100K

## Interactive Design–Agencies and Consultancies

- Junior information architect/educational in information design, plus some design experience: $50-65K
- Senior information architect/4 years experience: $75-100K
- Junior designer/salary dependent upon tech skills: $30- 45K
- Designer/1 year + experience: $40-55K
- Senior designer/2 years + experience: $ 55-75K
- Art director/conceptual development and presentation skills: $65-85K
- Associate creative director/management: $85-125K
- Creative director: $135–200K
- Executive creative directors/minimum 7-10 years experience: $200-250K

## Interactive Design–Corporate (In-house)

- Junior designer/depending on tech skills: $30-40K
- Designer/2+ years experience: $40–60K
- Senior designer/4 years + experience: $50–80K
- Creative manager/director/5 years managing a team: $100-150K
- Creative director/VP/wide range depending upon number of reports: $100-200K

## Production Artists

- Junior production artist: $35-45K (needs training in all programs)
- Mid-level production artist: $45-65K (excellent in at

least two programs and a good understanding of Quark, PhotoShop and Illustrator)
- Senior production artist: $65-85K (excellent Illustrator and PhotoShop skills, and some on-press experience)
- Junior print production managers: $35-50K
- Print production managers: $55-85K
- Studio managers: $85-120K
- Production directors: $85-120K+
- Director of creative services: $90-120K+

## Advertising

The range is very wide depending on the size of the agency and the billings of the accounts
- Entry level copywriters and art directors: $30-40K
- 3-5 years' experience: $40-75K
- 5-10 years' experience: $60-150K
- Associate creative directors: $125-200K
- Creative directors: $150-350K
- Executive creative directors: $300K-$1M+

# Moving On: When and How
# to Leave A Job

## 15

"It's time." That is the most common response I get when I ask an applicant why they want to look for another job. What does this internal clock signal? What are the signs that mark the moment to embark on such a career-altering process? Most often, it means there is "no place to go." The definition of this often-used phrase means the path forward and upward is blocked. It may be blocked by another person who occupies the position you want and that person shows no indication of leaving or being promoted. It may mean the size of the firm and its structure will not allow for a logical progression. It may mean that if you stay in the safety of your present position without being promoted you will stop growing professionally. "No place to go" often means, "no place to grow." It's a feeling of reaching a plateau and not being willing to stay there.

As design matures and changes over any given period of years there is, for some, a sense that their firms may not have kept pace with the times. Companies who have not set their sights forward find themselves in a perilous trap. Not only do they fail to keep up with the marketing trends or computerization but the result is often a creative brain drain. The employee's sense of frustration and the desire to be current will cause many individuals to recognize that the only way they will achieve a state of competitive professionalism is to change their job.

Now, not everyone wants to constantly move up, and that's fine. Many reach a position of contentment and comfort and stay in a firm for many years. But for the younger person still carving out a future from a collection of experiences or for the person whose ambition is frustrated, "it's time" has a powerful ring.

Nonetheless, other reasons exist for making a move. Money can often be a very compelling cause. Supporting a family, buying a home, and other personal motivations may cause dissatisfaction with the present work condition. Professional growth being thwarted or not rewarded inspires the need to change. A glance at the "frustrations" list in "The Candidate's Viewpoint" (pp. 149-152), will identify and confirm the many root causes launching the decision to move on. Work environment, lack of recognition, and the desire to move to another city can all be factors.

## HOW TO QUIT

For some reason we are often told how to educate ourselves, how to get a job, how to work, and how to design, but little is ever said about how to quit. Acting in a responsible and professional manner once you have decided to leave is just as important as your demeanor when entering a new office. How you leave and the impression you make will affect your relationships with the people involved for the rest of your life. And don't think that once you have left a place you have closed that chapter of your life and it's finished. We have discussed how "round" the world is and how closely people keep interacting with each other through the years. There are constant reminders in everyday conversations of how people seem always amazed to meet up with the past. The key factor is to "never burn bridges." It doesn't matter whether you are motivated by a desire to be considered a pleasant and likeable person or because you have the aspiration to maintain your people network. You should never block your access to anyone you might want to see again or have to be with again.

Maintaining your credibility and your professional relationships will strongly affect your performance in the workplace and your ability for future networking. There is nothing less productive than to leave a bad impression, or leave a place without grace and then find the same individuals working in the same firm with you years later. It happens! It happens with such frequency it pushes the point of plausibility.

You never know when you will need a recommendation, help of any sort, or perhaps even a job from individuals known through previous employment. The bottom line is, paths keep crossing, and we have witnessed these scenarios often in this game of professional musical chairs.

Let's consider a few amusing and sometimes not amusing examples. There was the young designer who left a firm with great hostility and anger. She left in a huff, telling her supervisor exactly what she thought of him!

(How many times did you only wish for such an opportunity?) You probably can guess the rest of the story. Two jobs later that same supervisor was hired as a creative director in her firm. It was a very uncomfortable situation, saved only by his understanding that people can make mistakes.

One person was hired for a three-month temporary position. The employer went out of his way to make an easy transition after the three months by having the person work part-time while looking for another position. As it was also over the Christmas holidays, the employee was still given presents and a small bonus. When the person left she informed the office manager of her last day, but never said one word to the employer, let alone a good-bye. How could she expect a good reference?

Knowing how to say good-bye is as important as saying hello. It is critical to say "thank you." You should say "thank you" for having the opportunity to work and grow, to learn, to partake of whatever success the firm represented has, to have accepted any gratuities that were given to you, any time that was spent on your behalf, and any effort the firm made to train you and allow you to reach the point that you could leave. Firms often recognize when "it's time" as well as you do and do not experience any animosity at your departure. Many times individuals are anxious and, perhaps, frightened over the imagined confrontation in the act of resigning. The result can be a relief, letdown, and even a humbling experience to learn that it may not be a big deal. Experienced and seasoned employers acknowledge the natural process of moving on. Your resignation may cause them some disappointment, but without question, they will find a method of replacing you. Leaving a job is another time when you must exhibit your sophistication with the process and show professional manners and polish. Remember, whatever you may really be thinking is not the issue.

This is also a point in time to understand you may have an employer who truly does not want you to leave and may make a counteroffer. It is a time to keep clear focus on your reasons for leaving. If they are purely monetary, the counteroffer may have a significance to you. However, remember that few people leave a firm only for reasons of money. Chances are that nothing fundamentally changes in most established organizations and people/business patterns are well established, so beware of promises that cannot be kept. I do not find counteroffers flattering or wise in the vast majority of instances. Consider: If your value to the firm is that much greater, why did it take this action for you to get an increase?

## AND IF YOU'RE FIRED?

Let's face it—it can happen, and does, as those who are going through the cutbacks of 2001 well know. Recessions and company restructuring have afforded too many people just that unpleasant experience. Y2K experienced the collapse of many dot.com companies and it is the first time since the recession of 1990 that there has been such fear about the state of the economy. At the time of this writing, no one knows how long the recession will last and while there are many who remember difficult times vividly, the vast majority of the workforce have never experienced a serious downturn. The first half of the 1990s produced huge layoffs due to corporate downsizing and merger activity as well as design firms restructuring to meet new electronic staffing requirements. It was estimated by a study conducted by the *New York Times* that one-third of middle management positions in corporations disappeared during those years—dramatically and, perhaps, forever changing the staffing profiles of these companies. Many euphemisms have come into the vernacular to try to alleviate the negative emotions attached to the words "fired." Some are kind, others represent corporate-speak that can be dehumanizing. So we experience a broad range of explanations of this action. Almost no one ever says "You're fired!" However, whether you have been let go, cut back, restructured, excessed, or reengineered, the effect is exactly the same. In 2001, the layoffs have been simply attributed to financial bottom-line requirements. It has been so sudden a downturn that many have not been prepared for it and corporate-speak has played a small role. Most large publicly traded companies have little flexibility and when the income is down the appropriate staff and overhead cuts are made by mandate. Some companies have been ingenious in managing the cutbacks, some offering employees temporary leaves or keeping some benefits or offering hiring bonuses if they can bring them back within a defined period of time. Smaller companies can be more flexible, cutting salaries instead of people's jobs as one solution.

Unless you were let go for a demonstrated reason there is little stigma attached to being fired. So many firms go through restructuring, especially when acquisitions are involved, that it is not a questionable event. The process of firms paring down has become all too common and acceptable. Other causes may be the lack of sufficient capitalization, especially with new start-up companies or lack of profitability even with lots of venture capital. Often if a client is lost, cash flow is immediately threatened, as the firm may not have a sufficiently broad or established client base. Agencies can have "Black Fridays" when a major account leaves, forcing them to immediately fire large numbers of people. Corporations, traditionally the slowest to react to a slowdown in revenues, will usually first seek to cut staff by attrition; however, as previously noted, they are no longer the bastions of employment security and are constantly subject to mergers and/or selling off divisions. The bottom line is, when interviewing, simply tell the truth about when and how you were laid off.

If you were let go for reasons relating to performance, you have a significantly different problem. If you have fallen prey to internal political fallout, you will have to be very tactful in how you will describe the situation to a future employer. But in either case, it is essential that you present a logical reason for your dismissal. Most often, we are confronted with explanations referring to a "difference of opinion" or "creative conflict" or simply company politics. Whenever you are faced with a problem of describing internal company conflicts be very general and beware of offering any libelous information. Remember, whatever you think about the organization you wish to leave or have left should not be reviewed in detail with future employers. If you have had negative experiences or observed business practices of which you don't approve, it is wise to keep it to yourself. If you are asked why you wish to leave or have left a position choose your words carefully. You could be inviting legal action by libeling another person or company.

If you feel you were wrongfully fired and you wish to protest in some manner, do not sign anything during your exit interview. If you are presented with any documents, show it to an attorney first. Your attorney may also advise you not to accept any severance pay.

Severance pay is often a way of compensating an individual who has been let go. Severance is not mandatory and the amount varies greatly from firm to firm. Most of the time it is based on the number of years you have been a member of the firm and many firms indicate the rules of severance pay in employee handbooks. Nonetheless, if you are not sure, always ask if you are entitled to severance pay or whether the firm would like to consider giving it to you. Often, this can be a negotiable item.

## FINISHING WORK IN PROGRESS

Leaving also means not leaving unfinished work or leaving the firm with a problem on their hands. You must be conscientious and professional about your assignments and responsibilities. Sometimes you may be pressured by the firm you are joining to come on board as quickly as possible. You may be the end product of a long search and you represent needed relief in their workplace. Their deadlines are their main priority. The proper notice of leaving is at least two weeks. (In Europe, it can mean one to three months.) The amount of notice you give your employer can be more or less dependent on workloads and the length of time you have been with the firm. If you have been there less than a year, one week is acceptable. Do not allow pressure to prevent you from finishing your work and/or handing it over to a coworker. Your new employer wouldn't want you to leave him or her in a lurch, either. Nonetheless, know that at some point it is important not to drag out the process through a misguided sense of responsibility, and you have a responsibility to your new employer and to your future.

We had one unusual example when an employer insisted the individual report immediately to work or lose the job offer. He needed her to join a team on a business trip to Japan immediately. He recognized that if she was not part of the original team, the Japanese would never fully accept her. She was, however, in the middle of a project that she did not feel should be left suddenly. The job offer was about to be rescinded when we were finally able to negotiate a compromise. She went to Japan for two weeks and upon her return finished the other project while working for her new employer part-time.

## OBTAINING PORTFOLIO SAMPLES

Industry practice dictates you should have accessibility to samples of all your work, including projects in which you have participated. It is your responsibility to present your work accurately, indicating the level of your responsibility, especially if the project is a shared one. Before and when you leave a firm you are entitled to be given samples of your work for your portfolio, barring confidentiality restrictions if products have not yet been released to the public. Some employers can make it difficult, and while there are no legal regulations per se (with the exception of proprietary or confidential projects), common past business practice indicates your entitlement to examples of your past experiences.

Upon exiting a firm, therefore, there may be recent samples you should be sure to request. You probably had updated your portfolio in order to seek employment, but don't forget to collect your most current samples. Perhaps it's new work that's at the printer and you will have to return in order to get them. You may have been working on sensitive projects that cannot be released until they are marketed. Make sure you get them later. These details are easily forgotten in the excitement of change and often are only remembered when you next seek a job and realize you require them for your book. By then, it's probably too late. Always protect yourself by keeping an archive of your work history (with duplicates), including your ideation sketches, up-to-date. The work that most often gets left behind or simply discarded are the preliminary sketches. It is these sketches that are a key component of your portfolio. (See chapter 12, "Your Portfolio.")

## EXIT INTERVIEWS

A segment of the departing process may be an "exit interview." It may be with a human resource person or with your boss. It should be a time of reflection and constructive evaluation. It may include a written questionnaire.

The purpose is twofold. First, it will give you tools in your search for a new job (if you are being let go), and second, it will allow you to evaluate the company from your point of view. If handled properly, it should give the firm an insight into their dealings with employees.

## REFERENCES

It is a very good idea to ask for a letter of reference upon departure. If you are leaving for another position, you may feel it's a moot point. It's a legitimate request in any case, and may turn out to be handy for the future.

## VACATIONS

The luxury of a vacation, be it short or long, between jobs is a terrific advantage. The physical and psychological breather refreshes your outlook and revitalizes your energy level. Of course, not everybody can take advantage of this possibility, but consider it an option. Every vacation day you can squeeze into your demanding schedule is a boon.

Some individuals prefer to quit after a vacation period or after a bonus period. This is manipulative but not surprising behavior. It is always questionable to me. If you want to factor in these often deserved and earned benefits, then do so, but don't quit immediately, at least for appearance's sake.

## GIVING NOTICE

While you may want to give the customary two weeks' notice, in some cases, quitting, may mean you'll leave before the day is out. In some business sectors you will probably be asked to leave the office the minute you give notice. This is mostly due to the confidential nature of the projects, and the proprietary nature of the work takes precedence over time considerations. It's particularly true in branding and packaging design. The sensitivity of the projects has to be protected immediately, especially if the designer is moving to another competitor. In that case, the two weeks' notice is forgotten and you will be wished good luck and told to pack up and leave. For the uninitiated it can be a rude shock. It is wise to be emotionally and professionally prepared for this possibility. However, this release can offer you a forced vacation or you may find yourself starting your new position sooner than expected.

After you have left, be careful not to discuss the confidential qualities of your former employer's projects. If you had signed a confidentiality agreement, read it again carefully. Make sure you adhere to its restrictions. Whether you signed an agreement or not, the work you did at your previous firm is considered confidential, as are the work procedures. Keep in mind that certain knowledge is proprietary and you must not abuse that responsibility. If you do so, in some extreme cases, you might be liable for a lawsuit under clauses relating to "trade secrets."

So you have remembered your professional and personal manners and you are leaving with your reputation intact along with your employer's good wishes for your future. It's a wonderful, exciting time. There is an element of risk as you assume new responsibilities and have to learn to work with a different set of personalities within a different company culture. But life is moving on—and so are you!

# In Search of Education

## 16

**W**hen a designer who is a recent grad contacts our office looking for a job, one of the first questions we ask is what school he or she attended. It's not a question of whether the designer has a degree but a question of where that degree was obtained, because the content and quality of design education is significantly different from one institution to another. For us, it may mean the difference between scheduling an immediate interview or asking the designer to drop off his or her portfolio. This is a clear indication of how significant the quality of education is for the designer in the job market.

## CHOICES IN DESIGN EDUCATION

Simply put, a common syllabus for graphic design education does not exist in the colleges of the United States. Design is a creative process, and, therefore, completely subjective. Design education is dependent upon the vision and insights of those who are responsible for hiring faculty and structuring curriculum and its content. It then relies on the day-to-day interaction and vision of the instructor. Each institution teaches design from a somewhat different point of view. To confirm this, one only has to examine the portfolios of graduating students. The educational focus and graphic style of these portfolios are, in most instances, so distinctive, it is possible to identify the graduate's college just by looking at them. It is easy to understand how selecting a college could very well enhance or limit future career choices.

Since design programs are different, let us examine some of the primary directions and choices. Initially, we need to acknowledge that almost every university has an art department; however, those departments' curricula focus on the traditional fine arts such as, drawing, painting, printmaking, and sculpture. Our analysis here is limited to "professional" programs—the education resulting in the requisite portfolio necessary to enter the graphic design field. Since the field is so competitive, it is necessary to value and evaluate the pressure put on graduates seeking their first job. We have acknowledged in previous chapters the importance of those first career steps, and how every advantage can help. The educational process is, naturally, the fundamental preparation for those first steps.

As stated, design, unlike mathematics or physics, does not have a fixed set of standards to follow. Each school has its own conception of the meaning and function of design. For the unsophisticated, these are subtle distinctions, and how to assess the characteristics of a curriculum are often only appreciated by professionals. This diversity is, from an educational standpoint, a healthy condition, but there exists a critical need, not always met by the various institutions, to communicate the essence of these educational differences to the public. Researching educational institutions may only compound the dilemma, for the jargon used in college or art school catalogs only confuses by the fact that they are defining the curriculum in what may sound like major areas of concentration—i.e., visual communications, visual design, graphic design, communication arts, or media arts, to name a few. It should be remembered that graphic arts is a term usually associated with the graphic arts industries, i.e., printing and pre-press. A distinguishing characteristic of all graphic design based programs is the fundamental concentration on problem-solving. Graphic arts and many interactive technology (IT) programs emphasize the technical needs of the industry. Therefore, in design, programs with identical or similar names and comparable fields of concentration do not necessarily have the identical course of study and may have wide variances in aesthetic philosophy and methodology. There are programs that offer two-year professional certificates, programs that exist in community colleges, graphic design programs within four-year studio degrees with majors other than graphic design, and graphic design programs within a four-year liberal arts program. Understandably, then, within the framework of a four-year degree program, there is no uniformity in degrees, so a bachelor of fine arts (B.F.A.), bachelor of arts (B.A.), bachelor of graphic design, or Bachelor of Science (B.S.) may be earned. Moreover, course requirements for the same degree will not necessarily be the same. Compounding the confusion, different programs even receive different accreditation. However, one key is the certification by the National Association of Schools of Art and Design. It is also important to remember that design education is not the same as fine arts education. The nature of design is that it is a business, servicing the client and consumer, not a self-fulfilling creative exploration. Therefore, the curricula of a design program should be focused towards professional goals.

What distinguishes graphic design programs, and how does one become an educated consumer in choosing a school? Furthermore, what is the net result or goal of the educational focus? Perhaps, more directly, what do the best graduate portfolios look like, and is it possible to control what kind of careers the graduates achieve? One excellent way to answer these questions is to ask practicing professionals, especially if they are in a position to evaluate newly graduated and young designers. It is often particularly helpful to know what their own educational and work background has been. They can then possibly be in a position to suggest which schools they might recommend on the basis of their own experience and hiring practices. While their responses will likely be highly subjective, they will nonetheless give a direction. Another direction is to talk with the placement office of the institution. First of all, it is highly desirable for the school to have an active placement office. Placement offices keep records of their activities and can provide information on the names and types of firms their graduates are placed in as well as the kind of positions. They also can provide details on what, if any, kind of co-op programs or summer placement exists for the undergraduate student. This is very valuable information in providing a key to what the future may hold for a graduate from that educational program.

My own preference is (1) a minimum four-year curriculum, (2) placing the utmost emphasis on the faculty associated with an institution, and (3) a program that integrates aspects of art history, liberal arts, and business or marketing with a strong concentration in graphic design. That means that more than half of the course work will be creative and the rest should have a balance as indicated above. When students choose electives, they need to be guided towards the realization that success is dependent on becoming a well-rounded individual (as stated in the beginning of this book). Too often, the student is so overwhelmed by our competitive society and the need to succeed in their chosen major, that this aspect of requirements for success is placed in a sidebar to be accessed at some other point in time. That access to educational time can be achieved in advanced degree programs, extra course work, professional conferences and seminars, or forever lost because of loss of interest or just "life" taking over. As a result, anything that can be achieved during those critical four years is absolutely essential.

# FACULTY: THE KEY INFLUENCE

The curriculum of any art institution is only as strong as the faculty, for in so many instances there is no written curriculum but merely a course outline. Therefore, the importance of the faculty input to the overall educational experience and achievement cannot be overemphasized. The teacher's own training and life experience will determine his or her aesthetic value system and may establish different desired levels of professionalism. The classroom situation rests on an ever-changing dynamic between students and instructors. Determining what is good, true, and right in art and design is a fundamental, recurring question whose answer is in constant flux.

It's common practice for most art schools located in a major metropolis to hire instructors who are working professionals for their day-to-day experience and insights. These part-time faculty are individuals that may teach only one class or one day a week. They often teach a specialized subject and bring into the classroom projects from their current work environment. The "real world" atmosphere of these classes simulates, in many respects, a working atelier. Students may be recruited by faculty to work as apprentices in their studios. These experiences can be priceless and offer a similar value-based level of experiences. Some institutions also actively and aggressively place their students into firms on co-operative work/study programs (co-ops) that offer actual work experience with college credit. The quality of these faculty/student relationships varies in direct correlation to the compatibility of their personalities. It is very hard to qualify the academic merit, but the pragmatic value becomes self-evident by the quality of the output. In gauging professional art schools, the term "professional" often refers to the number of design or advertising professionals on staff as visiting professors, compared to professional educators. Studying the listing of faculty and their accompanying bios can be more instructional than reading the class syllabus. It is these faculty members, and their point of view formed by their life experience, that will formulate the course content.

Schools may also call upon a sizable pool of professional talent that is not available for long-term teaching commitments, but represents a valuable resource for guest lectures, expert critiques, and intensive workshops. Institutions outside the main city centers use various techniques to flying in critics and guest lecturers, and organize field trips for students, but must rely on an established full-time faculty.

Frequent exposure to the diversified opinions of professionals, as well as their reinforcement of important underlying truths, will better equip the student to make intelligent, necessary career choices. The constant interplay with competent teachers who have specialized in different areas of design can provide desirable role models. The position role models can play in formatting a direction of education should not be undervalued. It is significant. The role-model process and the luxury of being exposed to superior talent in a formative period of life are some of the most enriching experiences any education can offer.

## IN SEARCH OF A CONTEMPORARY CURRICULUM

The importance of an academic curriculum should not be underestimated. The graphic designer is an arbiter of the times and must aware of cultural and political currents. The designer, therefore, must have a well-rounded education in order to be sensitive to these issues, and also needs basic business management course work. The graphic designer requires an educational foundation including the aesthetically directed creative studio work; a technological education that is up to current standards; a full grounding in liberal arts coursework, i.e., history, literature, mathematics, and social sciences; and basic business management. The graphic designer needs to be prepared to work as a creative individual with a knowledge of history, politics, and the arts, who can also communicate verbally and in writing, write a proposal, balance a budget, read a profit and loss statement, manage other people, and conceptually understand the functioning of their clients' businesses as well as their own. It is probable that in the future design education will formally be extended beyond a four-year span because of the amount of education required and the limitations within the period of time. In the meantime, it is critical to choose an institution that offers a balanced curriculum or recognize that the education of a designer needs to be augmented by other sources. Extremes in institutional approaches can be theoretical (Yale) or extremely practical. In the July/August 2000 issue of *Graphis*, in "The Design Business, Education and Preparing for the Future," Linda Bowen quotes Steve Heller, director of the Designer as Author program at New York's School of Visual Arts. Steve describes his program as "an entrepreneurial course where students learn how to turn their ideas into viable products. As maker/manufacturer of a product, students must determine what and where the market is, create both marketing and financial plans as well as learn how to legally protect the intellectual product in the business world. Our department simulates a design firm, not a lab or school."

With the explosion of information and technology, the need to manage it, the pressure of students to absorb everything before graduation, and the institutional administrators who can plan for only so many courses in four years, the only possible way is often continuing education. And as designers improve themselves and assume new responsibilities these required skills become evident. There is just so much on-the-job training can achieve.

The fact is, most firm owners or department heads were not trained to do their jobs. Designers sensitive to these rapid changes in design are forced to pursue conferences and seminars and find various methods of shoring up their business and management skills. A market response has been the tremendous growth of seminar programs by professional organizations and those whose business it is to develop conferences. The response from higher educational institutions is the recognition of the importance of basic business coursework in curriculum. At long last, courses and programs in business management and design management are appearing on the undergraduate and graduate level.

## POSTGRADUATE PROGRAMS

The master's degree is not required for professional practice. It can be effective for the student coming from a traditional fine arts/liberal arts education, who, by opting for a graduate-level or an advanced certificate program in graphic design, will achieve the specialized focus needed to develop a portfolio. It is also a solution for those pursuing continued career development into design management. The more obvious function of postgraduate work is its attraction to graphic designers who have an undergraduate degree in graphic design and some years of professional experience, and need to expand, revitalize, and refresh themselves. Today, designers are expected to keep current in the expanding world of digital media, assume research responsibilities, deal with far more complex problems than in the past, and need to understand the multifaceted business structures of their clients. Graduate programs can satisfy many of these needs and offer intensified study within a particular design philosophy or may simply offer a return to aesthetic goals after some years of work. Graduate programs can also offer the important business and management training mentioned that is most often missing in the undergraduate level course work.

In *Adobe* magazine's March/April 2000 issue, Carolyn McCarron quoted from Katherine McCoy's essay, "Education is an Adolescent Profession." Katherine is currently a professor at the Institute of Design, Illinois Institute of Technology, and formerly directed the graduate program at Cranbrook Academy of Art. Katherine wrote, "Four-year degree programs may not provide a sufficient grounding for this incredibly wide and complex field. Educators are beginning to consider a new model based on a four-year predesign program followed by a two- or three-year professional degree, similar to law or medicine."

While educators grapple with the future structures and models for achieving a fully rounded education, these current graduate programs result in professional enhancement and personal enrichment. Unfortunately, they do not represent recognized and critical educational requirements in the marketplace. At this point in time, the addition of a master's degree is rarely considered as part of a job profile or an incentive for an increase in salary. That will probably change. Designers in search of educational credentials for their profession sometimes seek out entrance to a masters of business administration (M.B.A.) program, which also has an unproven effect. There are several doctoral programs in the United States, the first one initiated in 1991 at Illinois Institute of Technology. While the need is recognized for designers to have a broader knowledge-base, the effect of a doctoral program is unknown at this time.

## A SAMPLE OF CHOICES

As demonstrated, the sheer number of choices in educational directions and institutions can be daunting. The following is a short and highly subjective list of schools, compiled and based on my observations during years of reviewing graduating student portfolios. It is a list of only those educational institutions I feel offer significant programs to prepare students to enter the graphic design field. Since the focus of graphic design education is crystallized in the graduates' portfolio, that resulting portfolio has become the hallmark of the educational success of the program as well as the vehicle of entry to that first job. As faculty and program leadership change so do the net effects (the relationship between faculty and syllabus having already been noted); thus, this factor must become a consideration to any educational survey.

The wild card in any design education process is always the talent factor, for no matter what the quality of the education is, ultimately, talent will out. Just as a mediocre student will not become a major talent no matter how superior the training, a great talent (with sufficient ambition) will overcome major obstacles. Individual creativity and innovative thinking is the overarching issue in any person's creative work, whatever the venue. Ultimately, it becomes very clear that this creativity has the power to surpass any educational dogma. The IQ that matters is the "individual" quotient. When a unique talent surfaces with all the requisite knowledge and personality, there are no boundaries. Any person in a position to review scores of portfolios cannot help but observe that, just as no two faces or no two fingerprints are alike, neither are two portfolios. For me, that is the mystery and beauty of the process.

## HOW TO CONTACT COLLEGES

The admissions offices are the entry point to receive detailed information about a school's programs, admission, tuition, and scholarships. The fastest way is through the National Association of Schools of Art and Design's Web site at *www.arts-accredit.org,* where you can search by name or location the current 226 accredited schools and hot link to many of the individual institutions. You can also order their directory from the site. As previously indicated, it is a good idea to ask the admissions office or the placement office about their data on graduates—where the majority find employment. Always check the faculty listings and read their biography. Try to get a sense of the ratio between tenured and visiting faculty. Full-time faculty offers stability and vision to a program; however, sometimes it is the visiting faculty (i.e., working professionals who teach) that gives a program its vitality and link to current issues. To get a more personal feel for the program's point of view I would suggest contacting the department chairperson. The competition for good students is keen and the admissions effort for many schools includes a major marketing drive. Keep in mind that, like any product or service, the schools are presenting themselves in an arena as competitive as any marketplace. Your choice has to be as objective as possible.

It should be noted that New York City, befitting its reputation as the Big Apple, has more graphic design programs than any other major metropolis. The unique quality of these programs is that they exist within the communications capital of the nation, including new and traditional media, which offers the most concentrated work environment, and thus provides these schools with a significant and wonderful teaching pool of design professionals. It is not unusual for a visiting professor to teach different courses at different schools. Most schools in New York and other metropolitan areas have extensive evening programs as well, which may offer specialized courses, degrees, or programs.

## AN EDUCATIONAL SHORTLIST

The following is a short list of schools with the focus on three classifications: undergraduate and graduate graphic design, and industrial design. Many institutions' design programs include advertising. Additionally, there are references to educational resources in the chapters on advertising (chapter 7) and production (chapter 10). The institutions offering both undergraduate and postgraduate programs will have a dot (•); important industrial design programs are indicated by an asterisk (★). New York City regional schools are separated because of their unique interrelationship. There is a separate list for doctoral programs. These are all institutions which hold significant enough status to be singled out. While these institutions do not guarantee success, they are at the forefront of design education. The bottom line is that the student attending a school of repute, who has the innate talent, curiosity, commitment, and passion for design and is willing to work hard, will succeed.

Academy of Art College

Graphic Design Program
79 New Montgomery Street
San Francisco, CA 94105
*www.academyart.edu*

Art Center College of Design • ★

1700 Lida Street
Pasadena, CA 91103
(626) 369-2200
*www.artcenter.edu*

Basel School of Design •

Schule Fur Gestaltung
Vogelsanstrasse 15
CH-4021 Basel, Switzerland
011-61-695-6770
*sfgbs@acess.ch*

Brigham Young University

Visual Communications Design
Provo, UT 84602
(801) 378-3890
*www.byu.edu*

California School of Arts • ★
and Crafts (Cal Arts)

1700 17th Street
San Francisco, CA 94103
(415) 703-9500
*www.ccac-art.edu*

Carnegie Mellon University

Design Department
110 Margaret Morrison
Pittsburgh, PA 15213
(412) 268-2828
*www.ccac-art.edu*

Cranbrook Academy of Art • ★

39221 Woodward Avenue
Bloomfield Hills, MI 48303-0801
(248) 645-3000
*www.cranbrook.edu*

Illinois Institute of Technology
Institute of Design

350 North La Salle Street
Chicago, IL 60616
(312) 567-3250
*www.id.iit.edu*

Kansas City Art Institute ★

4415 Warwick Boulevard
Kansas City, MO 64111
(816) 474-5224
*www.kcai.edu*

Kent State University ★

School of Art
Kent, OH 44242
(216) 672-2192
*www.kent.edu*

Portfolio Center of Atlanta

125 Bennett Street N.W.
Atlanta, GA 30309
(800) 255-3169
*www.portfoliocenter.edu*

Rhode Island School of Design • ★

2 College Street
Providence, RI 02903
(401) 331-3511
*www.risd.edu*

Rochester Institute of Technology

One Lomb Memorial Drive
Rochester, NY 14623
(716) 475-2411
*www.rit.edu*

Syracuse University

Department of Visual
Communications
102 Shaffer Art Building
Syracuse, NY 13244
(315) 443-4071
*www.syr.edu*

The University of the Arts ★

320 South Broad Street
Philadelphia, PA 19102
(215) 875-4800
*www.uarts.edu*

University of Cincinnati

2624 Clifton Avenue
Cincinnati, OH 45221
(513) 556-6000
*www.admission@uc.edu*

Yale University •

New Haven, CT 06520
(203) 432-4771
*www.yale.edu*

## New York City Region:

The Cooper Union

41 Cooper Square
New York, NY 10003
(212) 353-4120
*www.cooper.edu*

Fashion Institute of Technology
(State University of New York)

227 West 27th Street
New York, NY 10001-5992
(212) 760-7673
*www.fitnyc.suny.edu*

Parsons School of Design

66 Fifth Avenue
New York, NY 10011
(212) 741-8900
*www.parsons.edu*

Pratt Institute • *

School of Art & Design
Brooklyn, NY 11205
(718) 636-3600
*www.pratt.edu*

School of Visual Arts

209 East 23rd Street
New York, NY 10010-3994
(212) 679-7350
*www.schoolofvisualarts.edu*

SUNY Purchase
(State University of New York)

735 Anderson Hill Road
Purchase, NY 10577
(914) 251-6000
*www.purchase.edu*

# Past, Present and Future

## 17

**I**n the forward to this book I discussed why everyone should have the luxury of choice. I believe that the importance of recognizing life's choices and following one's intuition is key to realizing individual potential. Sometimes these choices offer surprising opportunities and directions never considered. It's always interesting to ask accomplished people, who seem to have a clear direction to their life, what they thought they were going to be when they began their careers. There are many surprises awaiting in those answers. (Certainly, no one grows up saying they want to become a "headhunter!") In the early stages of a career there is a sense that all the important choices are being made at that time and that the die is permanently cast. Of course, it is a very formative period in one's life, but, having passed through this phase, I can assure you your choices are not complete, and not over. It's no time to rest on past decisions and feel that the hard work is over. As you move into the mature periods of your career, know that the ability to make these transitions is a positive step. What a wonderful way to anticipate the future. It is a future full of choices, full of decisions, full of change—and therefore, full of promise.

## CHANGE: THE ONLY CONSTANT

It is important to perceive your career as a creative challenge, as one to be molded and formed by many sequential choices. The challenge of a creative career is the ability to achieve continuous progress and advancement. You should always have the sense of growing. The new should be wonderful and exciting, and faced with some apprehension—but not fear. We all know people, and role models, who continue to be vital influences and achievers late into life. And we all know those who seem to be beaten down, tired, and lacking a sense of purpose. Sustaining your intellectual curiosity, energy level, passion, and optimism for work and life are critical goals for all to attain. This is how we remain fresh and enjoy the unique gift of creativity.

Fortunately or unfortunately, nothing is forever. We all function in a state of flux and things never stay the same. Technology, demographics, and economics constantly change the landscape of opportunity. Business, by definition, is in a state of continuous flux. Firms form, grow, and change structure. Companies may downsize, or new partnerships may be formed. Clients change, move from company to company or sometimes, from country to country. Communications styles change, taste levels change—always moving in new directions.

Keeping up is, for most, the hardest chore. And some designers don't keep up. Relying on tried and true formulas, they unhappily learn their proven methods aren't so tried and true.  Somehow, they have fallen "behind," grown stale—and worse yet, dated. Creative "burnout" is a serious and dangerous problem in design and advertising. We work in a business environment that has an insatiable appetite for the new. The competition is keen (some would say brutal) and the workload very demanding. A continuous new crop of bright young talent entering the scene every year can easily create a justified paranoia for the insecure. This problem becomes an occupational hazard for the person whose talent has not continued onto new plateaus. Unless designers who have lost their spark can move into senior positions with administrative or marketing/sales responsibility, they become the casualties of our creatively driven business, for they can get "tired" without the excitement and enthusiasm of the new.

## THE FUTURE BELONGS TO...

Our graphic designer of the future is a fortunate person. This is an individual who will have wonderful resources to draw upon. It is an exciting time. The business keeps changing.

Graphic design has felt the same technological, demographic, and economic effects over the last ten years as every other segment of our society. The working structure within design firms has changed. Our technological age has released a revolution in the way we communicate and the manner in which we work. We have also witnessed the unanticipated and amazing demographic swing toward a workforce with a female majority and a workplace untethered by technology. Today's designer functions in a world compressed by technology. Tomorrow, that designer will be challenged by new options for communication and controlled, as always, by economics. The new horizons for design point to new applications of the process and systems, exploring how to use the strategic and organizational thinking in intellectual procedures.

The late 1990s have witnessed once again a period of intense merger and acquisition activity. Many advertising agencies and design firms underwent the sometimes painful transitions of unification. Now that partnerships have aged and buyout agreements have matured, a new structuring and a second generation of leadership are appearing. Companies are striving to become bigger and more global, yet think local, goaded on by their international clients. Product development and design is increasingly important in this mix as the look and feel of products is becoming a marketing reality. The integration of interactive media is still an ongoing event and no one is willing to second-guess who will be the successes and failures. It is interesting to note that only one company has survived to be listed on the stock exchanges of both the years 1900 and 2000. That company is General Electric. The only common agreement is that the Internet has already succeeded as part of our culture. The capability of the digital communications environment now and for the next few years is constantly challenging our perceptions of how to define the future. The net effect is that new opportunities are always emerging. What an exciting time to be a witness and participant!

As indicated by the merger activity, the global business order is a reality for most of the larger firms and rapidly evolving for some of the smaller. Global marketing is a driving force behind many products, services, and identity programs. Therefore, the ability to understand foreign languages and customs is increasingly important. New markets thoughout Europe, Latin America, Central America, and Asia are constantly being tapped to ascertain where opportunities may lie and where the economic or political conditions may be favorable.

It is hard to talk about the future because so much has changed already. The graphic designer is now and will continue to play his or her role all over the world. Adaptability and flexibility are crucially important personality traits. The graphic designer of the future will be required to have the necessary creative talent to demonstrate the intellectual savvy for the "big picture," be able to grasp the marketing strategies, possess the knowledge to access the latest technology, and exhibit the sensitivity to work with different cultures. This individual will have to wear many hats, and assume many guises. The graphic designer is and will become a true renaissance personality. Does this sound familiar?

So, always recognize the mark of the future. It is today!

# Appendix

## PROFESSIONAL SOCIETIES

In any discussion of graphic design groups, it is helpful to know which professional groups are associated with the area of specialization. These organizations promote their area of interest and offer its membership a variety of enriching programs. The following list represents some of the better-known groups. It may be helpful to contact them for information. Some have membership lists of firms that can be useful when you want to search for a job in another city. They may also be able to give you information about educational programs, seminars, newsletters, annual publications, and exhibition programs. These organizations provide the designer with the forum to keep up and current, as well as an opportunity to network and meet peer groups. The groups marked with an asterisk (*) have regional chapters; always check for those listings locally or with the national organization.

### American Center for Design (ACD)
213 West Institute Place, Suite 405
Chicago, IL 60611
phone: (312) 787-2018
fax: (312) 649-9518
e-mail: *acdchicago@aol.com*
*www.acd.org*

The American Institute of Graphic Arts (AIGA) ★
164 Fifth Avenue
New York, NY 10010
phone: (800) 548-1634 or (212) 807-1990
fax: (212) 807-1799
e-mail: *AIGAnswers@aiga.com*
*www.aiga.org*
(The AIGA has thirty-five local chapters.)

Art Directors Club of New York ★
250 Park Avenue South
New York, NY 10003
phone: (212) 674-0500
fax: (212) 228-0649
e-mail: *adcny@interport.net*
*www.interport.net/adcny*

(There are Art Directors Clubs in many cities, most of whom
incorporate the name of the city, or perhaps the state,
i.e., the Art Directors Club of New Jersey)

The Design Management Institute (DMI)
107 South Street, Suite 502
Boston, MA 02111-2811
phone: (617) 338-6380
fax: (617) 338-6570
e-mail: *dmistaff@dmi.org*
*www.dmi.org*

Direct Marketing Association (DMA)
1120 Avenue of the Americas
New York, NY 10036
phone: (212) 768-7277
fax: (212) 302-6714
e-mail: *dma@the-dma.org*
*www.the-dma.org*

Graphic Artists Guild ★
11 West 20th Street, 8th Floor
New York, NY 10010
phone: (212) 463-7730
fax: (212) 463-8779
e-mail: *paulAtGAG@aol.com*
*www.gag.org*

**Industrial Designers Society of America (IDSA) ★**
1142 Walker Road
Great Falls, VA 22066-1836
phone: (703) 759-0100
fax: (703) 759-7679
e-mail: *idsa@aol.com*

**Package Design Council International (PDC) ★**
481 Carlisle Drive
Herndon, VA 20170-4830
phone: (800) 432-4085 or (703) 318-7225
fax: (703) 318-0310
e-mail: *info@pkgmatters.com*
*www.packinfo-world.org*

**The Society of Environmental Designers (SEGD) ★**
401 F Street NW, Suite 333
Washington, DC 20001
phone: (202) 638-5555
fax: (202) 638-0891
e-mail: *segdoffice@aol.com*

**Society of Illustrators**
128 East 63rd Street
New York, NY 10021
phone: (212) 838-2560
fax: (212) 838-2561
*www.members@aol.com/si39th*

**The Society of Publication Designers (SPD)**
60 East 42nd Street, Suite 721
New York, NY 10165
phone: (212) 983-8585
fax: (212) 983-6043
e-mail: *spdnyc@aol.com*

# Bibliography

**BOOKS:**

The American Institute of Graphic Arts. *AIGA Professional Practices in Graphic Design*, edited by Tad Crawford. New York: Allworth Press, 1998

Chajet, Clive. *Image By Design From Corporate Vision to Business Reality*. New York: McGraw-Hill, 1997.

Crawford, Tad. *Legal Guide for the Visual Artist*. Allworth Press, New York, 1999.

Crawford, Tad and Eva Doman Bruck. *Business and Legal Forms for Graphic Designers*. New York: Allworth Press, 1999.

*Directory 92*. Reston, Virginia: National Association of Schools of Art and Design.

The Graphic Artists Guild. *Handbook of Pricing and Ethical Guidelines*, 10th Edition. New York: North Light Books, 2001.

*Graphic Design: USA*. New York: Annual publication of the American Institute of Graphic Arts.

Fletcher, Alan. *The Art of Looking Sideways*. New York: Phaidon Press, 2001

Heller, Steven. *Education of an E-Designer*. New York: Allworth Press, 2001.

Heller, Steven. *Graphic Design: New York*. New York: Rockport Allworth Editions, 1992.

*The Joint Ethics Committee Code of Fair Practice*. New York: Joint Ethics Committee, 1989.

Leland, Caryn. *Licensing Art and Design*. New York: Allworth Press, 1995.

*Art Directors Club Annual*. New York: Annual publication of the Art Directors Club.

*Typography*. New York: Annual publication of the Type Directors Club.

Wurman, Richard Saul. *Information Architects*, edited by Peter Bradford. Zurich: Graphis Press, 1996.

Wurman, Richard Saul. *Understanding USA*. The TED Conferences Inc., 2000

## PERIODICALS:

*The 100 Show*. Published annually. Chicago: American Center for Design.

@ *Issue: The Journal of Business and Design*. A periodical series. Boston, Massachusetts: Corporate Design Foundation.

*Communication Arts*. Published eight times a year. Palo Alto, California: Coyne & Blanchard.

*The DMI Journal*. Published quarterly. Boston, Massachusetts: Design Management Institute Press.

*The DMI Case Studies*. A periodical series. Boston, Massachusetts: Design Management Institute Press.

*Gain*. Published twice yearly. New York: American Institute of Graphic Arts.

*Graphic Design: USA*. Published monthly. New York: Kaye Publishing.

*Graphis*. Published bimonthly. New York and Zurich: B. Martin Pedersen.

*How*. Published bimonthly. Cincinnati, Ohio: F & W Publications.

*I.D.* Published monthly. Cincinnati, Ohio: F & W Publications.

*Multimedia Producer Magazine*. Published monthly. White Plains, New York: Montage Publishing.

*Print*. Published bimonthly. Rockville, Maryland: RC Publications.

*SEGD Messages*. Published quarterly. Cambridge, Massachusetts: Society of Environmental Graphic Designers.

*Statements*. Published bimonthly. Chicago: American Center for Design.

*Step-By-Step Graphics*. Published monthly. Peoria, Illinois: SBS Publishing.

*Wired*. Published monthly. San Francisco and New York: Condé Nast Publications.

# About the Author

Ken Hass

**Roz Goldfarb** is president of Roz Goldfarb Associates, a New York–based management, consulting, and recruitment firm specializing in the placement of design, new media, and advertising personnel. Ms. Goldfarb, serving as a management consultant, is also involved in establishing mergers, acquisitions, and new business ventures. Her multidisciplinary skills emanate from many years of hands-on business management and her early training as a sculptor and painter. During her tenure as the director of the Pratt Institute's associate degree program, she hired and trained numerous faculty and developed design curricula, seminars, and foreign programs.

Ms. Goldfarb is the author of *The Art of Consulting: The Design Management Journal* and is a contributor to *AIGA Professional Practices in Graphic Design*. She frequently addresses professional and educational institutions about career opportunities and the changing design environment. Her recent presentations have included an advertising conference for the Conference Board in 2001 and the *HOW* conferences "Design" and "Minding Your Own Business," both in 2000. Along with partner Jessica Goldfarb, she developed the "First Business of Design" conference for the Center for Visual Communication in Santa Fe in 2000 and the national conference for the AIGA in 1997. Ms. Goldfarb has been a visiting guest lecturer and critic at the Portfolio Center, the Academy of Art in San Francisco, Syracuse University, FIT State University of New York, Art Center College of Design, the Parsons School of Design, and Pratt Institute. She has juried the Package Design Council international awards and has participated in seminars for the annual meeting of the Association of Professional Design Firms. In 1998 she was toasted by Pratt Institute at the Hershel Levit Scholarship Fund dinner for her contributions to the design community. Since 1987, the Art Directors Club of New York has been the recipient of an RGA scholarship to further the education of talented design students who require financial aid.

Ms. Goldfarb holds an M.F.A. in sculpture from Pratt Institute and a B.A. from Hunter College of the City University of New York, where she studied painting with Robert Motherwell.

# Index

# BOOKS FROM ALLWORTH PRESS

**Starting Your Career as a Freelance Illustrator or Graphic Designer** by Michael Fleishman (paperback, 6 x 9, 272 pages, $19.95)

**Business and Legal Forms for Graphic Designers**, Revised Edition with CD-ROM by Tad Crawford and Eva Doman Bruck (paperback, $8\frac{1}{2}$ x 11, 240 pages, $24.95)

**Digital Design Practices**, Third Edition by Liane Sebastian (paperback, $6\frac{3}{4}$ x $9\frac{7}{8}$, 416 pages, $29.95)

**The Graphic Designer's Guide to Pricing, Estimating and Budgeting**, Revised Edition by Theo Stephen Williams (paperback, $6\frac{3}{4}$ x $9\frac{7}{8}$, 208 pages, $19.95)

**AIGA Professional Practices in Graphic Design** edited by Tad Crawford (paperback, $6\frac{7}{8}$ x $9\frac{7}{8}$, 320 pages, $24.95)

**Advertising Law Guide** by Lee Wilson (paperback, 6 x 9, 272 pages, $19.95)

**Design Dialogues** by Steven Heller and Elinor Pettit (paperback, 6 x $9\frac{7}{8}$, 272 pages, $18.95)

**Education of a Graphic Designer** edited by Steven Heller (paperback, $6\frac{3}{4}$ x $9\frac{7}{8}$, 288 pages, $18.95)

**Texts on Type** by Steven Heller and Philip B. Meggs (paperback, 6 x $9\frac{7}{8}$, 288 pages, $19.95)

**Selling Graphic Design**, Second Edition by Don Sparkman (paperback, 6 x 9, 256 pages, $19.95)

**Licensing Art and Design**, Revised Edition by Caryn R. Leland (paperback, 6 x 9, 128 pages, $16.95)

**Graphic Design History** edited by Steven Heller and Georgette Balance (paperback, 6 x 9, 352 pages, $21.95)

**The Education of an e-Designer** edited by Steven Heller (paperback, 6 x $9\frac{7}{8}$, 352 pages, $21.95)

**Legal Guide for the Visual Artist**, Fourth Edition by Tad Crawford (paperback, $8\frac{1}{2}$ x 11, 272 pages, $19.95)

Please write to request our free catalog. To order by credit card, call 1-800-491-2808 or send a check or money order to Allworth Press, 10 East 23rd Street, Suite 510, New York, NY 10010. Include $5 for shipping and handling for the first book ordered and $1 for each additional book. Ten dollars plus $1 for each additional book if ordering from Canada. New York State residents must add sales tax.

To see our complete catalog on the World Wide Web, or to order online, you can find us at *www.allworth.com*.